The
Pacific Horticulture
Book of
Western Gardening

Informal water garden with irises and primulas in Seattle

THE

PACIFIC HORTICULTURE

BOOK OF

Western Gardening

George Waters & Nora Harlow

David R. Godine, Publisher · Boston

IN ASSOCIATION WITH THE PACIFIC HORTICULTURAL FOUNDATION

First published in 1990 by *David R. Godine, Publisher, Inc.*
Horticultural Hall, 300 Massachusetts Avenue, Boston, Massachusetts 02115

Text and photographs copyright © 1990 by the Pacific Horticultural Foundation

LIBRARY OF CONGRESS CATALOGING IN PUBLICATION DATA
The Pacific Horticulture book of Western gardening / edited and
compiled by George Waters and Nora Harlow.
p.   cm.
ISBN 0-87923-763-5
1. Gardening.   2. Mediterranean climate.   3. Landscape gardening.
I. Waters, George.   II. Harlow, Nora.   III. Pacific horticulture.
SB454.3.M43P33   1990   89-46191
635.9′52—dc20   CIP

First edition
Printed in Hong Kong by
South China Printing Company (1988) Limited

The Pacific Horticulture Book of Western Gardening was designed by Christine Taylor and
set by Wilsted and Taylor in a digital version of Linotype Baskerville. Named for the
famous English printer, John Baskerville, the type reflects his interest in letter cutting
and engraving. It possesses fine hairlines, sharp, unaccented serifs, and crisp contrasts
between the thick and thin strokes, all prevalent elements among the "transitional
faces" of the late eighteenth century. Used by Baskerville for all his notable quartos,
and with great distinction in his folio Bible, it is one of the few faces that has successfully bridged the transition from letterpress to offset printing. Baskerville
can be instantly identified both by its total evenness of "color" and by its most idiosyn-
cratic feature: the open bowl of the lowercase g in both the roman and italic fonts.

CONTENTS

ACKNOWLEDGMENTS

The photographs in this book were provided by: Russell Beatty, 11, 12, 13, 17; Ed Carman, 227, 229; James Collatz, 260, 261, 262; Carl Deul, 135, 137; Karin Fintzy, 68; Ruth Gilkey, 93; Carol Greentree, 73, 74, 76; S. L. Gulman and H. A. Mooney, 153; Harland Hand, 86–7, 91; Pamela Harper, 159 (bottom right), 168, 170, 172; Lester Hawkins, 22, 23, 25, 27, 32, 35, 42 (bottom), 48 (bottom), 49, 52–3, 55, 114, 115, 123, 128–29, 184, 185, 186, 187, 195, 196, 210 (except bottom right), 217 (top), 233 (bottom); Barbara Hoshizaki, 164, 165; Ted Kipping, 48 (top), 149, 217 (bottom), 220 (bottom left and right), 240, 242, 246, 247; M. Landis, 60; Ron Lutsko, xvii, xix; L. S. Manning, 233 (top right); David Metheny, 233 (top left); NASA, 8; Robert Ornduff, 202, 203, 204; Robin Parer, 148; Christine Rosmini, 41; Sea World, 96, 97, 98, 99; Nevin Smith, 207, 210 (bottom right), 216, 220 (top); Joy Spurr, 281, 283; Art Tyree, 253; U.S. Weather Bureau, 5; W. G. Waters, cover, ii, viii, xii, 42 (top), 43, 59, 62, 89, 102, 103, 105, 109, 141, 143, 154, 156, 159 (except bottom right), 194; J. A. Witt, 177, 179.

The illustrations on pages 78, 81, 82, and 83 are from hand-tinted photographs made in the mid-1930s and reproduced here with permission of the director of the Santa Barbara Botanic Garden.

Drawings are by: Nancy Baron, 189, 190, 191; Marcia Cary, 243; Mary Coman, 244, 248; Connie Goddard, 218, 219, 221, 222, 223; Irina Gronberg, 146, 147; Kristin Jakob, 145; Malcolm Nobs, 263; Mimi Osborne, 271, 272, 273, 274; Elly Simmons, 208, 212, 213, 214; *Wild Shrubs: Finding and Growing Your Own*, 284, 285.

The map on page 4 is after Bartholomew's *Physical Atlas*, Vol. III, from Ronald Good, *The Geography of Flowering Plants*, Longman's 2nd ed., 1953.

Native trees and pastoral view in northern California

PREFACE

When, in the 1940s, Sydney Mitchell produced the first issue of the *Journal of the California Horticultural Society*, he also took the first step on a path that led in 1976 to the introduction of *Pacific Horticulture* and to the publication you have in your hands. *Western Gardening* is a selection from the first ten years of *Pacific Horticulture* revised for publication in this form.

In launching the journal, Mitchell and his friends were at the crest of a wave of popular enthusiasm for gardening. The California Horticultural Society they helped into existence was still young, the Golden Gate International Exposition of 1939 had generated great interest in gardening through the plants displayed there, and Eric Walther was planting the first few acres of a new botanic garden, known as Strybing Arboretum, at the corner of Golden Gate Park on Lincoln Way in San Francisco. Victor Reiter, Jr, another of the founders of the California Horticultural Society, wrote enthusiastically of Walther's work in the first issue of the journal. In addition, readers of the journal in that first year saw contributions by Elizabeth and Lockwood de Forest, Frank Reinelt, W. B.

Clarke, T. Harper Goodspeed, Hugh Evans, and Carl Purdy. Within a few years they were joined by others of equal renown, including Edgar Anderson, Lester Rowntree, Collingwood Ingram, Ralph Cornell, and Alice Eastwood. Clearly the journal deserved a larger readership, and in 1968 the Strybing Arboretum and Western Horticultural societies joined with the California Horticultural Society as publishers, distributing the renamed *California Horticultural Journal* to their members. The Southern California Horticultural Institute joined in 1970, and distribution was extended to the Los Angeles area.

In the 1970s another wave of gardening enthusiasm began to build, but there still was no specialist periodical devoted to the interests of gardeners in the West. In a climate so extraordinary that it is shared by only four other small areas throughout the world, too many were relying for information exclusively on eastern books and magazines. Ours is a Mediterranean climate suited to the cultivation of a great many plants only dreamed of by gardeners elsewhere in the country. And, of course, it is unsuitable for many plants favored by cold winters and rainy summers. The history of the West, its topography and native vegetation, and the special place of water in its life, all call for gardens of a kind quite different from those made elsewhere. But nationally distributed magazines and books have a homogenizing influence. Many gardeners, recent arrivals in the West, bring with them ideas of gardens from totally different climates. They need not the reinforcement of those ideas, but their replacement with others more in keeping with the reality of rainless summers and spring's equivalent experienced in fall. An antidote is needed; our gardening culture demands a regional literature.

In 1975, with enthusiasm but few other resources, the *California Horticultural Journal* was enlarged, redesigned, and with four-color printing was offered to the public on subscription as *Pacific Horticulture*. The new magazine was well received among gardeners, not only in the West, but in the East and abroad as well. The Northwest Horticultural Society, in Seattle, joined the publishing team, and the University of British Columbia Botanical Garden adopted the magazine for distribution to members of its Davidson club.

Periodic drought and increasing interest in conservation are encouraging a gradual recognition of the true nature of garden making in the West. More nurseries are offering native plants and plants from other Mediterranean areas that are appropriate to the West. Garden designers who specialize in the use of native and drought-tolerant plants are finding more willing clients. In *Pacific Horticulture* we have tried to encourage these ideas, and in offering this anthology of useful and inspirational writing from early issues we hope to reach more gardeners who feel, as we do, that reading about gardens and gardening is as enjoyable as the work of the garden itself.

The board of the Pacific Horticultural Foundation, representing the societies that distribute *Pacific Horticulture* to their members, has been steadfastly supportive throughout the preparation of this anthology. The authors, photographers, and artists whose work is reproduced here have shown their generosity once again by allowing its use without payment. Olive Rice has, since the magazine's inception, managed the circulation of *Pacific Horticulture*, and, as one of its members, has surmounted any number of difficulties on behalf of the board. Owen Pearce, editor of the *California Horticultural Journal* and its predecessor and first editor of *Pacific Horticulture*, also deserves acknowledgment, as does Elizabeth McClintock, dedicated taxonomist, friend, guide, and mentor to the editors. We wish also to thank Margedant Hayakawa, whose generosity, understanding, and advice made *Pacific Horticulture* possible and kept it going through the lean years; Richard Hildreth, president of the board at the inception of *Pacific Horticulture*, and inspiration for what came to be known as the format committee; committee members Emily Brown, Harland Hand, Charles Burr, Fred Boutin, Helen Markwett, and others who served from time to time; Laurence Hyman, designer, who realized the committee's ideas and set high standards for the publication; and Pat West, to whom we are grateful for the restrained layout and style of our advertising.

Friends of *Pacific Horticulture* have supported the magazine since 1980 with donations over and above their subscriptions. A list of names of Friends is published in the summer issue each year in acknowledgment of their help, but it is appropriate to say again how much their support is appreciated; it has, after all, made this book possible.

Christine Taylor, of Wilsted & Taylor, has shown extraordinary patience and understanding during typography and design of the book; David Godine's enthusiasm for the project has been a constant source of support. The editors offer their thanks to these, and to the many others not mentioned here who have helped *Pacific Horticulture* along the way, and thereby contributed to the production of this book.

George Waters and Nora Harlow
Berkeley, 1990

Oriental influence in a southern California garden

FOREWORD

For many years I have watched the row of *Pacific Horticulture* lengthening on my shelf. Occasionally I take one or two out and read them again to refresh my memory and to assure myself that the recent numbers have retained their quality. There is no doubt about it; the early excellence has been maintained, even improved. It is a horticultural magazine that may be described as a highlight in publishing. It is unsurpassed in presentation, printing, and in its ever varied content. There cannot be a keen gardener in the United States—or elsewhere—who would not find inspiration in its pages, whether his special interest might lie in trees or alpines, bulbs or succulents, tropical plants, hardy shrubs, or perennials; yes, and in ferns, annual and climbing plants, whether in gardens or in nature.

We in Britain grow many plants from western America, from Alaska to Mexico. One might think that a small European island lying in a latitude north of Vancouver, the Great Lakes, and Newfoundland could not find satisfactory homes for plants from so lengthy a strip of country, bounded on one side by the Pacific Ocean and on the other by the Rocky Mountains. But we do, and we value accordingly the views of the numerous contributors to *Pacific Horticulture*, presenting as they do so clearly their wide experiences in growing and knowing plants from many countries, to help us in our efforts to do likewise.

But all these benefits and interests, though they add up to a remarkable whole, would result in a mere jumble of an anthology were they not held together and supervised by an experienced editor. We have in George Waters one who is skilled in words, ideas, and presentation and who is a veritable expert—a wizard indeed—with his camera. Here again we should be lost were it not for the backbone of friends, benefactors, societies, and organizations who launched and have upheld the magazine with their generous financial help. To them we must all say a big word of thanks and hope that they, above all others, will welcome this volume of collected contributions to *Pacific Horticulture*'s first ten years. To them no less than to the magazine's staff we owe the luxury of this book.

George and I were both founding members of the Garden History Society; I have therefore known him for well over twenty years. From his wide knowledge he has put together a book of essays on many facets of horticulture. We shall not look in vain for hints and instruction in garden design, formal and informal; plants in the wild and in gardens; the restoration of historic gardens and the creation of new ones with completely fresh ideas; the scientific approach, the techniques and skills, or the botanical revisions, many of which have a significant value to all gardeners.

There is no doubt that he and his co-editor have achieved what so many would find difficult: the welding of an anthology of importance into a readable whole. It is not only a compendium of knowledge for all gardeners, but an inspiration in its presentation. I commend the book to all gardeners and hope that the word will go forth that it is unique in many ways, so much so that it will sell in quantity and be a constant reminder of the magazine from which it came, and the profits accruing will not only warrant a second volume in due course but may lead to the compiling from the biennial indexes already provided a combined index to all back numbers so that all of us can turn to our shelves and find easily the required information. Nothing would give the benefactors more pleasure than to know that this anthology will introduce yet more yearly subscribers to *Pacific Horticulture* and so spread the news that here in the western United States is one of the very best gardening magazines in the whole of the English-speaking world.

Graham S. Thomas, OBE, VMH

INTRODUCTION

When gardeners move from one house to another there is always the excitement of discovering what plants flourish in the new garden, and what ambition, thwarted by soil or climate before, can be realized with plants that may now be cultivated. This is never more true than when gardeners move to the West Coast, for here is found not simply a difference in the extremes, such as more or less rain and snow, higher or lower temperatures. Where climate is influenced by the Pacific Ocean, there is a dramatic change: winters are mild and in summer no rain falls at all. Even the high humidity that is the precipitation of summer days elsewhere in North America is lacking in the West.

In this favorable, essentially Mediterranean climate the rivers, fed by melting mountain snow, make possible tremendous agricultural production in the Willamette Valley in Oregon and the Central Valley in California; they also transform the opportunities for gardeners in the West. With a little summer irrigation, an extraordinary range of plants is cultivated. In gardens in the San Francisco Bay Area apples and citrus fruits grow side by side, and in the University of California Botanical Garden in Berkeley a magnificent collection of cacti and other plants of the New World's deserts can be admired from the shade of a grove of Asian rhododendrons. In the southwest, where weather is warmer, mandevilla, poinciana, and other tropical plants flourish; in the northwest ideal conditions are found for roses, Japanese maples, lilies, and most plants of temperate regions.

MAKING A GARDEN

The great variety of plants grown in the West, and a similar diversity of ideas in a population of recent immigrants drawn from all parts of the world, produce gardens of every imaginable kind. The most obvious influences on small urban and suburban gardens are English and Japanese. This is perhaps because immigrants from these countries brought with them strong gardening traditions. The influence is often seen in debased form—heaps of unkempt perennial plants offered as herbaceous borders; concrete lanterns and severely clipped junipers as oriental—but even these gardens are preferable to those where there is no attempt whatever at design. Thousands of acres of land in the most prominent places in and around every town and village, demanding many hours and much expensive material to maintain, display an almost complete lack of design and, in most cases, not a glimmer of esthetic feeling. Disappointing as it is, the lack of design is perhaps not surprising.

Much is written about what to put in our gardens, perhaps because there are so many people selling plants and garden furnishings, and they are always ready with advice. Much less is heard about how to arrange plants, paths, steps, pools, ornaments, and furniture into something like a garden. The accumulation of objects is not enough. We may have the largest collection of bellflowers and the rarest Himalayan poppy, but, interesting as they are, they haven't the magic of the garden at Sissinghurst Castle.

As in music, where sounds cleverly arranged are a symphony but randomly played are cacaphony, so it is in gardens; plants properly arranged may be memorable, but carelessly planted seldom are. Paths, pools, and other permanent fixtures, as well as hedges and trees, must first be placed to provide a good structure for the garden. The framework is then clothed with smaller woody and herbaceous plants that soften the outline and provide detail and variety. Magic comes, when all is well done, from the disposition and proportion of paths, steps, and pools; the height and breadth of borders and the harmony of colors; suggestions of secret places behind well trimmed hedges; memories stirred by the fragrance of flowers; the welcome shade of trees and the sounds of the birds they shelter; the liveliness that comes from variety and contrast; and the unity from appropriate choices throughout.

Gertrude Jekyll recognized that fine gardens are not made easily when she confessed that she had spent half her long life learning which plants were worth growing and the other half learning how to garden with them. Learning which plants are worth growing is the necessary first step, but not a difficult one; most of us come to gardening through a love of plants and an urge to make collections of them, and a collector's enthusiasm stimulates learning. The difficulty begins when it dawns upon us that our magnificent collection has not produced a garden. How do we transform this hodge-podge into a work of art? After years of collecting plants for their own sake it is difficult to discard those that have no place in a new design. Discipline falters and we look for places in which to tuck some favorite plant when we should be asking ourselves what is needed to fulfill the design. Every keen gardener is tempted in this way, and wants to try plants in his garden as they come to his attention. Whether or not these introductions harm the design depends on the gardener's skill in assessing their merit and finding the right place for those worth retaining.

Any residential garden design must take account of the activities and needs of the homeowner, the climate, and the character of the house that stands in the garden. If the garden is designed by the owner, it generally will accommodate his needs. A gardener with a passion for fresh vegetables will not fail to provide space in which to grow them, and parents of young children will consider the need for lawn and sandbox. More often overlooked in the design are the character of the house and the constraints of climate.

Very old houses, especially in Europe, draw character from local materials and the traditional methods of local craftsmen, but education, mass media, and modern transportation systems have changed these things, and materials and labor are likely to come from quite another part of

Entry to a private residence is made inviting with native plants in flower

the country. House designs, too, have been imported from other parts of the world and other times. Some are mere fantasies resembling Gothic castles, Palladian villas, and English Tudor mansions. Gardens for such houses can be contrived, but it is easier to design a garden for a house that has at least some roots in local history, since house and garden then can draw on the same historical, cultural, and practical insights. Here in the West, where the Spanish have been prominent since their explorations in 1542, many buildings reflect their influence. Because of similarities with the climate of Spain, especially in southern California, these buildings are appropriate. Harmony is achieved when a Spanish-style house is provided with a garden responsive to local climate.

The Arts and Crafts movement had great influence on building styles early in this century, and houses of rusticated design and finely detailed construction throughout the West are attributed to it. Garden styles associated with houses of this kind often draw from places in England such as Hestercombe, Barrington Court, and Folly Farm, where superb gardens were made about this time for houses inspired by similar ideas. Strong architectural lines extending from the house, with plantings, especially of hedges and herbaceous perennials, so lavish as to threaten the clarity of the design, seems to be the principal theme. At the heart of such gardens is the vital tension between rigid geometry and vegetative ebullience.

The California garden, the nearest to a western style we have, is recognized as the work of several landscape architects during the early and middle years of this century, but principally that of Thomas

Church. The style derives from Japanese gardens and early Spanish homesteads; from the domestic swimming pool and the tendency, encouraged by climate, to live outdoors; from increasing urban real estate prices, the automobile, and the consequent diminution in garden size; from the ranch-style house and the need for deck and paving rather than lawn in gardens that are to be used as outdoor rooms. These influences and ideas, in a designer of great perception and originality, produced, at their best, gardens in which decks, pools, paving, sculpture, and mainly evergreen plants were grouped within curvilinear lines reminiscent of much then seen in art and architecture.

Selecting Plants

But what shall we plant, and where should we plant it? In some places the commonest daisy is more beguiling than the rarest orchid, so choosing plants without knowing where they are to be used ignores the importance of the setting and the contribution it can make to our enjoyment of plants. Even so simple a thing as the size of the garden may influence our response to plants; cacti, prickly and threatening in small gardens, are dramatic and picturesque where greater space allows them to be seen at a safe distance. An appropriate setting can multiply the effect plants have: rush-like plants by a slight hollow or cleft create the impression of a stream even where there is no water, while the translucent petals of irises in early summer can be fully enjoyed only when viewed with the sun behind them.

Not only the position of plants but their companions must be considered. Irises of the tall bearded kinds need companion plants of mounding habit to allow their sword-like leaves to stand clear. If the mounding plants have leaves of grayish green similar to that of the irises, then the contrast of form will be most obvious, unconfused with considerations of color. Good companions for bearded irises are such plants as *Sedum spectabile, Geranium traversii*, some varieties of *G. cinereum*, and certain of the tree peonies. With leaves similar in color to that of the irises, these make up a planting at once unified and full of dramatic variety. What is more, their contribution to the garden continues well beyond the season of flowering, and none of the plants requires a great deal of water.

Here in the West, gardens that need little summer water have always been pleasing, if not popular. Now they are a practical necessity in some parts of the region, as economy is forced upon us by increasing population and greater use of water in industry. Despite the pleasure to be had from gardening with drought-tolerant plants, it is not until serious water shortages occur that attention is given to them. Most newcomers quickly learn to appreciate the mild climate on the West Coast and learn new ways of gardening with plants adapted to summer drought or needing only a little additional water to flourish. But some watch the hills turn from green to brown in late spring and find them ugly; the lack of rain is a defect in the climate that they must rectify on their own small plots. They make gardens with plants, no doubt old favorites from their gardens elsewhere, that must be watered often to keep them alive. The result is that half the water now used domestically in the West is poured on gardens.

Gardens suited to the West Coast climate are not difficult to make; certainly there are plenty of plants from which to choose. Of the five areas similar in climate to our West Coast, and therefore having plants likely to adapt to our gardens, some are especially rich in plants. The smallest of the

Garden plants require little irrigation and complement the color of the hills in summer

five is on the western side of the southern tip of South Africa, the Cape Peninsula, where an area of only 180 square miles has more than 2,200 species of native plants. This is almost half as many as are found in the whole of California, a state by no means lacking in beautiful native plants. Another of these regions, southwestern and southern Australia, has a rich flora as distinctive as is the country's fauna, but winter temperatures there are slightly higher than ours and some plants from those parts are reluctant immigrants. Nevertheless, there are many still to be tried here, and adventurous gardeners are having a good time experimenting with them. Besides our own West Coast, the other two regions of the world with dry summers and mild, wet winters are central Chile and the region around the Mediterranean, which gives its name to this distinctive and enviable climate. Between them they provide more than enough plants to make a paradise for any gardener.

PART ONE

GARDENING IN THE WEST

GARDENER'S GUIDE TO THE MEDITERRANEAN CLIMATE

LESTER HAWKINS

On the west coasts of all the great land masses of the world and on the warmer sides of the temperate regions (those that are farthest from the poles) lie those sunny lands that nevertheless are not deserts, but, instead, support rich and remarkable floras. There are five such areas of Mediterranean climate: the land bordering the Mediterranean on all sides, our own Pacific slopes, central Chile, southwestern and southern Australia, and a small western portion of the Cape of Good Hope in South Africa. In the northern hemisphere, these areas are roughly centered around 40° latitude and in the southern hemisphere around 35°, an important difference, as we shall see.

No two climates of the world are exactly alike, yet all these regions have much in common. First and foremost, these are, in the usual shorthand phrase, the winter-wet, summer-dry parts; it is a phrase, however, that needs a little spelling out.

As we have seen, all the Mediterranean climate zones are located on west coasts and the prevailing winds of the world are westerly; therefore these are all, in varying degrees, maritime climates where continental temperature extremes are rare. Thus we can say that these are areas with a cool season and a warm season, where sufficient rain falls to maintain a varied and often dense plant life and where it falls mostly in the cool season. Warm seasons are more or less extensive periods of drought with very little rain or none at all; they are sometimes hot but are more often tempered by westerly winds from the sea.

Many consequences follow from these facts and they are felt in all our areas. The most important for us here is that in all these lands spring is a time of an onrush of growth among native plants that later must endure drought, sometimes prolonged, with the corollary that the plants that survive this ordeal possess the means for doing so. This necessity gives rise to many of the characteristic features of Mediterranean plants, features that we gardeners often find so attractive, such as the nearly leafless green stems of brooms, or the gray-green or glaucous coloration of many shrubs, or as in our manzanitas, the ability of some shrubs to lose leaves in summer and thereby exhibit handsome trunk and branch patterns.

It is also worth noting that late in the dry season all our areas are threatened with fire. Spring plant growth becomes a potentially combustible mass as transpiration

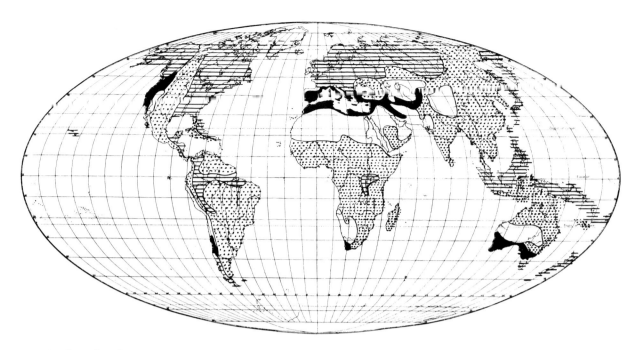

Regions of Mediterranean climate on this map of the world are shown with solid shading. Areas marked with horizontal lines have rain at all seasons. Dots mark areas of summer rain. Deserts are unshaded

falls to a minimum and atmospheric humidity sometimes drops to near-desert lows. The ability to resprout after fires is a feature of many of the plants we shall be considering.

It scarcely needs saying that so far I have been describing a median climate for the areas with which we are concerned; as we approach their edges, the situation, as we might expect, is less clear. On the poleward side, where there is land, Mediterranean zones give way to areas of year-round rainfall (France, Austria, the Balkans, British Columbia, southern Chile). On the equatorial side the period of drought becomes longer and more extreme, finally ending in deserts (the Sahara, Baja California, Namaqualand, the Kimberley, the Atacama). These gradual climate changes are particularly important to us on the Pacific Coast, because our winter-rainfall area has the greatest north-south extent of any in the world. Also, as we all know, climates have a

way of not keeping to absolutely regular schedules, and the borders of our Mediterranean regions are continually shifting, sometimes to bring winter rain to the deserts, sometimes to bring drought to the north. Nevertheless, it is possible to establish a demarcation by taking averages over an arbitrary period, say fifty years, or by defining an area as Mediterranean if it has the characteristics we have described for twenty-five years, say, out of thirty.

And, of course, all five of our regions differ from each other in ways only slightly less marked than the features they have in common. Here, the direction, height, and location of mountain ranges play the leading role. The mountains around the Mediterranean basin are latitudinally arranged (extend east and west); the basin can be considered therefore as a vast funnel for west winds and the sea itself a carrier inland of Atlantic ocean influence. This great extension of a typical west coast climate far into the great continental land mass formed by Europe, Asia, and Africa is unique in the world and it continues the winter rainfall pattern almost to the heart of Asia. As we might expect, continental influence, in the form of greater temperature differentials, increases as we travel eastward, and the climate of the heartland of Asia Minor is a mixture of Mediterranean and continental characteristics. Here plants must endure not only drought and heat but intense cold as well; this is the area richest of all in plants with bulbs.

By contrast, in our Pacific Coast region the mountains are longitudinally arranged (extend north and south) and are not far from the sea, two facts that give us a longer and less deep winter-rainfall area. As the traveler proceeds down the coast from the Canadian to the Mexican borders of the United States he finds that the summer-dry season gradually lengthens but that winter rains remain the rule throughout. Thus, we can say that southern California has an extreme Mediterranean climate with an admixture of desert zones. Western Washington, on the other hand, appears so green to summer tourists from California that they often think they are in a totally different climate, but this is still a summer-dry area, as anyone who tried a garden of vegetables on the Tacoma prairie without irrigation would soon discover. The annual rainfall in Seattle is thirty-five inches, of which only five inches falls from frost to frost in the warm season.

Because of this vast extension of our winter-rainfall area to the north, some authors have put western Washington and Oregon into a special class—the winter storm belt. I see no reason for this distinction, however, and would prefer to say that this is the coldest of all our Mediterranean climate areas, just as parts of Western Australia are the warmest.

A winter storm, which originated off the coast of Japan and has traveled across the Pacific in a great arc, arrives in the Northwest and is deflected toward California by the Cascade Mountains and the Sierra Nevada

All three winter-rainfall areas of the southern hemisphere also have their distinct peculiarities. The smallest of our regions is the western side of Cape Province in South Africa. The limited extent of this area is the result of abruptly rising mountains near the sea and the fact that the continent of Africa breaks off at 33° latitude (San Diego lies just below 33°). Despite its size, however, this is one of the richest floral provinces in the world; in approximately 150 square miles there are nearly 2,500 species of plants.

Our next smallest area is central Chile. Here the mountains extend north and south, as on our Pacific Coast, but they are even closer to the sea. Also, for complex reasons mostly connected with the narrowness of the lower reaches of the South American continent, the year-round rainfall part of Chile extends farther northward than similar areas in our hemisphere do to the south.

In Australia it is the absence of mountains and the shape of the continent presenting, as it does, a long front to the west winds that gives this Mediterranean climate area its depth. As you go eastward toward Melbourne you find the climate gradually changing to an east coast one of year-round rainfall and you see damp woods and tree-fern gulleys. Like western Washington, although in a different sense, southern Victoria is a borderline case.

Mountains are also important locally, perhaps nowhere more so than in a Mediterranean climate area where they determine the amount of maritime influence and protection from north winds a given microclimate will receive. As winter storms strike the coast of California, they encounter first the low coast ranges and later the Sierra Nevada, but even the hills near San Francisco Bay have an extraordinary effect on rainfall patterns. The west side of Mt. St. Helena, seventy miles to the north, has an annual rainfall of nearly ninety-five inches. Occidental averages fifty-six and a half inches, Kentfield near Mt. Tamalpais (and only ten miles from San Francisco) forty-six inches, San Francisco itself twenty-three inches, its suburb San Jose thirteen inches, and Walnut Creek, another suburb, nineteen inches. In summer, Walnut Creek will often experience temperatures of 100° F. while only about fifteen miles away, thermometers in Berkeley are in the sixties. This pattern is reversed on cold nights in winter when Walnut Creek can receive fourteen degrees of frost while temperatures in Berkeley are well above freezing.

I have said that Mediterranean regions are mild-climate areas and it is true that they have been widely celebrated by poets and talked about by laymen as genial lands,

but it is a statement that also needs qualification. In this respect, there are two marked differences between the winter-rainfall areas of the northern and southern hemispheres. One, which I noted earlier, is that the latter are all a few degrees closer to the equator than their counterparts in the north. More important, however, is the fact that the southern regions are more extensively exposed to ocean influences. Southwestern and southern Australia and the Cape Province are bounded on the poleward side by the Southern Ocean, and central Chile has only a narrow land mass lying to its south. In the north, however, great continental areas lie on the cold side of both the Mediterranean and our own Pacific slopes. As a result, the southern hemisphere areas have higher and more uniform minimum temperatures in winter. This is an unfortunate fact for gardeners on the Pacific Coast, because it places beyond reach of all but the few who have extremely favored microclimates a large part of the wonderful shrub flora of Western Australia.

There are even remarkable differences between the western Mediterranean and our Pacific Coast in this respect. The east-west mountain chains of Europe do a better job of protecting Italy, Spain, and northern Africa from north winds than do our north-south mountains. Periodic great freezes, such as those of 1932 and 1972, come down the Pacific Coast and devastate gardens; even the common rosemary died in many gardens with a north exposure near San Francisco in 1972. The climate of Greece and the Aegean is subject to somewhat similar cold conditions occasionally when the northeast wind from Russia, only barely warmed by its passage over the Black Sea, rushes through the gap between the mountains of Turkey and those of the Balkans.

SUMMER DROUGHT

The menaces of summer are more nearly equal in all five of our Mediterranean areas, but here our own climate has perhaps the edge on the others. When the desert climates widen to overcome parts of their Mediterranean neighbors, cities such as Perth, Capetown, Santiago, Rome, Athens, Los Angeles, and even, on rare occasions, San Francisco, can suddenly become burning ovens. At these times, plants droop, fires rage, and weathermen watch in awe as their humidity meters register lows almost unheard of even in the great deserts of the world. I remember one August of almost unbearable heat throughout most of California. Day after day temperatures in the high nineties were reported from the usually cool coast and the daily maximum hovered close to 120° F. in the Central Valley. This condition occurs more frequently in the Mediterranean basin as a hot wind from the Sahara, called the sirocco, engulfs Crete, mainland Greece, and sometimes Italy and Spain.

In general, however, westerly sea breezes in summer are happily the rule in all our regions. Without them, the many long days of clear skies would become unbearably hot and dry, and many of the plants that now endure this period would undoubtedly not survive. Travel brochures for Perth and Capetown stress the afternoon sea winds that afford relief on days that have begun with the threat of uncomfortable heat. The fact is that all our Mediterranean climate areas lie opposite great oceanic summer high-pressure areas and all have cold ocean currents off their shores, conditions that create cool winds but almost never bring rain. This circumstance is nowhere so marked as along the California coast, where it creates massive summer fogs that are one of the great anomalies of the world's climate structure, the product of California's peculiar topography. Our Central Valley is, in summer, a hot, low-lying area backed by high mountains and separated from the sea by lower mountains that flatten out into hills near San Francisco Bay, nearly in the center of the valley's western rim. Almost every summer afternoon masses of hot air rise from this basin, drawing cold air from the sea through gaps in the mountains and over the lowest of the hills. The result is the summer wind we know so well. Its regularity and strength set in motion a cold current along the coast, colder than similar currents along the coasts of the other regions we have been considering. The air above this current often condenses into fog, which is then driven inland as the cold sea air rushes into the afternoon low pressure zone of the valley. The resulting combination of wind, fog, and dry season is one that always surprises tourists to San Francisco.

It is instructive to consider our climate from a vantage point some miles up, say at the level of a low satellite or a medium order of angels. From here, if we look toward the equator we see cloud masses as hot air rises, condenses, and frequently drops its moisture. Still to the south, but closer, we see skies almost always clear as equatorial air returns to earth, warming as it descends and therefore never condensing water vapor into rain. (The air is, of course, being driven to the east by the rotation of the earth.) These are the deserts. In winter, if we look far to the west, across the Pacific, we can see storms gathering in a cyclonic pattern, as warm air from the south meets cold air from the north. The warm air rises and cools, condensing its moisture as rain or snow. These storms follow a great arc across the Pacific and descend along the Pa-

cific Coast. Sometimes, however, this pattern may be interrupted. Many of the storms fail to go south but instead head out across Canada toward the Great Lakes. In this case, the great Pacific high-pressure area, always out to sea opposite California in summer, has failed to gravitate southward with the sun in winter. California is in for a drought.

Now, if, in another winter, we look from our place among the angels far to the east, we can see clear sky along the entire East Coast. The Bermuda high has failed to gravitate south. Cold air from northeastern Canada is being forced through passes in the mountains to bring an unusual freeze to the Pacific states. On the night of December 12, 1972, when northern California was visited by what was perhaps its greatest frost of the century, minimum temperatures in Miami were 72° F. and in New York, 50° F. These, however, are the exceptions. Usually, above California, we see the descending storms in winter and clear skies in summer with westerly winds.

Such briefly are the basic facts of our Mediterranean climates—more or less the best and the worst they have to offer. To those of us who are gardeners and therefore also interested in landscapes—the earth's green mantle as it affords a home

for man—these regions of winter rainfall and clear summer skies have a significance that immediately separates them in our minds from other parts of the earth. No list of facts, however long, can supplant this intuition. At the very mention of the word Mediterranean any number of landscapes come to mind: the setting of Delphi with its wooded grotto and the rich maquis out of which rise the monasteries of Athos, for example, or, in paintings, the wilderness of Calabria by Salvator Rosa; Italy as seen by Corot; or Spain, always present in the backgrounds of Velasquez. All these (and thousands more) have their counterparts in the Sonoma hills or the Mendocino coast of California or the Umpqua valley of Oregon. And these again are duplicated—with some differences—in the magnificent brushland of the harbor at Albany in southwestern Australia or the tangle of plant forms of a ravine on Table Mountain. The traveler always knows when he is in a Mediterranean land.

Our purpose is to study the plants of these regions with a climate like, but never identical with, our own. If we want to enlarge our repertoire of beautiful plants, and if we hope to find those plants we can grow most nearly to perfection, then these are surely the places to look for them.

A finger of fog flows off the Pacific Ocean through the Golden Gate, drawn by hot air rising above California's great Central Valley. The photograph, provided by NASA, was taken at 65,000 feet on infra-red film. Areas of vegetation are red in the photograph. Golden Gate Park, including the Panhandle, two long, joined rectangles, runs west to east through San Francisco

BROWNING OF THE GREENSWARD

RUSSELL A. BEATTY

THE periodic crises of drought bring out two seemingly contradictory characteristics of human nature. The first is the incredible slowness with which we accept change. The second is the absurd speed with which we come to accept abnormal conditions. For years—decades, even a century—we have known that California has potential water problems and yet our lifestyles have not changed to reflect that fact. In fact, per capita water consumption has increased with the help of irrigation technology and the California Water Project, supplied by the bountiful Sierra Nevada.

But then we are cut off at the source. The rains don't come and all of us are hit directly in our daily lives. With the motivation of water rationing we change our lifestyles to adapt almost overnight. And to our amazement, it is not really that difficult nor all that detrimental, except, perhaps, to our gardens and the cultivated landscape. A flurry of conferences, hastily contrived research projects, and a flood of articles appear in quick succession to help everyone cope. Facts and figures inundate all of us to the saturation point. Madcap schemes (piping snow water from Alaska) are mixed with personal ingenuity (buying

barrels to store rain water). Everyone becomes involved, eagerly sharing his or her own ingenious water-saving devices. The scenario goes on, and approaches the bittersweet madness of a Marx Brothers film.

The mixture of serious concern and levity for the time being takes the focus off the long-range implications. Experts say the worst is yet to come. Even if the next few winters' rains are normal, the reservoirs won't be full for several years. And as the advertisement for an irrigation supplier asks, "But what if it doesn't rain?" The magnitude of the drought will be far greater than any of us can now predict. Then what will we do?

We are all being forced to consider the future whether we want to or not. The ability of human nature to adapt to abnormal conditions has been demonstrated. Whether or not we will be able to change or accept changing lifestyles in the long run remains to be seen.

In a time of crisis we need to gain perspective. To be aware of the origins of our predicament enables us to plan for future changes. One way to do this is to rediscover where in the world we live and where we have come from. We live in a lush landscape, a veritable paradise. What can happen to that landscape was illustrated to some extent in Marin County, California, which was hit especially hard by the drought of 1976–77. In many places the landscape turned brown under the hot summer sun and strict water conservation measures. The situation was temporary, but can we tolerate aesthetically unpleasant landscapes even for the moment? Or must we redesign our plantings? Is the alternative a brown and gray desert-like landscape?

The key question to ask ourselves is what is appropriate planting design for urbanized California? That is probably impossible to answer in any specific way. Nevertheless, we can take the opportunity to reevaluate our landscapes—gardens, parks, streets—and consider our tastes in landscape aesthetics. Where has our sense of beauty in landscape planting originated? Why do we demand a lush green landscape everywhere? What has led to the planting of acres of lawns in median islands and around commercial and industrial buildings where the only foot traffic is from the groundskeeper? Or why do we see the proliferation of heavily irrigated garden-like plantings as cosmetic settings for apartments, businesses, office complexes, and even freeways?

Origins

One of the first white immigrants, Juan Crespi (an associate of Padre Serra) described California as "this other Eden" and "the garden paradise." In fact, the name California originated in a sixteenth century Spanish legend describing a mythical place as a "wonderful island situated on the right hand of the Indies, an island rich in pearls and gold and very near to the terrestrial paradise." Therein lies the key—paradise, Eden—a fantasy to satisfy the human longings for a better place.

Not everyone who came in the beginning found California so inviting. The parched landscape of late summer was described as unhandsome and inhospitable. Yet in either case the tendency to create a lush, tropical paradise has been the hallmark of settlement. Gardens were planted either to fulfill the fantasy or to create a retreat from the seemingly hostile environment.

The Mexican padres and early settlers came from a similar landscape. They knew how to live in a land where rain falls in only

From the Moorish garden tradition the patio with its central fountain and limited garden is an expression of adaptation to a Mediterranean climate

Two median islands: one, planted with lawn, rhaphiolepis, crape myrtle, and pines, requires bi-weekly irrigation; the other, planted with dwarf coyote bush, arctostaphylos, ceanothus, and zelkovas, can require only bi-monthly irrigation. Maintenance costs as well as water waste are not justified for median island lawns

the few winter months. The missions were built around small central courtyard gardens. Rudimentary irrigation systems supplied water from wells, or *zanias* (ditches) from nearby streams, and enabled the growing of primarily utilitarian plants. Nevertheless, some flowers were grown to decorate the altar. The pepper tree from Peru, figs, olives, and other trees from similar climates provided shade as well as fruit. The abundance of wild roses reminiscent of the rose-of-Castile delighted the Franciscan padres as did the verdant valleys filled with wildflowers.

With them the padres brought their seeds and plants and horticultural expertise suitable for California. Many were trained horticulturists and most had copies of a horticultural guide published in Madrid. Even so, the establishment of gardens was not an easy task in the baked, untilled soil. Then, as today, there were

floods and periodic drought. Nevertheless, the padres were knowledgeable, persistent, and successful in developing their gardens. George Vancouver marvelled, ". . . the garden of Buena Ventura far exceeded anything I had before met with in this region . . ."

Sea traders brought new plants and seeds to the missions. Through the trial of growing those plants under such austere conditions numerous trees, shrubs, and flowers originated in these first California gardens to later supply the homes and farms of settlers. Even today this legacy is seen in the form of direct descendants (mission olive, fig, and grape) and in the use of pomegranates, oleanders, the pepper tree, citrus, and many others.

Following the demise of the missions in 1822, the gardens declined and were obliterated. The Mexican settlers who lived in the pueblos around the missions were retired soldiers or immigrants from northern Mexico. Neither they nor the ranchers were much interested in gardens and left little lasting effect except to allow the deterioration of a developing garden style.

In the 1840s another type of immigrant began to settle in California. The pioneers from the eastern United States mixed with the vaqueros, many intermarrying and assuming the title of a don. These people came to stay and brought with them the seeds of favorite plants from the East and Midwest. The Spanish-style garden was revived and adapted to the adobe houses, which were patterned after the Moorish houses of Andalusia. Shade trees, herbs, and flowers grew in the patio, the focal point of family life and hospitality. The vine-covered ramada became a symbol of the romantic age of the California don. The gardens were not large and represented an understanding of the climate and the landscape.

The vagaries of the climate in California during the 1860s—a period of drought followed by severe flooding and another drought—led to the demise of the great ranchos. Millions of cattle perished in two years because of the lack of sufficient grass. Pocket gophers and ground squirrels as well as insect pests and plant diseases compounded the misery and ruin. Unable to sustain such great losses, the vaqueros sold their immense tracts of land in small pieces. The newly arriving settlers from the East harvested a windfall in cheap land.

With the Gold Rush and later the completion of the transcontinental railroad in 1869, a tidal wave of emigration from the East began that has never quite ceased. It is this influx of immigrants from a completely foreign climate and landscape that has had the greatest influence on the gardens and urban landscapes of California.

For most Americans, then as well as now,

The origins in the romantic English landscape tradition are evident in this turfed office park in Walnut Creek, California. Mindless of the current drought, the sprinklers and ornamental fountains were going full tilt at the end of April 1977 when water rationing should have been in effect. This ostentatious display of water waste is inappropriate for California

the climate and landscape posed a sharp contrast to the temperate regions of their origins. Farmers accustomed to spring planting had to learn to plant in the fall. The native plants of this new land were unknown and the horticultural expertise learned in the East was of little value. These settlers brought many of their favorite plants with them and attempted to transform their California gardens into eastern-style landscapes.

In the boom years after the Gold Rush, the wealthy imported plants and seeds from eastern nurseries on a grand scale. Their taste in garden and park design had its origins in the romantic style of their northern European heritage. The picturesque style of the English landscape school was the *beau idéal*. They were accustomed, as today's newcomers are, to a greensward of lawn punctuated with groups of trees, shrubs, flowers. Thus, lawns became a ubiquitous part of gardens and parks. The newcomers found the parched brown summer landscape unpleasant and attempted to transform it.

At first the scarcity of water was a deterrent to many gardeners. Those who did not live near a stream or other water supply had to pay dearly for a water carrier. In Los Angeles it cost fifty cents a week for one bucketful a day, including Sundays. Obviously, little could be grown and plants that were used must have been drought tolerant.

The wealthy, however, were undaunted and were able to tunnel into the mountains or capture remnant zanias or nearby streams. With the development of irrigation techniques and well drilling, the use of irrigation water became commonplace. California was transformed into a paradise where plants from all over the world grew side by side.

Stories of the benign, healthful climate and the lush garden-like landscape were told in the East with great exuberance and no little exaggeration. California and paradise became synonymous. Writers such as Charles F. Holder of Pasadena lured easterners suffering with consumption or "wasting away with the vapours." He wrote: "When the blizzard blows in the East, the warm trade wind sighs through the orange blossoms here. When the ice is forming there, the birds are singing here. There is no lost time from one end of the year to the other. Nature seems always at her best, and the products of nearly every zone meet here. The banana and the pine, the palm and the apple grow in the same dooryard, and when the summer comes, and sunstroke and other ills visit the East, perfect immunity is found here in cooler days and perfect nights."

The railroad companies also enticed easterners away from the miseries of win-ter snows and summer heat. At first the influx was primarily in central California because of the completion of the transcontinental railroad to the San Francisco Bay Area. Later, with the completion of the Southern Pacific line to Los Angeles, settlement and the concurrent expansion of horticultural expertise in the south flourished. Cañon Crest Park in Redlands, designed by Franz Hosp, a German immigrant, became a showplace extravaganza of southern California horticulture. The Southern Pacific Railroad advertised it as a scenic wonder and encouraged travelers to visit Redlands by providing special trains and horse-drawn carriages to the park.

Visitors quickly succumbed to the charms of this tropical paradise. Many stayed on or returned later to bask in "the land of eternal spring." Once here they began to fulfill the fantasies dreamed during the long cold winters of the East. As Victoria Padilla says:

Many newcomers to southern California, excited at finding themselves living in a land of no snow and but little frost, liked to believe that they were actually in the tropics and grasped at everything that would make their gardens suggestive of the more torrid zones . . .
The average gardener had little real understanding of planting as practiced in a subtropical climate and little or no conception of the proper selection and arrangement of ornamentals . . .

Along with the plants brought with them—dahlias, lilacs, gladiolus, iris, chrysanthemums, hydrangeas, and privet—they discovered the fantastic array of exotics. Such plants were previously found growing only in greenhouses and conservatories. All of them could be grown outdoors in California. Plant introduction went berserk. Gardens and parks became more elaborate without restraint in the garish combinations and numbers of plants. Pampas grass, cycads, palms, deodars, and pines grew together in expansive lawns. Roses were everywhere, along with bougainvillea, trumpet vines, bamboos, and geraniums to create an orgasmic display of flower and foliage.

The design and planting of parks also followed the odd marriage of the English landscape tradition with the flamboyant display of tropical plants. Postcards of Piedmont Park in Oakland, around 1900, show this uncontrolled urge to celebrate the semi-tropical quality of the California climate. An account of a large estate was carried in a San Jose newspaper in 1877:

I was reminded of an English nobleman's park; there was such a wealth and variety of foliage in so small a space . . . Here I found evergreens from every climate, the Deodar cedar from the Himalaya Mountains; Cedar of Lebanon from Palestine; Chinese, Japanese, and Oregon cypress; the Sequoia gigantea; every conceivable variety of arborvitae and seventeen varieties of acacias. . . . The great palms were there in all their majesty. Enormous dracaenas, laurustinus, and all plants from New Holland [Australia] flourish there in the open.

Golden Gate Park represents a more restrained adaptation of the English-style park to the California landscape. William Hammond Hall, inspired by the work of Frederick Law Olmsted, was able to apply sensitively the design principles expressed in Central Park to the unique characteristics of the barren sand dunes of the western edge of San Francisco. Using indigenous California natives and many Australian imports, Hall checked the shifting sands, as well as the unrelenting wind, to create an essay in ecological adaptation. The result was the development of what is considered to be the most important park design of the nineteenth century.

Olmsted, a devoted student of the English landscape tradition, was appalled at the opulence of California gardens and cities. He grew to understand the nature of the California landscape and climate and deplored the eclectic styles evident in architecture and landscape design. He felt the semi-arid climate and the limitation of water should be basic constraints in landscape planning and design. In the design of the Stanford University campus he synthesized the special attributes of the California landscape and the Mediterranean climate. The shaded arcades and broad overhangs of the buildings were a response to the intense sun. Inspired by the early missions, he limited plantings to small beds in the centers of courtyards with only a single grass panel in the entrance court. Drought-tolerant trees and other plants were used as an expression of the scarcity of water. Compared with the elaborate, irrigated gardens of nearby estates, Stanford represented a departure from the accepted design style of the times. Unfortunately, Olmsted's example and concepts were not followed in further development of the campus or in the subsequent expansion of urban development of the California landscape in the twentieth century.

THE PRESENT

Fortunately, the ostentatious style of the Victorian era is gone. Refinements in garden and park design have been made during the twentieth century. Nevertheless, the landscape plantings we see today have their origins in the earlier styles imported from the East. The dominant theme is the picturesque style of the English landscape tradition. With twentieth century affluence, technological advances in the irrigation industry, and development of the turfgrass and nursery industries, the greensward has persisted as the accepted planting motif. Mixtures of drought-tolerant plants and thirsty species from less arid climates are combined with aesthetic effect as the primary concern. We have inherited, without question or reevaluation, a demand for highly irrigated landscapes. The simplicity and sensible fitness of the Mexican garden style have been largely discarded or forgotten. Newcomers are still lured to this benign climate by claims as exaggerated as those of the nineteenth-century writers. Television and movies influence every American and paint a picture of California as a sunny Eden (the smog notwithstanding).

From Maryland, Missouri, or Connecticut families leave their homes and the expanses of lawn to live in Novato or San Bernardino. Either they, or the developers, make the transition easy by duplicating the lush landscape of their hometowns.

In the past half century or so the phenomenon of the yearly garden show has helped homeowners by demonstrating garden design ideas. Invariably these temporary show gardens have little or no relationship to the reality of the California setting. Flamboyant, well-designed displays of fuchsias, azaleas, ferns, and similar "thirsties" are shown with "lawns" of sod laid upon asphalt.

People also tend to copy what they see in the public landscape. Freeways have become the most frequent landscape experience. Algerian ivy, African daisy, coast redwood, and liquidambar are combined with the more drought-tolerant eucalypts and acacias. For many people these combinations of plants represent a pleasing landscape. Frequently, the same combinations are planted in home gardens without regard for water compatibility. Similarly, irrigated parks become models for home gardeners as well as commercial and industrial complexes. Thus lawns and gardenesque plantings proliferate. Georgian colonial bank buildings rise amidst rolling mounds of grass and trees as though transported wholesale from Atlanta. Mission style architecture is aped in new office buildings surrounded by English ivy—the ultimate aberration of eclecticism.

The net result is that we have forgotten, or have never really discovered, where in the world we live. We have become so detached from nature through dependency on modern technology that we have developed a lifestyle largely independent of the climate and landscape. Air conditioners cool us, furnaces warm us, and a pipeline at the end of modern man's most audacious control over nature, the California Water Project, has supplied us with unlimited water. The great nursery industry has provided a cornucopia of plants from all over the world. Sod farms produce instant lawns. We are an impatient race and we expect instant results, instant gardens. Real estate developers know this and now spend millions to produce instantly green landscapes for new residential complexes. Landscape architects, many trained in the East, have contributed to this transformation of California into a green landscape. Without knowing it we have become trapped in the dilemma we now experience. We have attempted to irrigate the entire state. The 1972 freeze and the 1976–77 drought combined in a quick one-two punch at the landscape industry. More importantly, these examples of a capricious climate are forcing us to reckon with nature.

Three possibilities seem apparent. First, we can regard drought as an ephemeral event and make do. The rains will come

California poppies and dwarf baccharis combined with drought-tolerant trees and shrubs produce a lush green and colorful effect appropriate for a California landscape. This scene, in the Rancho Santa Ana Botanic Garden, could be easily adapted for corporate or private landscapes

sooner or later, and we can adjust temporarily to a brown landscape.

A second philosophy would support arguments for depending more heavily on technological solutions. Supporters of the expansion of the California Water Project have good evidence to justify building more dams and reservoirs and perhaps extending taps to the Northwest or beyond.

A third approach seems more plausible in the long run. That is to develop a new landscape ethic and aesthetic consciousness. By considering drought as a welcome opportunity and a challenge, we can be more effective in dealing with it directly, as individuals, and with longer lasting, more satisfying results. By learning anew or relearning what it means to live in a Mediterranean climate where water is a precious limited resource, we can all develop a new consciousness in planting the landscape.

Does this mean that the greensward will turn brown—that our gardens will look like desert scenes? Or will we return to the austere gardens of the padre and the vaquero? Not necessarily. The touchstone is ecological fitness. This does not mean aesthetic satisfaction need be sacrificed. Nor does it imply a renunciation of exotic plants for the sole use of California native plants. Care must be taken that we are not driven heedlessly into new fads.

There are several positive alternatives to consider. First, extensive plantings of trees, shrubs, and ground covers should follow what Professor Bob Perry of California Polytechnic, Pomona, calls "the ecological alternative." Mesophytic (high water-using) plants should not be mixed with those that are xerophytic (drought tolerant). He calculated net savings of $5,722/acre/year when comparing a consistently drought-tolerant planting (the ecological alternative) with a mixed planting of mesophytes and xerophytes on a freeway interchange in Pasadena.* In mixed plantings water-demanding plants become the common denominator, and drought-tolerant plants are overwatered.

With sensible plant selection and arrangement, landscapes at all scales from home gardens to parks and freeways can be both aesthetically pleasing and ecologically sound, not to mention economical.

Second, thirsty plants should be limited to small areas where such plants can be justified on either a functional or an aesthetic basis. Turf grass is the only plant tolerant of foot traffic. Its use should be restricted primarily to that function—playing fields, home lawns for children to play on, park and campus lawns for recreation. Even with such economics of limited planting, turf grass selection can be based upon water conservation principles. Some grasses such as tall fescue require less total irrigation than shallower-rooted species.

*The figure is based upon a reduction of 1.55 acre feet/acre/year in supplemental irrigation. The freeway planting would have required 1.95 acre feet/acre/year compared to 0.4 acre feet/acre/year for a similar visual effect using only drought-tolerant plants.

Unfortunately it must be seeded because it is a bunchgrass. The demand for instant landscapes using sod must be tempered with long-range conservation policies. Another modification in turf practices could be to break away from the fine, precisely clipped lawn in large parks in favor of a meadow-like turf. The latter would require less frequent mowing and watering. In natural settings its appearance would certainly be more appropriate aesthetically.

Another way to limit the use of thirsty plants is to rediscover the charms of the California patio. In residential neighborhoods and to a certain extent in business areas so many plantings are purely cosmetic—exterior window dressing. Building ordinances force a setback of twenty feet for suburban houses. That strip frequently becomes a piece of unused landscape and is usually planted in lawn or flowers with little or no function. A front patio enclosed by a fence or wall would be a more useful family space as well as a pleasant entry forecourt. Here small beds of flowers, azaleas, and other "thirsties" could be grown satisfactorily. Such interior gardens would be low water users compared with planting the entire front yard. The exterior could be planted with suitable Mediterranean plants selected for both appearance and drought tolerance. Lawns could be eliminated or relegated to a small patch in the rear garden. Combinations of broadleaf evergreen shrubs such as rock rose (*Cistus*), rosemary, lavender, ceanothus, arbutus, photinia, and dwarf baccharis could be accentuated with California poppies (from seed) or the similar-looking gazania for a brilliant floral display. The possibilities are endless and the visual effects every bit as delightful as shrubs and lawn.

A third and perhaps less tangible approach to water-conserving planting design is to consider the visual fitness of plants relative to the character of the California landscape setting. This concept is more important in areas where the natural or rural landscape predominates as compared with an urban landscape. Again, the sole use of California native plants is not suggested. For lack of a better term, "visual ecology" comes closest to an appropriate label. This means what is planted fits the setting both ecologically (low water demand, not invasive, and so on) as well as visually. Some plants such as purple hopbush (*Dodonaea viscosa* 'Purpurea') and New Zealand flax (*Phormium tenax*) are certainly drought-tolerant. But when imposed in a setting dominated by oak woodlands or a mixed evergreen forest, these plants suddenly become eccentric oddities reminiscent of the Victorian era. Less ostentatious and equally drought-tolerant plants could be used more satisfactorily—strawberry tree (*Arbutus unedo*) or the native toyon (*Heteromeles arbutifolia*) or *Photinia serrulata*, which is somewhat reminiscent of a shrubby madrone.

Monterey pine and coast redwood in interior valley landscapes are examples of the use of natives outside their natural range. Visually they contradict settings dominated by the rounded forms of oak, bay, madrone, and buckeye. What many of us have not realized is that most native plants available in nurseries come from cooler coastal plant communities. Some can be grown in the hotter interior areas; some are visually incompatible; and many are horticulturally unsuitable. There are many plants from other Mediterranean climates that are both horticulturally and visually compatible in the various landscapes of California.

We now have an opportunity to achieve a new beginning in the planting of the California landscape. There is much to be done—research, education, and revised maintenance techniques. The foresight and maturity with which we deal with drought now will have long-lasting effects on the landscape of the future. We can retrofit our irrigation systems for more efficient water usage. We also need to retrofit our attitudes and aesthetic tastes. We need not sacrifice the image of paradise, "this other Eden."

AUSTRALIA—A SOURCE OF PACIFIC COAST PLANTS

LESTER HAWKINS

A LIMITED number of Australian plants have been cultivated in the West for more than a hundred years, and, looking back, I think it has been an unfortunate history. That this is so is certainly not due to the nurserymen who introduced these strange and marvelous plants, nor to the careful gardeners who used them, as we can see from the remains of their work in the city of Santa Barbara, California. The real culprits are those who planted hastily and in ignorance of the behavior of these plants. Greed, as embodied in Modern Economic Man, also played a part. The blue gum, for example, grows rapidly even in our Mediterranean climate. "What better use, then," said the entrepreneurs, "for these useless hills that dry up in the summer than to convert them to timber plantations and to inaugurate a fashion for gumwood interiors and furniture?" It was, as we all know, the wrong eucalypt for the purpose, but those responsible for the damage to the landscape were, by the time this was discovered, involved in other, far different speculative schemes.

Many subsequent settlers in California thought the blue gums were native trees, even though they often occurred in square plots and occasionally in straight rows. As they were handy, farmers planted them for windbreaks, although they are not particularly suitable for this purpose either. Again, being handy, they were planted in housing developments for quick effect. Homeowners in the hills destroyed their own and their neighbors' views with them, and they were planted in parks and to control soil erosion. Why? Because they were there. *Eucalyptus globulus* is a most notorious example, but similar histories could be traced for acacias, bottlebrushes, and many other Australian plants; there are now several times as many plants of the bottlebrush, *Callistemon lanceolatus*, in California as in the whole of Australia.

In the meantime the number of people to whom California is something more than orange groves, Yosemite Valley, and mild winters is growing. These people are developing a deep and lasting commitment to our grassy knolls, our brushlands, and our wild, foggy coast. Quite naturally they resent the large-scale intrusion of alien plants with different growth patterns, color, and scale. This is an unfortunate situation, as it tends to obscure the fact that the Australian flora contains a great number of flowering shrubs of distinction, beauty, and utility for our gardens, provided that they are used with modesty, discretion, and some semblance of the gardener's art. The Australian flora is distinct; for the most part, Australian plants do not look like other plants. Special care is needed for their placement in the garden, but the effort can be extraordinarily rewarding.

The Australian bush contains an almost unbelievable profusion of evergreen flowering shrubs. It is no exaggeration to say that there are at least two thousand species that are well worth cultivating, most of them picturesque or showy. Undoubtedly more such plants can be found there than in all the rest of the world. If we consider the protea family alone, we find that there are more than 200 grevilleas, 100 hakeas, nearly fifty banksias, fifty dryandras, and numerous species of *Adenanthos, Conospermum, Isopogon, Lambertia, Petrophile, Synaphea*, and other picturesque genera. Only a few gardeners have ever suspected the existence of such a wealth of new and marvelous garden plants.

Nearly as important as its sheer aesthetic impact is the large number of garden uses to which these plants lend themselves. One significant attraction is their ability to withstand drought and still look good; in fact, many Australian shrubs are far tougher in this regard than our own natives. They demonstrate most of the means woody plants have developed to withstand the absence of water for long periods. These include: tiny leaves; phyllodes or flattened branchlets replacing leaves altogether; fewer stomata or pores on leaf surfaces, reducing transpiration; thickened outer covering or cuticle to the leaves; stiffer cell walls; and, frequently, an overall coloring that reflects light and heat. It is true that the appearance of plants with these xerophytic qualities accords poorly with large and soft-leaved plants from more humid climates, but they have their own peculiar grace and luxuriance.

Particularly desirable for gardeners are the dwarf evergreen flowering shrubs. These plants are easy to accommodate and can be used in many ways—to edge paths and steps, to furnish odd corners, the spreading ones to clothe banks and the more upright ones to create those mounds and hummocks that so delight the eye. Australian shrubs are of all sizes, but the bush is particularly notable for its high percentage of dwarfs. A native plant nursery near Melbourne once listed in its catalog 550 species and varieties of shrubs averaging around two feet in height and an additional fifty that were completely prostrate.

The number of shrubs available to gardeners for badly drained areas is small and few of these are evergreen, but a number of Australian flowering shrubs naturally occur in temporary winter bogs, many of which dry out totally in summer. All of these are useful plants for low-lying garden areas; in fact, I have found them almost the only plants of suitable size and aspect for furnishing poorly drained areas on housing projects.

Similarly, there are Australian shrubs, often most attractive ones, for windbreaks, for brackish seacoast conditions, and for unusually rocky or impoverished sandy soils. It is, therefore, understandable that some western gardeners have devoted a good part of their professional lives to the introduction and cultivation of these plants. Here is a reservoir of often odd, rare, and useful plants even more voluminous for us than the Himalayas were for British gardeners in the epoch of great plant explorations.

Unfortunately, many otherwise remarkable plants are not suitable for introduction to the West; they grow in highly specialized conditions that are difficult or

The Stirling Range, low but dramatic mountains in Western Australia, supports a dense and diverse bush flora: above, Bluff Knoll and Kingia australis; *top right,* Isopogon formosus, *which has been grown in northern California; center right,* Dryandra nivea, *a dwarf spreading shrub with coarse, fern-like leaves that may prove well suited to conditions here; bottom right,* Lechenaultia formosa

impossible to duplicate or they are not hardy. To discover why this is so and where we should look for plants most likely to succeed, we should glance briefly at the whole of the island continent and its flora.

CLIMATE

Australia measures about 2,000 miles from north to south, about 3,000 miles across, and about a third of this area lies above the Tropic of Capricorn. It is a flat country with only a few low mountains to intercept the flow of moist air from the sea. The interior of the continent is dry range land and desert, and the areas of appreciable rainfall are all coastal strips varying from only a few miles to about 300 miles in depth. The southeast trade winds bring summer rain to a northern coastal strip and to the seaward side of the mountains of Queensland and part of New South Wales. Westerlies from the Indian Ocean are intercepted by the mountains of the southwestern corner of Australia, South Australia, and Victoria; these are the regions of Mediterranean climate with winter rains. The Sydney area benefits from both these air streams and has year-round rainfall. The island of Tasmania also has rain at all seasons—heavy on the western side of the mountains and light on the eastern side.

Broadly speaking, the flora of Australia is of two types. Tropical and semi-tropical rain forest dominates the vegetation of coastal Queensland and continues in pockets down the coast of New South Wales and even into Victoria. The chief characteristic of these areas is their dampness; they retain sufficient moisture even during dry seasons to support epiphytes, ferns, and a wide variety of evergreen, moisture-loving trees. No one family, and especially no one genus, of trees dominates the rain forest; eucalypts almost never grow there, although they are a dominant feature of the flora of most of the rest of Australia. The rain forest never knows fire; unlike the bush, to burn it is to destroy it, for these plants have never known the need to resprout. Here, the traveler is struck by the great age and size of the plants. *Tristania conferta*, a tree often planted in California, is a giant 250 feet high with an awesome buttressed trunk. *Nothofagus moorei*, one of the southern beeches, becomes an enormous multi-trunked tree with Gothic-looking, free-standing buttresses where suckering sprouts have grown around a long dead and decayed mother tree. High above are masses of the great orchid, *Dendrobium speciosum*, and alongside the trails a profusion of ferns and club mosses. There is a strong feeling of dampness even at the end of the dry season, and, although the eye grows accustomed to the dim light, it is necessary to use time exposures to take photographs even on the fastest film.

In the Blue Mountains west of Sydney there are pockets of rain forest, and their sudden appearance is startling to travelers. One moment you are in eucalyptus woodland with a dense growth of shrubs and the next you are in this entirely different, shadowy world with its wealth of trees. There is no gradual transition, no mixture of the two types of vegetation; the dividing line is clear and unmistakable.

All the rest of the flora of Australia has a surprisingly uniform character, excepting such areas as grasslands and alpine meadows, of which there are a number even in these low mountains. It consists of brushland or woodland or a mixture of the two that is sparse or dense depending upon the rainfall. Whether you are on the Queensland plateau, inland from the rain forest, where summer rains are the rule, or in the

Pultenaea capitata, *an erect shrub about a foot high, from the sand heath north of Perth*

Stirling range of southwestern Australia nearly 4,000 miles away, where the climate is Mediterranean, you see a dense mass of shrubs of many species; their heights and overall aspect in these widely separated locations are similar, and many of these are from the same genera. Or, again, as you travel inland away from the more heavily watered coastal areas, plants become sparser and the trees and shrubs take on an obviously xerophytic appearance. For all these differences, they are still trees and shrubs very similar to those seen near the coast. The eucalypts of the interior may have white trunks and light gray leaves, but they are still trees of roughly the same shape and form as those near the coast. There are no cacti and almost no succulents; indeed, there are few of the changes

we expect here when we leave the coastal woodland and chaparral to travel to the desert. There is also nothing like the change from the Cape flora to that of the Karoo in South Africa. The Australian flora is poor in both succulent and bulbous plants; we might say that in their place the trees and shrubs have developed an extraordinary range of adaptive devices to endure hardship. Also this flora is not rich either in annual or perennial herbaceous plants; colorful flowering plants that from a distance seem to be herbaceous, prove, upon closer inspection, to be woody.

Such is the Australian bush, the world's most extensive and intensive chaparral. At times the march of shrubs seems inexorable, invading swamps, salt pans, and sandy wastes that in other parts of the world are bare of vegetation or given over to grasses and sedges, stopping only at the edge of the sea, and, even here, overhanging outlying rocks as though to challenge this final obstacle. Low-lying swampy ground is the home of *Grevillea acanthifolia* and many other beautiful shrubs near Sydney, and a large number of well-known plants—*Boronia megastigma, Beaufortia sparsa, Banksia verticillata, B. occidentalis*, and the great Albany bottlebrush, *Callistemon speciosus*—in southwestern Australia. The rocky seacoast below Albany is the home of a profusion of such handsome shrubs as *Dryandra formosa, Banksia baxteri, B. speciosa*, and *Calocephalus brownii*. On the east coast, the Hawkesbury sandstones near Sydney form a low-lying area between the hills and the sea with numerous bays, inlets, and river mouths, the shores of which are entirely clothed with intertwining shrubs among which can be found the native rose, *Boronia serrulata*, the gray spider flower, *Grevillea buxifolia, Actinotus helianthi*, and many other delightful flowering shrubs.

We must keep in mind the vast extent of the Australian bush when we select shrubs for Pacific Coast gardens. The more knowledge we have of the native environment of a plant, the greater will be our chance of success in growing it. Of course, it is not always possible to predict with total accuracy on this basis; some alpines, for example, can be cultivated at low elevations and others resist the change. Nevertheless, there are some factors it is well to keep in mind, particularly those that have to do with hardiness.

Australia is an island. It has no great land mass on its poleward side and therefore is not subject to periodic great freezes. In general the plants, unlike our natives, are not much hardier than the average winter lows of their locality would suggest. And it is important to remember differences in latitude. For example, the whole of Western Australia lies on the equatorial side of 35°, which is about the equivalent latitude of San Luis Obispo, California. A third or more of the Mediterranean climate area of the state has never known frost. Inland, however, there are frosts and in the southern part of the region there are numerous frost pockets.

In general, winter temperatures in the states of South Australia and Victoria are lower than those of Western Australia; in fact, almost all the eastern plants I've grown have proved hardier than those from the western side of the continent. Plant hunters should look also for plants from higher altitudes. For complex reasons, altitude has more effect on temperature in the southern hemisphere than in the north; plants growing at 2,000 feet will generally be far hardier than those found at sea level.

An abundance of data on frost tolerance can be found in publications of the Society for Growing Australian Plants. Members of the society living in the colder parts of Australia have kept careful records and sent them to their editor. Also, all plants growing in the Canberra Botanic Garden are fair game; temperatures in the Australian capital city, which is in the mountains, drop to 10° F. almost every winter.

Here on the Pacific Coast, and especially in California, we are interested primarily in plants from the winter-rainfall parts of Australia. However, it should be noted that most Australian shrubs are drought tolerant, even those that come from areas of summer or year-round rainfall, all shrubs that is, except those found in the rain forest. Much of the continent has known occasional severe droughts which, like our occasional freezes, have resulted in plants that in this respect are far tougher than need be in average conditions.

One of the many dryandras found in Western Australia

PART TWO

WESTERN GARDENS

PLANTING THE PLANTSMAN'S GARDEN

LESTER HAWKINS

For all serious gardeners 1983 was a significant centennial, for it was in November 1883 that William Robinson's *The English Flower Garden* was published. This event was important not only for the English, but for gardeners everywhere who enjoy and want to grow a wide range of plants.

It is difficult to pinpoint revolutions in taste. Already, by 1883, Great Britain had seen a tremendous influx of plants from all over the world, and there were many gardens that were also sizable collections. However, Robinson's great work was at once a strongly worded manifesto and an enthusiastic spelling out of the possibilities of the plantsman's garden. It describes in considerable detail almost everything we need to know to plant at least one kind of informal and graceful garden in which a diversity of plants could be made to lie down in harmony.

Robinson's title is misleading; he covers not only flowers but every conceivable aspect of the gardener's art: hedges, trees, evergreen shrubs, even garden structures, rock gardens, and ponds. So complete is this remarkable book that the works of virtually all subsequent garden authors, from Gertrude Jekyll to Frances Perry and Graham Stuart Thomas, can be thought of as so many marginal notes to it. Thirty-six years before the appearance of Farrer's *English Rock Garden*, Robinson was urging a more naturalistic laying of rock and deep and gritty drainage for a truly successful alpine garden. Here, twenty-nine years before Miss Jekyll's *Colour Schemes for the Garden*, were many of the ideas for perennial borders that she carried out and expanded. Most astonishing, perhaps, are Robinson's lists of plants for various purposes. A hundred years later I am hard put to think of a vine, a fragrant plant, or a good perennial that he did not mention at least by genus.

Robinson and Jekyll both hated formality and were fond of describing their plantings as "natural" or as similar to "painting pictures." I don't think these authors were aware how odd their choice of words was. Most often, the plant combinations they mentioned were unlike anything found in nature; even as "pictures," there is nothing on earth they could be said to represent. By a curious inversion, Robinson makes the extraordinary claim that if English gardens were as well planted as he would like them to be, artists would prefer them to nature as subject matter.

An area planted with stachys, lavender, valerian, and furcraeas by the pool in the author's garden

The idea of nature is obviously large and many-faceted. It has been variously defined, and at different times differing choices among its many faces have been emphasized. Most often words like "natural" are the rallying cries of those in revolt against what they see as the excesses of artifice and the stilted fashions that threaten to gain a stranglehold on the morals or tastes of a civilization. We can, therefore, best discover what these authors meant not by asking for definitions, but by examining what they were rebelling against and how they proposed to remedy it.

VICTORIAN ARTIFICE

In mid-Victorian times, before Robinson's influence began to be felt and after the late-eighteenth-century fashion of landscape gardening, there was a long period of return to formality. Parterres, hedges, fountains, bedding-out schemes, long, straight avenues, and abundant terracing were the order of the day. Judging from all the descriptions, it was deplorable, lacking as it did the grandeur of French formal gardens and the grace and intricacy of their Italian counterparts. There were statues, but they were awful statues; fountains, but they were ugly; pergolas and gazebos, but they were ungainly. In the growing prosperity of the British Empire, most of these things were bought by the newly prosperous to impress rather than to charm. Robinson's descriptions of all this are exasperated; he hated it so. This is, in a way, unfortunate, because it made him an uneven and crotchety writer. To discover his remarkable world, we must fight again a battle that has long since been won, and it is difficult to discern the peaceful beauty he expounded through the turmoil and dust of his struggle.

Robinson particularly hated excess terraces, which he compares to railway embankments and to fortifications "made by Uncle Toby and an army of Corporal Tims." He writes:

The landscape gardener, too often led by custom, falls in with the notion that every house, no matter what its position, should be fortified by terraces and he busies himself forming them even on level ground, and large sums are spent on fountains, vases, statues, ballustrades, useless walls, and stucco work out of place.

The plantings are, if anything, worse:

On top of all this formality of design of our day were grafted the most formal and inartistic ways of arranging flowers that ever came into the head of man . . . Bedding out, or marshalling the flowers in stiff lines and geometrical patterns, is entirely a thing of our precious time and 'carpet' gardening is simply a further remove in ugliness.

Much of this folly, Robinson says—and this I think is still true today—comes from giving architects too much power and from the "too facile labors of the drawing board artist." It would be difficult to exaggerate the depth of his feelings on this score:

Any pupil in an architect's office will get out a drawing for the kind of garden we see everywhere . . . It is the difference between life and death we have to think of, and never to the end of time shall we get the garden beautiful formed or planted save by men who know something of the earth and its flowers, shrubs, and trees.

In Robinson's mind, the natural was a clear and beckoning goal that rose above all considerations of style, a word he hated and usually put in quotes. Criticizing a garden writer who talks about style, he says:

What is the result to anybody who looks from words to things? That there are two styles; the one straitlaced, mechanical, with much wall and stone, with fountains and sculpture; the other the natural, which, once free of the house, accepts the ground lines of the earth herself as the best and gets plant beauty from the flowers and trees arranged in picturesque ways.

And there we have it; the common conceit that one has risen above all fashion and all history into the light of the truth.

The natural and the picturesque are not the geometrical, the architectural, and the formal. What, then, are they? Robinson's efforts at definition are vague, but we can infer much from his descriptions of his favorite garden projects, his flower borders, shady walks, rock arrangements, and bog gardens; from his notes on the placement of trees and shrubs; and from his ideas of light and shade and the circulation of air in the garden.

THE ROBINSON IDEAL

Central to his thinking is the use of an abundance of plants; a feature of nature is said to be variety, and "the question is, how the garden lover is to enjoy as many of these treasures as his conditions allow of." Apart from the woods where there is natural leaf mold, there is no bare ground, and in all the descriptions there is a feeling of luxuriance, sometimes even a riot of foliage, flowers, and plant forms.

Robinson quotes with approval the artist and gardener, Frank Miles, who writes:

Well, supposing the back of the border filled with delphiniums, phloxes and roses, pegged down, and other summer and autumn blooming plants. . . I should carpet the ground at the back with spring blooming flowers, so that when the roses are bare and the delphiniums and phloxes have not pushed above ground, the border should even then be a blaze of beauty. Crocuses, snowdrops, aconites and primroses are quite enough for that purpose. The whole space under the roses I should cover with the common wood anemone and the golden wood anemone, and early cyclamens and the earliest dwarf daffodils. And among the roses and paeonies and other medium-sized shrubs I would put all the taller lilies, such as require continual shade on their roots; and such as pardalinum and the Californian lilies generally, the Japanese, Chinese and finer American lilies. Now we come to the front of the border, and here I would have combinations, such as the great St. Bruno's lily and the delicate hybrid columbines, primroses planted over hardy gladioli . . . carnations and daffodils planted so that the carnations form a blaze of blue-green for the delicate creams and oranges of the daffodils. . . .

The picture gradually unfolds: densely planted borders, vines on pergolas and walls (and sometimes on trees and shrubs as well), rock and dry-wall gardens chock full of plants that thrive there, ponds edged with reeds, water irises, cannas, and much more. As we walk into the woods, the paths are bordered at first with closely planted sun-loving plants, then those that like the shelter and frost protection of dappled shade, and finally to the genuine shade lovers. Some tropical plants are bedded out—bananas, tender palms, and philodendrons.

Any feeling of congestion is relieved by broad, rolling lawns, and all is contrived to fit into its setting with as little alteration of grade as possible. Above all, there is geometry only near the house.

We have, in short, what the world now knows as the English garden. In England, there has been no real revolution in taste since the appearance of *The English Flower Garden*. Writers such as Christopher Lloyd, Margery Fish, and Beth Chatto have laid more emphasis on selectivity, refinement, and unity of effect, but they all stress variety in planting—though none would urge, as Robinson did, that the gardener plant "as many of these treasures as his conditions allow of."

Alas, we cannot say that William Robinson superseded all styles and found his way to the ultimate truth of the natural mode. He is, we must say it, very *fin de siècle*, or late Victorian in his opulence. Natural would be a strange term to apply to the garden feature for which he and Gertrude Jekyll are most famous: the long, straight, double flower border backed on both sides with hedges. Or to what Robinson approvingly called "one of the brightest colored beds I have ever seen," consisting of *Sedum acre* 'Elegans', creamy white; *Sedum glaucum*, gray; *Herniaria glabra*, green; *Aptenia cordifolia* 'Variegatum' (*Mesembryanthemum cordifolium*), light yellow; bright orange and scarlet alternantheras; the central plants being *Grevillea robusta* and variegated abutilons. Clearly, for all his protestations, Robinson was a product of his time.

I am sometimes appalled by Robinson, but I far more often agree with him and the feeling of communion and rapport runs deep. I agree that plantings should be graceful, well-rounded, and informal, and that they should charm rather than impress. I agree that plans on paper drawn up in offices do not make gardens. And I too like to use a wide variety of plants, al-

Above: brooms and rock roses cover a bank with achilleas, pinks, and other herbaceous plants at their feet in the author's garden at Western Hills Nursery; left: martagon lilies, variegated grass, and lavenders at Knightshayes Court, Devonshire, England

though perhaps not with quite the same abandon. Even before I read *The English Flower Garden*, Robinson's world in many ways was mine as well. In our changed circumstances, I hope I have kept something of his spirit if little of his letter in the following observations and suggestions of my own for creating effective plantings.

First, however, I should like briefly to compare the "natural" plantings of Robinson, Jekyll, and their disciples with those other "natural" plantings of the great landscape gardeners a hundred years previously. On the one hand we have a crowded canvas bright with colored foliage and flowers; on the other there is quiet, uneventful serenity. But that is not all; there is also an extreme difference in scale. Gertrude Jekyll spent her life earnestly tending a ten-acre plot. "Capability" Brown had hundreds, sometimes thousands, of acres at his disposal, and, once planted, they were never to be dug again.

The differences are there for all to see at Stourhead, in Wiltshire, where the followers of Robinson and Jekyll have planted colored foliage trees and flowering shrubs in a sparse and serene eighteenth-century landscape. There are many, even today, who find these additions excrescences that should be removed. To Brown, the "natural" was a landscape stretching as far as the eye could see, similar to one that might be found in some privileged place undisturbed by man. To Jekyll and Robinson it was bits and pieces of nature—the edge of a pond, the crowded verge of a copse, or a riot of wildflowers—to be imported, laboriously cultivated, and used to grace a well-trodden path. There are many other differences, of course. We also have to consider such factors as the great plant introductions into England in the nineteenth century, the late-eighteenth-century taste for classical simplicity, and the Victorian

taste for opulence. Nevertheless, it is plain that nature is an alluring but varied guide, and now, a hundred years later still, we shall try again to capture the natural, and on plots that have become even smaller.

Mixed Plantings

Perhaps the most useful planting for small gardens and one that can be extraordinarily handsome almost anywhere is a border that mixes, more or less deliberately, the basic categories of plants—basic, that is, in the gardening sense. Perennials, shrubs, bulbs, and grasses can be combined in ways reminiscent of memorable scenes in nature and capable of providing interest the year round. I remember in Greece in late spring, on the island of Evia, a mixture that could well be copied just as it was. In the middle ground were euphorbias, lavenders, and campanulas (some of which were twining through the lavenders). These were backed by brooms and rock roses with low meadow annuals and bulbs—mostly anemones—in the foreground. For a garden we might want to extend the flowering season by adding later-flowering bulbs—*Allium christophii* (*A. albopilosum*) and *A. pulchellum*, perhaps—and some summer- and fall-flowering low perennials—origanums undoubtedly, and helichrysums.

Along a path at Knightshayes Court in the west of England there is a sizable drift of white martagon lilies with, in the foreground, a silvery and blue grass interplanted with dwarf lavenders. This planting has the merit of great simplicity. The totality was a memorable picture (as Gertrude Jekyll would say), but it also was effective in displaying the individual beauty of each of these plants.

One obvious advantage of the mixed border is that it is the best possible home for bulbs, which are often difficult to place in the perennial border and by themselves leave bare ground for considerable periods. In another English garden *Allium rosenbachianum* was in flower among *Stachys macrantha*, with its deep rose panicles, both in front of a shell-pink dwarf rose. Without detracting from the whole effect, it is possible in such a planting to leave bits of bare ground for bulbs such as nerines, after carefully calculating whether the neighbors on all sides will be compatible at flowering time.

Innumerable plants are available for the mixed border, but it is important to keep them all more or less within the same general scale (a useful cue one can take from nature). By scale I do not mean only size; it is not always a thing you can measure, but it is something we can generally agree on. A mullein, for example, may shoot skyward out of a bed of thistles by the roadside. The mullein has larger leaves, greater height, and a thicker stem than the thistle, but both are obviously lush, lowland plants, and neither looks out of scale. If, on the other hand, we make the mistake of planting a diminutive dianthus (which belongs in the alpine garden) with artemisias and lavenders a foot or more high, the dianthus not only will eventually be overrun, it will look out of place from the start. I have found that a good way to judge scale is to allow one or preferably two of the plants I intend to use to stand as a measure against which I judge the others—*Origanum hybridum* and *Salvia officinalis*, for example, or *Alchemilla vulgaris* and *Geranium macrorrhizum*.

There are many shrubs that can be used with plants of the stature of a medium-sized dianthus for pathside plantings. Among my favorites are the elegant *Arctostaphylos nummularia* 'Anchor Bay', many hebes of the size of *Hebe menziesii*, and *Rhododendron racemosum*, one of the best small

rhododendrons for general planting in the garden. Many barberries are possibilities, including *Berberis calliantha*, with its graceful hanging flowers and the dwarf red-leaved *B. thunbergii* 'Atropurpurea'. Dwarf brooms are not only showy in flower but offer a variety of picturesque evergreen forms for year-round effect. And most of the well-known deciduous flowering shrubs have dwarf species or forms—*Syringa patula* (*S. palibiniana*), a dwarf *Viburnum plicatum* 'Mariesii', or *Philadelphus × purpureomaculatus* 'Nuage Rose', to name a few.

Candidates for the herbaceous parts of our pathside can often be found among those plants that are beautiful, but too large or too rampant for the rock garden, which should be reserved for diminutive gems from the high mountains. Such plants are *Omphalodes cappadocica*, *Gypsophila repens* 'Rosea', *Lithodora diffusa* 'Grace Ward' (*Lithospermum diffusum*), *Helichrysum* 'Moe's Gold' (which blooms in October), and *Diascia cordata*.

Grasses somewhat on the same scale are the Japanese blood grass, *Imperata cylindrica*, the bulbous grass, *Arrhenatherum elatius* 'Variegatum', and *Hakonechloa macra* 'Albo Aurea'. There are also many colorful sedges, particularly from the New Zealand Alps. All of these plants are ideal in size for the average garden path, for mixed plantings in front of larger shrubs, in front of small trees on the sunny side, or for islands in lawns that do not obtrude far above the grass.

One way to start thinking about such a planting is to begin with two plants that are extraordinarily handsome together—*Trachelium caeruleum* and the pink stokesia, for example—and gradually add plants that will further enhance the effect, such as *Aster × frikartii* 'Mönch', the beautiful deep red grass, *Pennisetum setaceum* 'Cupreum',

Picea glauca 'Montgomery', and *Allium pulchellum*. Another way is to choose a geographical theme, a mixed planting of Mediterraneans, for example, or of California natives.

The mixed planting is ideal for displaying plant collections, provided the plants are of a size to be accommodated. A collection of dwarf grasses or sempervivums, for example, can be planted along a curving path together with bulbs, small perennials, and alpines of the right size in a way that gives a natural touch without detracting from the enthusiast's interest in the plants themselves.

Here I have been thinking of more or less ordinary pathside plantings, since I agree with Robinson and Jekyll that all spaces in the garden should be utilized. When I see gardens that are primarily roses, perhaps, or rhododendrons, and the paths are either not planted or given over to a dull ground cover, I always wonder at the lost opportunities. It is true that many people see only plants and not gardens, but I have always considered this a curable deficiency.

Many variants of the mixed planting format are possible—those of larger or smaller scale than the above, for example, depending upon the plants to be used and whether delicacy or boldness is the aim.

PLANTING THE PLANTSMAN'S GARDEN: HERBACEOUS PERENNIALS

LESTER HAWKINS

Iᴛ is an axiom that serious gardeners love plants for themselves. They want to possess them, to grow them, to look at them, and, more generally and simply, to have them around. Here I am concerned with that aspect of gardening that consists in growing these plants well and displaying them well in association. Therefore I should like to put aside for the moment not only such peripheral matters as stones, statues, ponds, and gazebos, but also the various functions that plants may serve as privacy screens, as settings for houses, and as something more orderly than nature usually provides by way of ground cover. It is no doubt true that plants may serve certain useful functions and be beautiful at the same time, but I want to talk about planting as we would about music when we go to a concert and simply lend ourselves to the performance. In other words, I want to reverse the usual order that starts with garden design and ends with planting. If we begin instead with plants and their associations, perhaps we can then work back to the scheme of the garden as a whole with new insights.

In the last chapter I noted that William Robinson and Gertrude Jekyll initiated a modern style of gardening using an abundance of plants informally disposed, which they thought of as natural. Their use of this word has come under scrutiny and various substitutions have been suggested, such as "in the natural style" or "in the language of nature." I think we could clarify this matter by saying that the garden plants we buy or propagate have necessarily been torn from their origins in plant communities in nature and that we try to arrange them in our gardens in a way that will give them new homes—an art whose final aim is to appear artless and natural in that sense.

HERBACEOUS PLANTINGS

Earlier in this century the heart of the English garden was the herbaceous border, an elaborate arrangement of non-woody flowering plants, often well over two hundred feet long and about fifteen feet—or sometimes much more—deep. As brought to fruition in some of the famous gardens, this represented the most tenuous and difficult project in the history of gardening. To be successful, the border had to fulfill a staggering number of conditions. It had to present, in succession, a satisfying and sizable number of plants in full flower over a considerable period of time. All the plants had to be arranged so as to be visible from the front of the border, which was usually a lawn path. As the plants came into flower they had to be compatible with their neighbors and with the border as a whole. Above all, the entire border had to present a diversity of plants with a unity of overall effect—from every angle of vision it had to be a "living picture," as Miss Jekyll was fond of saying. And all this was just a beginning. The great borders also had to qualify as distinctive works of art; they had, in other words, to offer the viewer plant combinations and, if possible, plants themselves that could be found nowhere else.

Some gardeners tried to plant a border that would put on floral displays from spring to fall, but Gertrude Jekyll considered this feat impossible. Her own border was at its best in late summer and was considered satisfactory from July until October; other parts of the garden were used for spring and summer displays. Even so, a considerable amount of tinkering was involved in keeping the border going for three months. Many and devious were the contrivances used. One of them might be called plant substitution. Thus, if we want to grow *Gypsophila paniculata* with its starry flowers in magnificent heads four feet across, we have the problem of four feet of blank space until this great flowering event occurs. Accordingly, in this space we grow oriental poppies. They, however, rather soon leave brown seed heads; therefore we also grow nasturtiums in this plot to cover the "greater part of the brown seed spray."

Another device used we might call successive plant hiding. Thus, the bare stems of delphiniums are covered by the everlasting pea, and when this goes out of bloom, *Clematis × jackmanii* takes over, followed in turn by *Clematis flammula*. And none of this is simple. Miss Jekyll explains:

It must not be supposed that they are just lumped one above another so that the under ones have their leafy growth smothered.

They are always being watched, and, bit by bit, the earlier growths are removed as soon as their respective plants are better without them.

Still another trick is to pull down plants whose natural habit is tall and upright to cover the plants that are past flowering. Finally, when all else fails, it was considered wise to have a stock of perennials growing in pots for rapid transplantation to the border. In no event should holes be allowed to threaten the totality of the "living picture."

Of course, keeping the border going in summer was only a small part of what had to be done. Elaborate procedures were devised, many of them by Miss Jekyll, for staking plants that needed support in a way that would not show, and this was done in late winter. The habits and requirements of all the plants had to be known well. It was important to know, for example, the volume of roots required for maximum performance. *Eryngium* 'Violetta' needs to be left undisturbed for five years or more to give rise to a showy clump of flowering stalks. *Macleaya cordata* (*Bocconia cordata*), on the other hand, spreads widely and most of its roots will need to be dug up and thrown away every year. All this is in addition to soil preparation, top dressings, mulches, drainage preparations, and other gardening practices that will guarantee maximum healthy growth of a close planting of large-scale plants.

Difficult and intricate in both its inception and its maintenance, the perennial border was strictly for intrepid gardeners. Said Miss Jekyll:

Good gardening means patience and dogged determination. . . . Those who do not know are apt to think that hardy flower gardening of the best kind is easy. It is not easy at all. It has taken me half a lifetime merely to find what is best worth doing, and a good slice of the other half to puzzle out the ways of doing it.

In the course of time, ingenious British gardeners found many ways to heighten the originality and elegance of their borders. Differing placements of plants according to size were attempted, sometimes with signal results. Early in the history of the border it was realized that a simple scheme using low plants in front with a gradual rise to very tall ones in the rear could be improved upon. A more compelling form and apparent artlessness could result from placing an occasional bold plant in front, from massing tall plants here and there to prevent a too-uniform skyline, and from carrying a carpet of low plants all the way from the front to the rear in a few places. Considerable attention was paid to the form of plants—whether, for example, they sent up flowers in rounded masses or in spikes. Sometimes tall grasses or colored-foliage shrubs would be introduced to create a backdrop for certain flowers or to give a formally bold effect.

Most important, however, was the arrangement of plants according to flower and foliage color. Miss Jekyll's most influential work is a volume that covers many aspects of gardening but is symptomatically entitled *Colour Schemes for the Flower Garden*. Here, with a few omissions, is how she describes the color scheme of her own border:

At the two ends there is a groundwork of grey and glaucous foliage. With this, at the near or western end, there are flowers of pure blue, grey-blue, palest yellow and palest pink. The coloring then passes through stronger yellows to orange and red. By the time the middle space . . . is reached the color is strong and gorgeous, but, as it is in good harmonies, it is never garish. Then the color strength recedes in inverse sequence through orange and deep yellow to pale yellow, white and pal-

Double herbaceous borders at Bampton Manor, Oxfordshire

est pink; again with blue-grey foliage. But at this eastern end, instead of pure blues, we have purples and lilacs.

Today we can still see in England a number of beautiful borders with pronounced color themes. One has only blue and yellow flowers; another simply eliminates all strong colors; still another consists entirely of warm colors. There are carefully blended borders and others with deliberately contrasting flower tints. It is true that perhaps an equal number of famous borders are not based on such color themes, but even here I have noticed that plants have been carefully placed among their neighbors to display their colors to advantage. The effect of these borders as a whole is that of a giant Victorian bouquet, a wild and seemingly careless arrangement of plant forms and colors that in reality demands extreme care. Anyone who gardens can see that none of this is easy. A great

Achillea *'Moonshine' with a background of* Salvia nemorosa

Bay of perennials with Macleaya cordata *at left and* Salvia uliginosa, Phlox maculata *'Miss Lingard', and* Linaria triornithophora

Recently planted border in the author's garden with alstroemerias in foreground

many years often went by before most borders reached the degree of perfection their creators were seeking.

Such is, or perhaps I should say was, the English perennial border. I have tried to describe it at some length for a number of reasons. One is that some gardeners still plant borders of this kind. But far more important here is the fact that the English border was the last great garden form in our history to have won wide acceptance, and the surviving examples are works of almost incomparable beauty. There are many reasons, however, why I cannot in all honesty urge gardeners today to set out on the laborious path outlined by Gertrude Jekyll. In part this is because they are apt not to have the time and resources to carry this great art form to new heights and the results therefore would be likely to fall short of achieving the magic and charm needed to be truly successful.

There is another more complicated reason to search for other ways of using perennial plants in the garden. For all its compelling beauty, I find that the grand border subordinated plants too much to overall effect. In the case of those plants that flower profusely but otherwise are of no interest, little is lost. But many superb herbaceous plants from the prairies, low mountains, valleys, and streamsides of the temperate world have great beauty of form as well as flower. They deserve better than simply to serve as ingredients in a bouquet. Today we must find new homes for the large lowland flowering plants that most of us find such an essential ingredient in our gardens.

Herbaceous perennials, together with large deciduous bulbs and grasses, are the most difficult of all plants to site. Because of their long-lived roots or other parts below ground, these plants need more or less permanent homes. But since at certain seasons their parts above ground are small or nonexistent while at others they are siz-

able, considerable foresight and planning are necessary to visualize their effects both at maturity and in dormancy. We do not like bare spaces in winter here on the Pacific Coast where gardens are enjoyed year round, and in summer a sudden growth of lush foliage risks shading out neighboring plants.

The easiest of all gardens to maintain is one made up of long-lived, mostly evergreen, well-behaved shrubs. Such a garden needs a minimum of pruning, weeding, and cleaning and no cultivation at all; it is, however, uneventful even when some of the shrubs are briefly showy in flower. Perennials, on the other hand, need a maximum of pruning, weeding, and cultivation, even sometimes staking and additional managing, but they are marvelously eventful. Some of them spring out of the ground with the advent of warm weather, grow rapidly to prodigious heights, and flower for half or more of the time they are above ground.

This is, of course, a somewhat simplified picture. There are some evergreen perennials that behave more like shrubs and vice versa. It is, however, a useful image to keep in mind when allocating spaces. We need to decide, and decide quickly, how much of the garden we wish to give over to plants of a highly eventful character and balance this against our resources for maintenance. Having accomplished this imaginative exercise, we can then find places in the garden to site perennials that will show off these plants to advantage and give us many of the qualities of the great border with far less labor.

Perennials in Bays Among Shrubs

Planting perennials in small groupings in a number of plots among shrubs and small trees seems to me one way of managing the problems associated with the grand flower border. Because of their smaller number, it becomes vastly more feasible to imagine how certain associations of plants will look at maturity. Also, many of the problems of maintaining a continuous succession of flowers will be solved simply by assigning shorter periods of duty to each plot; thus, when the full flowering of one such bay is diminishing, another somewhere along the path is preparing to take over. With enough care, no special contrivances other than deadheading will be necessary to keep these plots looking garden-worthy.

What we are to imagine is a continuous series of flowering events throughout a larger area of the garden to replace the concentrated show Robinson and Jekyll demanded. The drama of these events, of course, depends upon our skill as gardeners—whether, for example, we find the most striking combinations or site our enclaves for maximum effect. Even the sizes and shapes of the plots we create are important.

In a bay in our own garden, we decided to plant only perennials that flower in late summer. Spring and early summer interest in this part of the garden is already provided by nearby flowering shrubs and trees, two clematises that have been trained over supports, and mixed pathside plantings above and below.

The primary objective was to show off *Artemisia lactiflora*, a beautiful and statuesque but untypical member of its genus. This plant grows to over five feet, has dark green foliage topped by graceful panicles of creamy white flowers, and needs semi-shade to perform well. To allow the full stature of the plant to be appreciated, it is surrounded with much lower, blue-flowered geraniums, for which this exposure is also ideal in our climate.

In the foreground of this arrangement is a large mound of three plants of *Nepeta*

gigantea. Probably a hybrid, this looks like the plant often sold in nurseries as *Nepeta × faassenii*, but it grows twice as high and wide (three by three feet). Beyond this mound and well to one side of the artemisia is perovskia, with spires of light blue over silvery gray, finely divided leaves. Beyond this again is the tall, late-flowering *Campanula latifolia*. Off to one side is a group of *Phlox paniculata* 'Norah Leigh', which has delicate pink flowers and equally delicate cream and pink variegated leaves.

Between the phlox and the artemisia is the big, globular, soft-yellow thistle, *Centaurea glastifolia*. On the other side of the artemisia is the tall *Rudbeckia nitida* 'Herbstsonne', which has primrose yellow flowers with green centers. This would also be a good place to site the giant annual rudbeckia, *Rudbeckia maxima*, with its magnificent display of thousands of small black-eyed-Susan daisies.

The only other important part of this planting is a stand of *Aster × frikartii* 'Mönch', with its great mound of blue asters produced over a long season. There are a number of other single, smaller plants. One is *Potentilla* 'Gibson's Scarlet', which blooms sparingly over a long period, and there are a few plants of *Aquilegia longissima*, which flower in the spring and whose foliage seems to survive the crowding of larger neighbors.

Of course, this late-flowering enclave is not bare in spring and early summer. The plants chosen for it have good foliage, and the plot forms part of the general leafy garden background until it flowers.

Just beyond our perennial enclave is a patch of *Helleborus foetidus* for late winter flowers, a stand of Evansia irises for early spring, and alstroemerias for late spring and early summer. There is a succession of flowering shrubs from *Daphne bholua* in mid-winter to *Hydrangea aspera* (*H. villosa*) in late summer.

The deliberate stage management of the plot I have just described is not typical of the garden as a whole, as we can tell if we enlarge our vision to include the neighboring trees, shrubs, and other plants. If I ask myself how these plants came to be where they are, the answer has perhaps more to do with their well-being than with any purely aesthetic considerations. Soon after publication of the works of Robinson and Jekyll a schism among their followers became apparent, dividing those whose primary concern was "the garden beautiful" from those who, above all, wanted to grow a range of plants to perfection. E. A. Bowles was one of the latter, and in 1914 he wrote:

I fear I am a little impatient of the school of gardening that encourages the selection of plants merely as artistic furniture, chosen for color only, like ribbons or embroidery silks. I feel sorry for plants that are obliged to make a struggle for life in uncongenial situations because their owner wishes all things of those shades of pink, blue or orange to fit in next to the grey or crimson planting. . . .

In my own case, my habit of trying important new additions to the garden in three locations to give the plants a fair trial more or less precludes total control and unity of aesthetic effect. This says nothing of the anarchy caused by planting out seedlings of shrubs and trees I cannot even find described in the books. All this does not mean, however, that plants are placed just anywhere among their neighbors. Many agonizing decisions are made in an effort to combine a desire for experimentation with a longing for a harmonious garden. Speaking of his own method, E. A. Bowles writes:

The distribution of plants in this garden has been governed chiefly by a sort of extra sense that seems to be developed by many enthusiastic gardeners, a sympathetic understanding derived from a new plant's appearance only when the power is perfected. . . .

In general I would say that it is because so much of the garden is planned only in this intuitive way that I welcome the occasional opportunity to try self-consciously to bring off a well planned coup, and, of course, the herbaceous perennial with its varying heights and floral mass is the ideal plant for this purpose.

Another, somewhat smaller bay, also given over to late-flowering plants, is ideally situated in front of a sizable group of *Melianthus major*. This much maligned shrub forms a beautiful background for herbaceous plants with its great, jagged, blue-green leaves that themselves have the look of a giant perennial. Here have been planted several of a pink form of *Sedum spectabile*, which has foliage of the same blue-gray and whose large, flat flower clusters remain beautiful in the autumn when they have darkened to a deep rosy brown. Behind the sedum are a few plants of the late-flowering *Cimicifuga racemosa* with, in front of these and among the sedums, an aconite, *Aconitum carmichaelii* (erroneously known as *A. fischeri*). These are all lovely and majestic plants.

In front of this display is a brilliant blue patch of late-flowering *Ceratostigma plumbaginoides*. These flowers provide the climax to a long season in this part of the garden, where there are also early bulbs, early-summer-flowering lilies rising out of the melianthus (which is cut back severely every spring), and a somewhat later-flowering dierama off to one side.

PLANTING THE PLANTSMAN'S GARDEN: MORE HERBACEOUS PERENNIALS

LESTER HAWKINS

I N the preceding chapter I mentioned a division between, on the one hand, those gardeners who are primarily plant collectors and are more interested in the plants themselves and their health than the total effect of their various associations, and, on the other hand, those who are more concerned with the beauty of a path, a view, and, ultimately, of a garden as a whole. I should like to think of these not as two irreconcilable stances but as two opposed moments, the systole and diastole, of gardening. It is true that when I stand in one of these positions I only dimly see the other. Either I am trying to improve a view and am busily planting or transplanting to that end, or I am trying to find the ideal conditions for a plant I can see in my mind's eye as a magnificent specimen.

These two poles of the gardening activity ought, however, to be self-correcting. Too much concern with planning—color schemes, foliage similarities or contrasts, floral combinations—and the plants become no more than material for the garden, like ornaments or paths. But too many specimens and the result is bewildering; views disappear, and, worst of all, the plants cease to provide the necessary setting for each other. Planting is always problematic (as time goes on it causes me more, not less, anxiety) and this is one of the contradictions whose solution (or transcendence) I think of as inspiration. I believe that what is finally most distinctive about a garden owes far more to hundreds of these inspired decisions than to the basic idea, however grand, that was its starting point.

PERENNIAL ISLANDS

Two modern English authors, Alan Bloom and Graham Stuart Thomas, have written extensively on perennials and their books have become standard works of reference. As we might expect, both have made valuable suggestions for using these plants in the garden.

Alan Bloom, who owns the world's largest perennial nursery, has developed the idea of islands of herbaceous plants in lawns. This can be an attractive format and has become quite popular in Britain where sizable lawns are common and easy to maintain. It allows for small, manageable groupings of perennials and for a three-dimensional composition that can be viewed from all sides. Where the idea has been put into practice, as in the extensive grounds at Mr Bloom's nursery, the lawns

Penstemon *'Hidcote Pink'*

Eryngium *'Violetta'*

Eryngium pandanifolium *by a path in the author's garden*

are converted into wide, grassy paths that meander among flowering plants.

Since most perennials are considerably less than head-height, it is possible to look across a nearby island to others in the distance. This offers the prospect of going down directly into a garden—a kind of idealized meadow—of flowering plants, which, no longer ranked in borders, become intimately present to us. It is the ideal home for these plants, many of which are native to meadows, and it allows their individuality to be displayed to its fullest extent.

There is, however, a consequence of the idea that is not usually spelled out. Since several islands can be seen in one sweeping view, the serious gardener would want to make the most of this circumstance. He would want to introduce some thematic order into the entire complex of several islands and to intensify the effect of these continuously shifting, kaleidoscopic views. Seen in this light, the format coud be still more demanding than that of the grand border, and we can onl imagine the strictures Gertrude Jekyll would have placed on it had the idea occurred or appealed to her.

Here on the Pacific Coast the comparative rarity of large lawns and the difficulties involved in their maintenance severely limit the applictiton of Alan Bloom's idea. Usually, our lawns are valued for their open space and those who can afford them are not apt to want them pitted in winter with beds of largely dormant perennials, although that problem could be partially solved by planting their edges with low evergreen plants. Still I think we should keep the island notion in our vocabulary of gardening. Elsewhere I have urged the use of islands of low, mounding shrubs for the hillsides of country gardens in place of lawns, and here I think it is worth contem-

plating the possibility of beds of perennials among the shrubs that are treated in this way. The versatility of new irrigation systems that allow the watering of separate plots at different times makes such plantings possible, and the combination of a basically evergreen effect with interspersed masses of summer-flowering plants is inviting.

MIXED PLANTINGS:
GARDENING IN FOUR LAYERS

We have so far not mentioned one obvious possibility for placing perennials in the garden—that they should be planted here and there to rise above ground covers, mingle with shrubs, form specimen plantings against fences, and so on. "The place of perennials in the garden," says Graham Stuart Thomas, "is *everywhere*, to act as complements to the greater or lesser things about them." In place of the laborious perennial border, Thomas urges the return to an earlier style of gardening when plants of all kinds were grown together. It is a kind of gardening sometimes called gardening in four layers, with emphasis on blending the plants of the garden by height. Thomas describes such a garden as one "where there are some trees giving retreats for shade-loving shrubs and plants, and casting their dappling of shade across the lawn; groups of larger shrubs on corners and elsewhere to give shape to the views and to create surprises; and a general mixture throughout of dwarf shrubs, perennials and groundcovers, with bulbs to provide added interest."

This, too, is an inviting prospect and one can easily imagine cimicifugas growing behind daphnes or some aconites or campanulas arising among dwarf shrubs that have flowered in the spring. In Graham Stuart Thomas' gardens (he has made three) photographs show the format carried to a kind of perfection. I, too, am fond of mixed borders and think they should comprise a large portion of any plantsman's garden. However, I have two objections to using perennials only in this way. One is that whereas I can imagine certain plants as ideal components of such borders, others seem less well adapted and are better seen among other herbaceous plants. A far more important objection, however, is that, if at all possible, one does not want to forego those displays of certain combinations of perennials that Miss Jekyll called variously "brilliant" and "gorgeous."

Gardening in four layers is a useful image, but it is also useful to think in terms of the creation of habitats. Part of a garden, even a small one, should be reminiscent of a woods, another part should be open hillside or a clearing, and, where we can manage it, there should be north slopes, south slopes, dry areas, and bogs. The function of mixed borders would be primarily to blend these areas together. Thus, there are many low ground-cover plants and subalpines in the garden, but somewhere these coalesce into a true rock garden where the best high alpines can be grown. Similarly, there are numerous herbaceous perennials growing in places that suit them best and in mixed borders, but these in turn become massive displays here and there, like pieces of a meadow of pure flowers.

THREE PERENNIAL BAYS

With all these possibilities in mind, I should like to take another brief look at the idea of bays of herbaceous plants among shrubs. In a less miscellaneous garden than our own, one where all the principal plantings were specified on a plan and the woody plants were mostly California na-

tives, three bays were left for perennials. The object was to provide summer flowers in an otherwise spring-flowering garden that has a minimum of irrigation in an area of limited water supply. This garden is near the coast and these particular shrubs were planted on its westward side as a windbreak. Originally I had thought to plan a perennial border along the entire length of the plot with the windbreak as a backdrop, but the maintenance that would be required seemed excessive. The alternative of three bays not only solved this problem, but also allowed us to increase the evergreen effect of the entire planting in winter.

After considering an enormous range of possibilities, we finally decided to use late-flowering plants in the center plot and those that start flowering in early summer on the two sides. Since there were many unusual specimen plants in other parts of the garden, we thought we could give this plot over simply to decorative color schemes. In the late-flowering center are the deep blues of *Salvia guaranitica* and *S. azurea* subsp. *pitcheri*, and, in front of these, several plants of *Chelone obliqua* and a few brilliant red spires of *Lobelia splendens* (*L. fulgens*). In the foreground is *Limonium perezii*, a feathery, spreading artemisia, pink-flowered *Sedum spectabile* 'Autumn Joy', *Penstemon* 'Hidcote Pink', and some late-flowering, low astilbes.

The earlier-flowering side bays are mostly of plants with pink, blue, and violet flowers, but both have a pure white centerpiece. In the far bay, there is a single plant of *Crambe cordifolia*, a cousin of the common cabbage, which gives rise to a mass of tiny white flowers five feet high and as much across. This is surrounded by numerous plants of *Salvia* × *superba*, veronicas, campanulas, and pink phloxes. The nearer bay has three plants of *Gypsophila paniculata*

Verbena bonariensis
at Western Hills Nursery

'Pacifica' to match the crambe. Noteworthy among the pink plants in this section is a California native, a plant of *Achillea borealis* collected by Wayne Roderick on Santa Cruz Island, that makes a near-perfect dome of rose-colored umbels and is a vast improvement over *A. millefolium* 'Cerise Queen'. There are displays in the three bays from June to November.

PLANT FORM

So far we have been following the modern tradition of color in the garden for which perennials with their long flowering period are a principal source. There is also, however, a sizable number of perennial plants that are more notable for their habits of growth and their formal properties than for the color of their flowers. For example, many umbelliferous plants—giant heracleums, ferulas, and *Angelica archangelica*—have dingy flowers but are well worth growing for their imposing stature, remarkable foliage, and stalwart flower panicles. These plants can be used to create bold effects.

A large number of flowering plants

spires of some South Americans, such as *Eryngium pandanifolium*, to the silvery, spiky knobs of *E. giganteum* and the beautifully colored, sharply pointed ornaments of *E.* 'Violetta'.

Probably many euphorbias belong here and *Anchusa azurea*, cephalarias, scabiosas, *Catananche caerulea*, and many bulbs such as *Allium giganteum* and *Urginea maritima*. Such a border or bay would be a good home for an occasional dahlia, otherwise a difficult plant to place in the garden, and for such stately plants of the lily family as grass trees and furcraeas. It is apparent that if we add the combinations that are worth trying on the basis of form alone to what we learn about flower color over the years, the possibilities for novel and satisfying plantings are indeed endless.

TENDER PERENNIALS

In general, perennials are known as hardy plants; if the roots live from year to year in a garden they are by definition hardy. However, the word "hardy" has come to be somewhat ambiguous as it is often used to denote those plants that are hardy on the average in a given area, very often the British Isles, the source of so much of our garden literature. Plants that are hardy only in the milder parts of such an area are referred to as half-hardy, while those that cannot be grown at all, except perhaps as annuals, become tender perennials.

For those gardens in the West with few frosts, any number of so-called tender perennials are hardy and can be used to enlarge the repertoire of effective herbaceous flowering plants. Most of these come from the Canary Islands, South Africa, and parts of Central and South America. A special study would be necessary to do justice to these plants, and a survey of any class of plants is not our purpose here. Never-

called thistles by laymen are frequently effective forms to be used by the creative gardener. The best known of these are the stately white hairy plants of *Onopordum nervosum* (*O. arabicum*), which is really a biennial, and the cardoons and artichokes, but there are many more plants of similar stature and interest among the genera *Cnicus*, *Cirsium*, *Carlina*, *Carduus*, *Echinops*, and *Sonchus*. Their leaf forms, flowers, and particularly the flower buds of several centaureas can make beautiful additions, as can the marvelously spiky forms of eryngiums, from the very tall and gracefully slender

theless, we should point to the existence of this wide range of plants for our garden planning, many if not most of which have been cultivated but not used—in the sense of creating effective plant combinations—in our gardens.

Californians are familiar with *Limonium perezii* from the Canary Islands, a plant similar to *L. latifolium* except that it is larger in all its parts, has an extended flowering season, and is evergreen. This is an excellent example of this class of little-used plants; there are also other beautiful limoniums from the Canaries, culminating in that giant of them all, *L. arborescens*. *Sonchus* is a genus that flowers with large yellow daisies. The species that occur in western Europe are weedy, but in the Canary Islands they have developed into beautiful, large-leaved plants with distinctive brown-toned golden flower heads in green clusters.

The Mexican salvias, of which an increasing number are now being grown in California, are most often huge perennials with outsized flowers (those of *Salvia gesneriiflora* are nearly three inches long, and the spikes of some species are nearly a foot high). The great blue-flowered salvia, *S. guaranitica*, is easy to use among other perennials; it is like a larger, deeper colored *S. azurea* subsp. *pitcheri*. Most of the others, however, have such lush foliage and are so overwhelming that I have yet to find a place for them that is in scale and shows off their qualities to advantage.

A newly discovered perennial from South Africa has proved to be a veritable gem. It is *Diascia rigescens*, which makes a more or less evergreen mat three feet across from which arise an abundance of nearly foot-high spikes of pink pentstemon-like flowers throughout the summer and well into fall. Still more remarkable, perhaps, is the fact that the plant hides its spent flowers and seed heads and always looks its best with no attention at all. There are other, smaller diascias that are useful as path edgings and ground covers. Among these are *Diascia cordata* and the larger-flowered cultivar, 'Ruby Field', both very popular in England, and the untried *D. hanaganii* and *D. feltonii*. All are lesser plants than *D. rigescens*, and apparently less tolerant of hot situations.

Also from South Africa is the orange-flowered, sun-loving *Leonotis leonurus* and its coarser relative, *L. nepetaefolia*, as well as three remarkable shade lovers, *Plectranthus behrii*, *P. saccatus*, and *P. fruticosus*, which combine beautiful foliage with very large heads of salvia-like flowers in shades of pink or violet blue.

All of these tender perennials differ from most of their hardy cousins in being evergreen, and some of them flower in winter. They are best used among plants with similar qualities such as quasi-tender evergreen shrubs and in warm, frost-protected places in the garden.

DROUGHT RESISTANCE

Verbena bonariensis and *Gaura lindheimeri* are two tall, handsome perennials that flower from midsummer to late autumn, and will lighten up any usually dull, unwatered, or seldom watered garden in the late dry season. Among the best very tough plants for earlier flowering are *Achillea borealis* in the rose-colored Santa Cruz Island form, *Corethrogyne californica* (also a California coastal native), and many such Mediterraneans as *Centranthus ruber*, *Catananche caerulea*, *Stachys olympica*, lavenders, origanums, and Jerusalem sages.

PLANTING PERENNIALS

Reginald Farrer, in his introduction to *The English Rock Garden*, speaks of the "natural interwoven carpet" of a garden and goes on to ask a rhetorical question about alpine gardens that could, *mutatis mutandis*, be asked about plantings of larger plants. "What can be uglier," he says, "and less harmonious than the large unbroken stretches in which you sometimes see alpines laid out, each species in a broad irregular space to itself, with each plant inserted at a neat distance from the next, quite regularly like bedded out stocks, and with the bare ground between picked clean of weeds, and raked as tidy as a tablecloth?" A bed of perennials should, I think, be even more informal than a rock garden, and the plants should be even less regularly spaced and less obviously cultivated. There should be as little bare ground as possible, and this without resorting to what are usually called ground covers.

How this is done, it is usual to say, is a matter of individual taste and judgment; nevertheless, experience has suggested a few generalizations that may be of some interest. In his book on perennials, Graham Stuart Thomas has quite accurately given their ultimate height and spread. It is a case of deciding how many plants we want to use. Part of the answer is given by the plants themselves: some plants, especially those with an imposing formal structure, are best used singly as specimens; others, *Phlox paniculata* for example, seem to demand to be used in fairly large numbers for good effect; still others seem to appear at their best in fair-sized clumps, and for these three or four fairly closely spaced plants will do.

For the rest, we must visualize several things at once: the specimen plants that will dominate the plot; the plants we shall use many of and that will set the tone of the plot or dominate the *mise en scène*; the plants that may mean little by themselves but add interesting complexity; and, fi-

Diascia rigescens

nally, the plants that tie this plot into its neighbors or to the garden as a whole. When we have made these decisions, the number of plants to use will more or less fall into place. In an earlier chapter I mentioned a group of about two hundred martagon lilies, part of a planting at Knightshayes Court, in Devonshire, England. If we look at this and imagine perhaps only five, we should see an entirely different picture and one far from the intentions of the masterful gardener who created this scene.

CULTIVATION OF PERENNIALS

Although our topic is basically where and not how to plant, this occasion perhaps should be used to say something about the general cultivation of perennials and other large herbaceous plants. Unlike rock garden plants, most of the larger perennials come not only from the lowlands but from areas with a comparatively rich, loamy soil. They are good plants for what are often called ordinary garden soils, a term that covers a wide latitude of soil types and drainage conditions. What it means is that perennials do not need the exquisite drainage most alpines and other rock garden plants find necessary for their existence. We should not be misled by this, however. Most plants, other than those that make water or bogs their home, thrive on good drainage, and the average perennial is no exception.

Where possible, therefore, it is a good idea to cultivate perennial plots deeply before planting. Sawdust or other organic matter should be worked into the soil— any soil—and particularly one that is either silty-sandy or clay. If possible, it is desirable to lighten and aerate the soil to a depth of two feet or so, although the earthworms and moles will often do much of this for you.

Like good vegetables, healthy perennials are usually sizable. Whether the ideal is one of large flower trusses or noble form and foliage, it can best be realized when the plant is growing with its utmost vigor. The tight, starved, exquisite buns of the rock garden belong to a different world. Good fertilization programs are in order, and if a plant that is supposed to put on a magnificent display fails for some reason to do so, it is a good idea to check one's procedures and perhaps seek advice.

RECOMMENDED PERENNIAL PLANTS

The Northwest

From a list as short as this many fine plants that command attention during their moment of glory are omitted in favor of those with a longer season—usually extended by their foliage. But within a framework of the dozen listed, others not on the list, which might be described as prima donnas, may be accommodated.

Hostas and astilbes have fine foliage that contrasts in striking fashion; both enjoy conditions in which rhododendrons thrive and make good backgrounds for them.

Primulas are also excellent; there are many of them, but a start can be made with *Primula denticulata* and *P. polyantha*. Siberian irises will be happy in the moist conditions enjoyed by primulas, and their leaf shapes contrast well. Tall bearded irises like drier soil and a more formal setting, but are also easy to grow. Start with these two kinds and expand into others.

Most hybrid peonies flower with the irises in June, but don't limit your garden to these; discover the handsome spring-flowering species and the Saunders hybrids.

The spiky blue stems of delphiniums are the traditional complement to roses, and they do best in the Northwest. Asters, like delphiniums, have a short season and their leaves are not remarkable, but they are the mainstay of late summer. Start with a few Michaelmas daisies (*Aster novi-belgii*), of which there are many cultivars, and graduate to *Aster ericoides* and *A. cordifolius*—rarer, but worth the search. Geraniums are workhorses of the spring and summer perennial border, and they are rich in pink, rose, lavender, blue, and white.

Pinks, old-fashioned or modern, need plenty of sun and good drainage if they are not to succumb to Puget Sound's damp winters, but their leaves and scent make all efforts worthwhile.

Euphorbias I find indispensable in a good perennial scheme, because they are great flatterers of their neighbors. Rodgersias, however, are obviously superior; among them are the dark handsome strangers with foliage worth dying for that many gardeners have yet to meet. They are plants for moist soil.

Among anemones are some wonderfully permanent and dependable plants. Begin with *Anemone nemorosa* and *A. japonica* for late summer and fall.

Marvin Black

Northern and Central California

Garden conditions in northern and central California vary enormously depending mostly upon distance from the coast. Where there is abundant ocean influence and where wind protection can be provided, perennials flower for very long periods. Midway between the Northwest and southern California, our region has the advantages of both, but also the disadvantages: it is in a sense a more extreme and seasonal climate, experiencing the hot, dry summers of the south and the rainy and windy winters of the north.

More perennials can be grown even in hot, inland areas than is usually supposed. *Phlox paniculata*, for example, puts on a brilliant but comparatively short-lived display in warm areas. However, if the plants are cut back after bloom, they will flower again. A long season of bloom can be assured by planting the beautiful and disease-free white hybrid of *Phlox maculata* and *P. carolina*, 'Miss Lingard', in front of the white *Phlox paniculata* 'Mt. Fuji'. 'Miss Lingard' is cut back after flowering, whereupon the larger phlox blooms. It then is cut back, to be replaced by the reblooming 'Miss Lingard', which again (with luck) is followed by 'Mt. Fuji'. In this way, months of bloom are assured for the white garden.

In general, plants from the central and southeastern United States have proved more reliable for hot areas than those from the Himalayas. Some familiar examples are stokesia, echinacea, rudbeckia, lythrum, liatris, physostegia, and *Gaura lindheimeri*. Plants that fall apart in hot spells should be ruthlessly discarded. This includes such otherwise useful plants as the larger geraniums, *Centaurea montana*, *Sedum maximum* and *S. telephium*, and even Shasta daisies.

When the year comes to its end and the garden is subject to heavy winter rains and wind another group of problems appears. One can be illustrated by the gorgeous Mexican sages. Whereas the early-blooming *Salvia uliginosa*, *S. guaranitica*, *S. involucrata*, *S. cacaliifolia*, and others are superb garden plants, the huge winter-blooming bushes of *Salvia gesneriifolia*, *S. madrensis*, *S. holowayii*, *S. mexicana*, and their like are so often broken down by rain and wind as to be of dubious garden value.

Another winter problem in the wetter areas of central California comes from the combination of mild weather and saturated soils. Since most herbaceous perennials come from regions of snow and cold winters, they often are subject to fungal and bacterial attacks in warm wet winters. In a sense many perennials are less winter-hardy here than they are in the continental areas of the country.

Lester Hawkins

Southern California

Gardeners all over the world talk of having something to enjoy in their gardens twelve months of the year, and in southern California, even more than the rest of the generally mild Pacific Coast, we expect every month to be equally interesting. Even when gardeners take the sensible approach of designing a number of plantings, each to take the stage for a limited period and then fade into the background, year-round visibility puts a high priority on good-looking foliage and long season of bloom as factors in choosing perennials. Our arid climate and lack of winter chilling limit the use of many of the traditional perennials, but there are others. Here, in no particular order, are some I have found useful and accommodating in coastal and valley gardens of southern California.

These are for sun and any reasonably well-drained soil:

Limonium perezii—perennial statice with purple flowers and good leaves, will naturalize along the coast.

Penstemon gloxinioides hybrids—tall with pink, red, or purple flowers all year if old stems are cut to the ground.

Tulbaghia violacea—society garlic, an eighteen-inch onion with lilac flowers all the warm months.

Achillea taygetea—pale yellow small yarrow with fern-like gray foliage (I like this better than the brighter cultivar 'Moonshine').

Hemerocallis and bearded irises—both have many re-blooming cultivars, which may not be as spectacular individually as the latest introduction, but give better value in the garden.

Salvia 'May Night'—twelve- to eighteen-inch spires of deep purple flowers that will often re-bloom if cut back to basal leaves after first flowering.

Geranium sanguineum, G. sanguineum var. *lancastriense, G. ibericum*—excellent plants for a sunny place in good soil; *G. macrorrhizum* will make a splendid ground cover in light shade.

Euphorbia characias subsp. *wulfenii, E. rigida, E. epithymoides* (*E. polychroma*)—all green-flowered, gray-leaved, and bloom in winter or early spring. *Sedum* 'Autumn Joy'—for its gray leaves as much as its pink to russet flower clusters.

Centranthus ruber—valerian, a fixture on wild hillsides in southern California, but good in gardens too; cut spent stems to ground for all-year bloom.

These will take some shade:

Heuchera maxima—white coral bells on a grand scale; Rancho Santa Ana hybrids come in red and pink in the same size.

Justicia brandegeana 'Chartreuse'—a shrimp plant with yellow-green bracts; blooms all year in shade.

Some good plants wouldn't bloom or look good for a long enough season to list but for their willingness to time-share space in the garden, either by one plant growing through the other and both blooming together, such as *Verbena rigida* and *Convolvulus mauritanicus*, or by one plant replacing the other completely. *Alstroemeria ligtu* hybrids come up through the early foliage of *Physostegia virginiana*, flower in early summer and disappear completely in time for the physostegia to put on a display in August. *Ceratostigma plumbaginoides* has intense blue flowers in fall, after which the twelve-inch stems turn brilliant red and die back completely, leaving space for sprawling winter bloomers such as *Euphorbia rigida*.

Chris Rosmini

HERBACEOUS PERENNIAL BORDER IN OREGON

FAITH P. MACKANESS

COMBINATIONS and permutations of color, form, size, texture, line, and habit in the hardy perennial border are a constant source of surprise and pleasure. Its plants put on a continuous show. With planning they hold one another up and smother most of the undesirable weeds. They have no mechanical supports and need little cutting back except where necessary to reduce stature. Their flowers and

A mid-summer group: purple siberian iris, red-hot poker, and yellow daylily

decorative fruits beautify our home and the homes of flower-arranging friends. There will even be a surplus for fall and spring plant sales.

True, the overall effect has been a far cry from the carefully designed and manicured British perennial borders. Ours lacks the large masses of choice cultivars (most of which are unavailable in this country). Too many items have been included for their botanical or horticultural interest. If the clumps had been dug, divided, and replanted regularly, they admittedly would have shown better growth, but there have been many pleasures from it.

Sometimes by design, more often by accident, plants consort in unforgettable combinations.

SPECIAL EFFECTS

It is early May, with only *Bergenia crassifolia* (pig squeak) blooming among the rosettes and spears of things to come at the south end of the border. Then one day, a colony of *Dicentra spectabilis* (tall bleeding heart) extends arching stems of rosy hearts over a mist of the tiny blue forget-me-not flowers of *Brunnera macrophylla*.

Thalictrum delavayi 'Album' (tall white

The well maintained yew hedge provides an ideal setting for the author's perennial border in early summer

meadow rue) is another early riser; its clutch of buds explodes to reveal mauve sepals subtending masses of cream-colored stamens. Simultaneously *Salvia × superba*, in the front row below, erupts in a low wall of rosy lavender fireworks.

My favorite season is mid-May when staggered fluffy mauve drifts of *Thalictrum rochebrunianum* make a background for the early geraniums (*Geranium maculatum* and *G. cinereum var. subcaulescens*) and paired architectural leaf-fans of *Iris pallida* 'Variegata'.

In mid-June interrupted spikes of mauve-colored flowers of *Phlomis tuberosa* are held up by the tall false indigo in sea green and dusky blue. This is also the time that *Adenophora confusa* (lady bells) on the edge of the border sends up controlled spikes of hanging bells that echo in hue the extravagantly floriferous display put on by the royal blue *Campanula latifolia* 'Brantwood' beyond and above it.

The October border can be glorious with *Aconitum carmichaelii* towering above *Aster cordifolius* 'Silver Spray' and *Aster × frikartii*. *Helenium* 'Moerheim Beauty' fans out between the asters and the tall monkshood. Single pink, white, and old rose Japanese anemones flutter all around like huge butterflies.

Traditional hardy herbaceous perennial borders have declined in popularity over the past fifty years. Could their reputation for requiring a great deal of work have something to do with the reluctance of gardeners today to make them? Although our own perennial border began in the traditional way, its intensive labor requirements soon made me rethink the whole operation.

New approaches described by experienced gardeners such as Alan Bloom (*Perennials for Trouble-Free Gardening*), Marjorie Fish (*Carefree Gardening*), and Graham Stuart Thomas (*Perennial Garden Plants, or The Modern Florilegium*), have been inspirational along the way.

The overall plan for our flat acre of country garden in the Columbia River Gorge was designed by Desmond Muirhead in the mid-1950s. It provides for a herbaceous perennial border roughly twenty by 180 feet, the long axis extending north and south. Backed on three sides by a clipped English yew hedge, it faces the house and an east lawn and parking area but is generally approached from the south.

The landscape blueprints designated the foundation trees, shrubs, and ground covers, but left the contents of the border to me. I visited gardens by day and pored over books and catalogs by night. My gardening friends came bearing gifts. These plants and subsequent largess over the years have given the creation of this part of our garden a special importance.

Many of the first plants in the border came from the old Wayside Gardens of Mentor, Ohio. Others were grown from seed obtained from the Royal Horticultural Society or Major V. J. Howell's Seed Exchange in England.

Some of the early acquisitions have proved to be long-lived perennials and form the backbone of the border today. Over the years, many more plants have qualified to join this select company. On the other hand, there were those that succumbed to our climatic extremes; that resented competition from their border associates; that exhibited weedy characteristics; that resented my cultural methods; or that were innately short-lived. The cemetery section of my garden files expanded as they were added to the compost pile.

RENOVATING THE ORIGINAL BORDER

Five years after the border was planted, my husband, a Briton, announced that renovation was long overdue. That fall we dug everything up, divided the clumps, and replanted the divisions in nursery plots. The next spring, after the emptied border had been re-dug, limed, fertilized, and cultivated, there was a massive replanting.

The arrangement of the original border had been quite unsophisticated. All of the tallest perennials had been positioned in the rear rows, the medium-sized ones in the middle, and the smaller plants along the front, creating an all-too-obvious stair-step effect. The color schemes throughout the changing seasons were, at best, incidental. Design was practically nonexistent. Such faults would have to be righted in the new border.

I had chafed in the past over the time and energy devoted to twigging, pegging, staking, tying, and cutting back spent flowers, and this revitalizing operation had been the last straw. I decided then and there that I was extremely allergic to all such time-honored, time-consuming gardening practices. Henceforth, I would do things my way—the lazy way.

My first strategy in the new border was to position massive subjects in front of spiky ones with tendencies to lean or fall over after rain or windstorms. The larkspurs, hollyhocks, and Russell lupines rebelled. They were already threatened by the burgeoning yew hedge behind them and were doomed anyway. An initial move was to plant the candelabra-like *Verbascum chaixii* in place of the once incomparable larkspurs. A biennial in our climate, this mullein, as is the nature of mulleins, always leaves enough seed behind to ensure an adequate supply of its lovely woolly rosettes

Globe thistle (Echinops ritro) *and plume poppy* (Macleaya cordata) *in midsummer*

for producing the following year's flowers. After judicious thinning, the magnificent leaves produce a most effective ground cover.

To prevent their becoming rangy late in the season, the tall phloxes, sneezeworts, and Michaelmas daisies were sheared back in late June or early July. Keeping these erect had been one of the most onerous tasks connected with the original border.

Over the years, the entire bed has been raised enough with compost to allow for a low sloping bank above the lawn. This makes it possible to grow plants more often found in rockeries—small bluebells, dwarf hardy geraniums, and so on.

A few selected shrubs: *Lavandula* 'Munstead Dwarf' and *L.* 'Hidcote Purple', *Perovskia atriplicifolia* (Russian sage), and *Romneya coulteri* (canyon or Matilija poppy) have slipped in over the years. However, no bulbs and no peonies have been included. These seemed to be easier to handle in beds of their own.

In the great European perennial borders, such as those at the Royal Botanical Garden, Edinburgh, large groups of each plant are employed to give staggered masses of color all through the season. This is virtually impossible in a small border. One way of overcoming the lack of color, in certain areas and at certain times, is to introduce quantities of annuals, but this makes more work and is anathema to one who prefers form, line, and texture to color.

ARCHITECTURAL PLANTS

Fortunately, there is a large group of border subjects that possess architectural qualities. Many of them are even more attractive in fruit than when immature. Topping the list is *Miscanthus sinensis* 'Zebrinus' (zebra grass). A veritable fountain of green and gold most of the season, it shoots out glistening crimson panicles in late September or early October. Eventually these explode into fluffy beige plumes. If one has room for them, *Acanthus spinosissimus* and *A. mollis* (bear's breeches) are impressive plants, albeit somewhat somber. *Morina longifolia* is a prickly teasel whose tubular white flowers turn from pink to crimson after fertilization. The fragrant thistle-like rosettes put out a succession of flowering stems from June until frost. Globe thistles and sea hollies always elicit comment. The sea holly *Eryngium giganteum*, another biennial that leaves a host of offspring, glows in the twilight and has the popular name Miss Willmott's ghost. *E. alpinum, E. bourgatii*, and *E.* 'Violetta' are steel blue and spiny. Others like *E. agavifolium* and *E. variifolium* are green, but all are flower arrangers' delights if picked when still in bloom. So too is the blue-balled *Echinops ritro* (globe thistle) and its various cultivars. The Jerusalem sages (*Phlomis tuberosa* and *P. russeliana*) display interrupted spikes of hooded flowers. Those of the former are rosy lilac—of the latter, butter yellow. The pagoda-like fruiting stems, which turn from beige to brown to black with weathering, are lovely both outdoors and in. Besides being beautiful in flower, *Baptisia australis* (false indigo) has the most amazing fruits of all. Its oddly inflated gunmetal-colored pods are overtopped somewhat, until after the first frosts, by luscious glaucous blue-green foliage. One plant will increase in circumference to spectacular proportions in twenty years. The gas plants are long-lived too. *Dictamnus albus* and *D. albus* 'Purpureus' have crimson velour-covered starlike capsules that mature to eject BB-like projectiles with the aid of yoke-shaped valves. The flowers are so spectacular and long-lasting that no border should be without them. All of these architectural plants can be used in the front to middle rows of a border.

BORDER PLANTS

FRONT ROWS:
Aurinia saxatilis 'Citrina' (madwort)
Geranium nepalense
Geranium sanguineum var. *prostratum*
Echioides longiflorum (prophet flower)
Iris pallida 'Variegata'
Phlomis russeliana
Veronica latifolia (*V. teucrium*) 'Crater Lake Blue'
Dianthus plumarius (garden pinks)
Lavandula 'Munstead'—*L.* 'Hidcote'
Campanula carpatica
Eryngium bourgatii—*E. alpinum*
Buphthalmum salicifolium—*Inula ensifolia*
Sedum 'Ruby Glow'
Sedum spectabile 'Meteor'—*S.* 'Autumn Joy'

MIDDLE ROWS:
Thalictrum rochebrunianum
Dictamnus albus—*D. albus* 'Purpureus'
Hemerocallis lilioasphodelus—*H. fulva*
Geranium pratense—*G. sylvaticum*
Geranium × *magnificum*
Cephalaria gigantea
Lythrum salicaria 'Morden's Pink'—*L. virgatum* 'The Rocket'
Hemerocallis 'Hyperion'
Campanula latifolia 'Brantwood'
Monarda 'Croftway Pink'—*M.* 'Violet Queen'
Anemone 'White Giant'—*A.* 'Whirlwind'

BACK ROWS:
Thalictrum speciosissimum
Filipendula rubra 'Venusta'
Verbascum chaixii
Artemisia lactiflora
Helenium 'The Bishop'

CENTER:

BACK ROWS:
Large clumps of Siberian irises, seven hybrids.

MIDDLE ROWS:
Heuchera Bressingham hybrids
Malva moschata
Echinacea purpurea

FRONT ROW:
Morina longifolia

To help achieve a feeling of unity, identical or similar plants have been repeated on opposite halves of the long border. Thus paired, masses of the same approximate height, shape, texture, or color attract attention as the seasons change. In the accompanying list, where no paired plant is given, the same plant is used in both ends of the border.

With between fifty and eighty kinds of perennials in bloom at any one time between mid-May and mid-October, repetition lends stability to the inevitable kaleidoscope.

ROUTINE MAINTENANCE

By the time of the first frosts in the Columbia River Gorge, putting the garden to bed for the winter has already begun. Between rainy spells, the remaining stems and leaves are attacked with grass shears, pruners, snips, and a saw. The lavender and other shrubs are merely given haircuts. Meanwhile, the adjacent bulb bed is a blaze of glory, so there is no sadness.

Every winter one and one-half buckets of commercial 15–15–15 fertilizer are broadcast over the border. At four-year intervals about a hundred pounds of dolomite is spread over everything to counteract acidity.

On our return from vacation, the debris of winter is raked up and perennial weeds are dug out. As soon as the first shoots and rosettes emerge, the spaces between them are lightly cultivated with a blunt-tined scratcher to eliminate and discourage germinating annual weeds.

After this, one to three inches of ripe old compost is applied around and between the rosettes. If last season's garden notebook suggests that a plant was out of hand, it is now cut into halves or thirds with a sharpened spade and the excess material

removed. Alternatively, hunks are shaved off the outside of the offending clumps and good compost is used in filling the holes. Zebra grass confinement requires the use of an axe.

I invite covetous gardeners to help themselves to difficult-to-divide items, and to large plants that need eliminating. The ploy usually works if I hand them the tools and show them where to operate. Excess *Physostegia virginiana* 'Vivid' (false dragonhead), *Lysimachia punctata*, *L. ephemerum*, and *L. clethroides* are merely pulled out. On the other hand, *Lythrum virgatum* and *L. salicaria* hybrids are effective as quite large clumps.

Some plants out of place are of a more serious nature, particularly the striking *Alstroemeria aurantiaca* and *A. ligtu* hybrids. Their wandering ways are difficult to keep in check. Apart from trench warfare, the only control is to pull the shoots out where they are not wanted. When they reappear, repeat the process, and plant over with tough customers like sidalcea hybrids. The prime adversary, of course, is twitch or couch grass (*Agropyron repens*), which requires constant vigilance lest it invade everything in the border. Fortunately, healthy border perennials smother most other kinds of weeds.

PESTS

Perhaps the most insidious enemies of the border are slugs and snails. The tall delphiniums were their primary targets in the original border, but every few years they concentrate on one of the paired gas plants. This spring they destroyed the flowers of the lacy white one. Leaves eventually reappeared, but there have been no flowers this year. Every known bait has been tried but, where annual rainfall may reach seventy inches, no bait is entirely effective.

Spittle bugs sometimes descend *en masse*, lending unity if not beauty to the total picture. Some years aphids and leaf hoppers are bothersome—this is the year of the grasshopper. I seldom have to resort to sprays because the natural controls appear to keep pests in check. Grazing and digging wildlife (chipmunks, rabbits, possums, moles, and the neighbor's livestock) can play havoc overnight. Last season the rabbits finished off all the tuberous rhizomes of *Platycodon* (bellflower). Sometimes they attack lily bulbs. Three young bald eagles from the nearby Sandy River Canyon devoured the rabbits eventually, so the story has a happy ending, at least for the bellflowers.

Perhaps the most essential adjunct to the herbaceous perennial border is a wide path between the border and the backing hedge or wall. Besides furnishing ventilation, it offers access for weeding, cultivating, attacking predators, and the addition and subtraction of plants. More importantly, it provides growing room for the roots of the yew hedge and a base of operations from which my husband and son have kept the hedge pruned to a stunning six feet.

is an incurable addiction. I confine myself to hardy subjects and so need only simple equipment.

All of my seeds have been sown in used tin cans, sterilized in the dishwasher and punched with holes for drainage. The standard growing medium is a mixture of half perlite and half vermiculite. Sometimes for liliaceous and ericaceous subjects I add a covering of milled sphagnum moss. Once the seedlings have appeared, their containers are placed together and watered with weak Rapid Gro—strength increasing as the seedlings develop. When they are large enough to be handled, a table knife is run around the inside of the can and the contents dropped gently into a plastic tray. The seedlings are planted directly in rows in the nursery or brought on to larger size in plastic or clay containers in a cold frame. Success has exceeded my wildest expectations these past twenty-odd years.

Because the plants grown from seed do not always match the name or description on the packet or in the plant dictionaries, it is best to let them flower in the nursery before transferring them to the border. Sometimes an entire planting of seeds has to be discarded if the plants are not up to expectation.

ASSEMBLING THE PLANTS

Assembling a collection of compatible perennials is a never-ending adventure. Checking over the new catalogs, looking up the offerings listed in the annual exchanges of the plant societies and botanical gardens, and swapping plants, bulbs, and seeds with like-minded gardeners over the world are among the more exciting aspects of the hobby.

Raising new plants from seed, of course,

SHORT-LIVED PERENNIALS

Whereas the majority of the denizens of the border have been long-lived, many of the well known favorites have not. Thus gardeners choosing to continue including them must remember to put seeds or cuttings or divisions in the frame or on nursery plots. The garden pinks and the bergamots must be restored once they have been in the border for a few years.

Lobelia (*Lobelia siphilitica*, *L. fulgens* and

L. cardinalis, and their hybrids) are notoriously short-lived. Once acquired, the brown-leaved forms must be cosseted and offshoots rooted.

Linum (flax), *Chrysanthemum coccineum* (pyrethrum), *Aquilegia* (columbine), *Anthemis*, *Achillea*, *Lychnis*, *Digitalis*, *Anchusa*, *Penstemon*, and *Delphinium* have had comparatively limited life-spans in the border here, but there are always new and untried plants to replace them. These substitutions lend spice to making a border. It is a good idea to keep a diary of unsatisfactory combinations and needed renovations.

Creating a hardy herbaceous perennial border has been an intellectual and an aesthetic exercise. It has given me a reason for growing a great many plants from all parts of the world. It has offered me a chance to study their relations with and reactions to one another in an interesting, if essentially artificial, environment.

William Robinson, in *The English Flower Garden*, writes,

To the good gardener all kinds of designs are good, if not against the site, soil, climate and labors of his garden—a very important point the last.

That was in 1883. It is even more relevant today. Gardening with hardy herbaceous perennials can be high adventure when one remembers always to keep the mechanics of maintenance from taking the fun from it.

LONG-LIVED PLANTS

Long-lived and trouble-free plants now forming the backbone of the border:

Acanthus spinosus (bear's breeches)
Anemone 'September Charm', 'White Giant', 'Whirlwind', 'Prince Henry' (Japanese windflower)
Artemisia lactiflora (mugwort)
Asphodeline lutea (Jacob's rod)
Baptisia australis (false indigo)
Bergenia crassifolia (pig squeak)
Campanula latifolia 'Brantwood' (tall bellflower)
Campanula latifolia 'Alba' (tall white bellflower)
Dictamnus albus (gas plant)
Dictamnus albus 'Purpureus' (gas plant)
Echinops ritro 'Taplow Blue' (globe thistle)
Eryngium 'Violetta' (sea holly)
Filipendula rubra 'Venusta' (queen of the prairie)
Geranium × *magnificum* (tall geranium)
Geranium sanguineum (bloody crane's bill)
Geranium sanguineum 'Album'
Helenium 'The Bishop', 'Moerheim Beauty', 'Butterpat' (sneezeweed)
Helianthus 'Coronation' (sunflower)
Hemerocallis lilioasphodelus (*H. flava*) (yellow daylily)
Hemerocallis fulva (orange daylily)
Hemerocallis 'Hyperion'
Iris pallida 'Variegata'
Iris sibirica 'Eric the Red', 'Caesar's Brother', 'Periwinkle', 'Snow Crest', 'Summer Sky', 'Turquoise Cup', 'Tycoon'
Lysimachia punctata (yellow loosestrife)
Lythrum salicaria 'Morden's Pink' (purple loosestrife)
Miscanthus sinensis 'Zebrinus' (zebra grass)
Papaver orientale 'May Curtis' (oriental poppy)
Phlomis russeliana (Jerusalem sage)
Solidago 'Golden Wings'

A CANYON GARDEN

KARIN P. FINTZY

THE garden has been developing in the shelter of Santa Monica Canyon, near the Los Angeles beaches, for some twenty years. Many parts of it appear older and one area derives great maturity from a tree that has been on this spot for over three hundred years.

It is the home of Marian and Karl M. Wagner. Mr Wagner is a landscape architecture graduate of the University of California at Berkeley who some years ago traded the drawing board for the privilege of traveling, collecting, developing, and marketing plants. He and Mrs Wagner operated a nursey and retail store on Santa Monica Boulevard in North Hollywood where they specialized in exotic plants for interior use. Here, nearly every morning, the nursery counters were lined with expensive jardinieres from the finest homes in Beverly Hills, waiting to be filled with the latest in exotic plants.

The Wagners' travels in Central and South American countries resulted in a fine collection of unusual plants, many of which the Wagners introduced. The hybridization of spathiphyllums, now widely grown indoors, was a specialty of theirs. One of them, a cross between *Spathiphyllum clevelandii* and *S. cochlearispathum*, is appropriately named 'Marian Wagner'.

So it happened that, when the Wagners were ready to retire from the nursery business, they realized that they would need a special site to accommodate several hundred of their favorite plants.

They couldn't have found a more fortunate spot. Protected from the extremes of winter and summer by the nearby ocean and surrounding hills and blessed with deep soil, the canyon provides sanctuary for a wide range of plants—from the rarest bamboo to the ubiquitous impatiens. Some volunteer themselves with abandon, even among the shingles on the roof.

The Wagners needed the proper environment for their collection of indoor tropicals. Most important was adequate light, the lack of which has caused many indoor gardeners much grief. Thus, Cliff May designed the house to most exacting specifications, including huge skylights, massive interior planting islands, pebbled concrete floors for ease of maintenance (surprisingly warm to the touch due to embedded radiant heaters), a glass-enclosed plant room, and an aviary for Mrs Wagner's canaries, which she breeds as a hobby.

Both the horticulturist and the landscape designer would find much to admire in the garden. The first would be fasci-

Sycamore branches and reclining trunk filled with bromeliads and ferns

nated by the variety of plants here, many of which are unlikely to be found elsewhere in this part of Los Angeles. The landscape designer would want to know how this disparate collection has been arranged so as to be simultaneously stimulating and peaceful.

A visitor finds himself approaching down a long drive and across a bridge that spans what remains of Las Lagrimas (The Tears) de Santa Monica—a spring-fed stream that had been one of the original attractions of the site. Years of winter storms and flooding caused much damage and Las Lagrimas is now diverted into a concrete flood control channel to the ocean. Canyon residents have come to accept this as necessary for their survival. The garden has matured gracefully around the fringes of the culvert, the hard edges of which are camouflaged with *Iris*

douglasiana, a native western iris, and its hybrids. The decomposed granite of the drive is shaded on the southwest by a wall of southern magnolia, native California sycamore, and copper beech (*Fagus sylvatica* 'Atropunicea'). These have grown happily and melded so well that the effect is that of a collage of large, leathery, bright-green magnolia leaves with their tawny undersides, contrasted with fresh, green, maple-like sycamore leaves, all accented with the shimmering foliage of the European copper beech (growing well but rarely seen in this area). Of sycamore leaves Vita Sackville-West wrote, "they may not inaptly be compared to an Isfahan carpet, with their depths of rose-madder and violet, and the tips of young growth as sanguine as a garnet seen against the light."

The feeling and purpose of this garden are established immediately upon entry.

This is a plantsman's garden. And it is one case where such a garden is more than a collection of plants.

Not an inch is wasted on lawn. Beds of trees, shrubs, and ground covers line the paths of decomposed granite that form the backbone of the garden. A stroll through the garden shows that the paths, while unpretentious and informal, have strong purpose. They provide separation and circulation, of course. They provide interest and texture by repeatedly leading us through dappled shade and then into sunlight. Their artful design also provides the excitement of never quite letting us know where we are going, but showing enough to make us want to take the trip. If any landscaping rule has been consciously employed here, it is surely that of expectation and surprise.

Expectation is rewarded and surprises are pleasant. There are many points of interest: the allée of flowering peach trees with its graceful underplanting of Louisiana irises—one of the loveliest features of the garden in spring; a sheltering hillside planted with *Koelreuteria bipinnata*, whose flame-colored papery fruits are a sight enjoyed by residents far across the canyon; a planting on the same hillside of a chusquea, a rare bamboo from Guatemala with arching, filmy growth that appears from a distance much like a very large, very delicate fern; the carefully tended vegetable garden at the foot of the hill; a special, shaded place featuring a Mexican fountain and graced by a head-high (and then some) fibrous-rooted begonia; at a turn of a path, the appearance, unexpected in these parts, of *Aesculus carnea* 'Briotii', the red horse-chestnut tree, in radiant blossom. And there is the focus of the garden, the space to which all paths lead eventually, the sycamore-shaded patio.

The site for the patio is not the usual left-over space. The house, in fact, was designed around this place. The three-hundred-year-old native California sycamore that forms a bridge-like arch over the patio was one of the attractions for the Wagners when they first saw the undeveloped property. The heavy, beautifully mottled trunk leans so that its far end touches the ground. It has rooted and another sycamore grows from that spot. The arching part of the trunk is dead, but secure enough for the Wagners to hollow out as an overhead planter—one high enough to provide a feeling of shelter, yet low enough for a close-up view of the plantings.

A social place has resulted that is exciting to pass through and pleasant for lingering.

Now, years later, the combination of sycamore branches and reclining trunk filled with bromeliads and ferns provides a marvelously rich pattern against the sky. The bromeliads are in perfect surroundings. Being epiphytes, they almost take care of themselves. They need little moisture at their roots and these plants hasten the decay of the sycamore less than would other plants in their place. The dappled light provided by the trees is just right for the fullest development of bromeliad color which, in this garden, ranges from green, pink, red, bronze, to almost black. Volunteer impatiens and ferns, such as *Aglaomorpha coronans*, also an epiphyte, add to the rich texture.

The patio area provides another horticultural surprise. *Loropetalum chinense*, that gracefully arching evergreen shrub with small white flowers like shredded coconut, is described in *Sunset Western Garden Book* as growing "possibly up to twelve feet in great age." Here is one lusty example, although it is surely not of great age. The loropetalum in a corner of the Wagners' patio, admittedly grown in a slightly raised bed, is over fifteen feet high and at least that in width, providing a delightful umbrella for those fortunate enough to be seated on the benches that encircle the trunk. It is an especially decorative plant because of the touches of red throughout the year in its new growth and in the maturing foliage. It grows in the sun as well as in half shade and is so versatile and amenable to shaping that it is a shame we are rarely able to find it in the market. Fortunately, it is quite easy to propagate from cuttings.

Other plants that distinguish this area are the palm-like *Cycas circinalis* from the Old World tropics, a relative of the common *Cycas revoluta* from Japan, both primitive cone-bearing plants. A substantial shrub of *Michelia figo*, relative of the magnolias, is by a path entering the patio where the scent of its small pale yellow maroon-centered flowers cannot be missed. On a warm day they smell much like ripe bananas.

Also providing fragrance is a handsome bed with three cultivars of *Brunfelsia pauciflora*: *B. pauciflora* 'Floribunda', called yesterday-today-and-tomorrow because it changes color from purple to lavender to white in about three days; *B. pauciflora* 'Eximia', smaller and equally charming; and *B. pauciflora* 'Macrantha', which has larger flowers of deep purple that do not change color and are not fragrant. All of these flourish in the shade and shelter provided by the sycamores here.

Elsewhere in this garden are found additional plants that are not in the market now, yet grow successfully and contribute so much to the landscape that one wonders why nurserymen no longer bother with them. An example is the royal trumpet vine, the mauve-colored *Distictis buccinato-*

ria 'Rivers', which is even more vigorous than plants of *D. buccinatoria* with orange trumpets and which retains a better appearance in winter. It is virtually disease- and pest-free, and is displayed to advantage here on a sunny fence bordering the entrance drive.

Another vine that has served the Wagners well, and that is beginning to be appreciated again by nurserymen in this area, is *Lonicera heckrottii*, the coral honeysuckle, with silvery gray leaves, red stems, and pink-and-cream-colored flowers all summer. Hummingbirds love it.

Just about nonexistent in the market is *Cibotium schiedei*, the Mexican tree fern, which is very sturdy despite the elegance of its arching, chartreuse fronds. It is grown in the ground here where it hasn't yet, after many years, reached its possible height of fifteen feet. It can also be used to great effect in a large tub.

To the extensive list of plants found here that are not often seen in this part of the city we can add: *Picea abies* 'Nidiformis', the bird's nest spruce, which after twenty-two years is still an inviting cushion no more than two feet high; *Cleyera japonica*, a camellia relative with fragrant, un-camellia-like flowers in fall, followed by red berries; *Caryota ochlandra*, the Canton fishtail palm, most often used as a houseplant but successful outdoors here; *Stenocarpus sinuatus*, the firewheel tree, said to be an unreliable bloomer near the coast, but not so in this garden; and numerous other uncommon cycads, ferns, palms, and perennials.

This is a garden in which a variety of plants has been assembled without confusion—a lesson for those who make gardens and for those who collect plants.

THE MOOR IN OUR MIDST: ANDALUSIAN INTERLUDE

CAROL GREENTREE

THE romance of Spain and Latin America threaded itself into the architecture, gardens, and popular music of California during the early years of this century and blossomed again in postwar years as a renaissance of Mediterranean styles. Under the lacy mantilla of imitated Andalusian charm there is a sturdy heritage of culture and custom that seems tailor-made for California. Doughty padres who scouted the first trail north from San Diego marveled at the similarity of the country to their native land. Tawny, oak-studded hills, rainless summers, and temperate winters reminded the Franciscan missionaries of southern Spain. (Conversely, today, first-time California visitors remark with amazement at the likeness of Andalusia to their native scenery.)

Cave drawings at Altamira and elsewhere in Spain attest to societies nearly twenty centuries old. Tides of invasion swelled and receded: Celts, Carthaginians, and Romans preceded Vandals and Visigoths. Vestiges of fine Roman aqueducts, cisterns, baths, and sewer systems astonish tourists even today.

In the early 700s Arabs made themselves at home in southern Spain, and by the ninth century had transformed Córdoba into a center of learning and culture. Called the Athens and sometimes the Baghdad of the West, Córdoba gleamed with palaces, mosques, baths, libraries, and gardens during Europe's Dark Ages. For almost eight centuries, Andalusia attracted linguists, historians, poets, and scholars from every part of the known world.

Agriculture in southern Spain benefited from intellectual progress. Mountain water was channeled to the plains; fields and gardens were terraced; a network of irrigation channels created a lush, productive landscape, and fertile farms were made to support an affluent society. Spain was the most powerful and wealthy country in Europe.

Eventually Christian factions cracked the Islamic stronghold. Ironically, in the same year that Columbus sailed to the New World, the Arabs were routed forever from Iberia. Large farms and great landholdings fell into disuse, water systems were neglected, and Moorish customs abandoned. Yet it is impossible to erase completely the results of centuries of culture. Crenelated medina walls remain. Fragments of rabbit-warren cities still lure visitors. Cool Moorish patios offer refuge from a *clima muy fuerte*—a very intense climate.

Blank-faced houses with only a few small windows hug narrow streets, revealing nothing of their inhabitants. Packed close together, ancient buildings are giant neighborhoods like honeycombs, dotted with pockets of personal privacy, not one like another, yet each patterned with the same motifs, bequests of the Moors and Romans. Within the walls, there are also courtyards and patios—roofless rooms for family life.

A patio is a précis of a garden. With utmost economy, few plants, little water, and simple design, an Iberian courtyard conjures an illusion of cool, leafy luxuriance.

The family patio also serves practical purposes. It can be a sunny drying yard for laundry. It can be an outdoor parlor for entertaining guests. It can be an open-air living room for sewing, snoozing, or gossiping.

A patio is a nice place to bathe the baby or peel potatoes. Strings of peppers and onions may hang under the eaves. In a climate that provides blue skies most of the year, Spanish gardens integrate the civilized amenities of outdoor and indoor living with consummate geniality.

Spanish patios beckon one to enter, to stroll and explore hidden corners. They are often disarming blends of order and artless insouciance. Even in neglect, patios have charm. Most appear well tended; they are seldom over-groomed. Four solid walls may be pierced by gates, doors, or windows. In some, colonnaded walks along the sides provide a periphery of deep shade. Small pockets of soil may accommodate trained vines or trees at the paving edges. Clusters of potted plants surround the most salient and ubiquitous of all patio features—the water source.

Supplied by hidden cisterns, fountains create a humidified microclimate in each protected courtyard. Water spatters, dribbles, and spits on the leaves of nearby plants, keeping greenery fresh. Glazed tiles—or *azulejos*—line the fountain basin, where their sheen and color give even greater liveliness to the sparkle of moving water. Embossed tiles create riffles in the water channels, to catch the light and amplify the motion of the thinnest film of water.

Parsimony is the key to water use in a thirsty land. (Imagine life without a hose bibb at the corner of the house; if we had to draw our water from a well we'd be more frugal ourselves.) Centuries of refinement allow Andalusians to have their cake and eat it too. A ripple of water is as effective as a cascade when its spangles can be seen and its murmurs heard throughout the patio in its travels. Water vanishes and reappears. Clever underground channels deploy it first to the patio fountain, then into a catch basin, finally down through drains and tiles to the vegetable garden, or *huerta*, and perhaps to a nearby orchard. In the rainy season, well-placed water spouts spurt runoff from roofs into basins and runnels which fill out-of-the-way wells for future use. The sound of water is good company. Its music creates a serene atmosphere for contemplation. The intimate acoustics of a small enclosed space enhance the sound of trickling water and induce a mood of tranquility. Indeed, the musical quality of Spanish gardens has inspired compositions such as Manuel de Falla's *Nights in the Gardens of Spain* and Francisco Tarrega's *Recuerdos de la Alhambra*.

Most patios have white walls, but other colors are also used on colonnades and walls. Subtle combinations of soft yellows, pale blues, and sienna tints emphasize the shadows behind thick pillars and low arches. Sometimes deeper pastels are

Remnants of thick-walled Moorish fortifications in Córdoba bear a strong resemblance to those in Marrakech and Rabat—mementos of the powerful link between Spain and Morocco

used: dusty violet, leaded green, and earthy ochre. Only once, in Seville, did I see an intense color used. A patio tucked nearly out of sight had walls of rich, Marrakech rose. The plants were young and their leaves pale green; the combination of colors was breathtaking.

In some patios, brightly glazed pots are the only contrast. Picture six brilliant blue aspidistra-filled pots encircling a diminutive fountain set into a gray pebbled floor. Or imagine the exquisite simplicity of plain terracotta pots on a clay tile pavement in a peach-walled garden hallway; saffron ceramic cache pots against old-gold walls.

Each patio appears to reflect its owner.

Some seem playful, cheery, and artless. Others are tailored and dignified—even restrained and formal. A few are rustic and unpretentious; straightforward in their use of rough stone paving and plain pottery. Many are lighthearted and romantic, with touches of lacy wrought iron and trailing, fragrant jasmine. There may be tile-edged corner beds and cruciform paths reminiscent of Moroccan *riads*. The fountain is often placed precisely at the center of the court. And there may be bands of colored ceramic tiles in the walls and benches and catch-basins—legacies from ancient mosques and palaces.

The choice of plants also reflects Mos-

Above: simple beauty is integrated into the mechanics of moving water through a patio. A single bubbler fills a fluted coupe, which spills into a channel-rimmed catch basin. Overflow drains away through the water groove at right. Paving patterns are of edge-set pebbles and gray stone. Left: water-stairs that imitate pedestrian steps can tumble water noisily into an unseen network of underground channels in this ancient Moorish garden of the Alcázar in Seville

lem heritage. Tall dark cypresses spike the skies from the corners of path crossings, just as suggested in early Arab horticulture manuals. An affection for scented flowers and aromatic herbs endures in today's patios. Some courtyard walls are curtains of jasmine or wisteria grown on painstakingly espaliered vines. Violets, mint, and thyme border paved walks. Oleanders and roses bring color and fragrance to closed courtyards, just as they did in the twelfth century, when Abu Zacaria, an Arabian horticulturist, recorded traditional guidelines for making Moorish gardens.

The Moslems introduced citrus plants, via Persia, from southeast Asia, and today the very name Valencia conjures images of oranges and marmalade. Lemon trees perfume numberless Spanish patios and yield fruit for refreshing sangria.

Dozens of our favorite plants are found in Andalusian gardens: pendulous datura flowers, bright geraniums, pale plumbago, and cheery lantana. Spider plants and aspidistra and ivy make green-on-green compositions. The ventures of Columbus and his followers yielded to the Spanish great botanical riches from the New World, and many of our own American plants now grow in the Mediterranean region like natives.

Patios never seem cluttered in Andalusia. To keep them open and uncrowded, just a single specimen plant may be chosen—perhaps a pomegranate or orange, for its flowers and fruit. To conserve space, vines are kept flat against walls by tying and pruning into light, informal espaliers.

Because they are so small and use so few plants, patios and balconies always seem tidy. They are undemanding and maintenance is easy. Regular watering, some pruning and sweeping seem to be all that is required.

Thick, high protecting walls insure early morning and late afternoon shade. They also permit full use of a lot by screening outdoor areas from public view. No front lawns demand regular mowing, and every square foot of land is kept for private use.

Tall walls divide some large gardens into a series of separate patios, each different in atmosphere and treatment from its neighbor. Part of the charm of such gardens is the adventure of moving into and through closed spaces from one compound to the next, through narrow cypress corridors, under deep arches, behind thick walls, down steps, up terraces, past pools and fountains, in and out of little rooms and big rooms. Proportion and style may vary widely from court to court. Surprising vistas and unexpected touches of humor encourage exploration in the hope of discovering yet another attraction beyond the next gate or archway.

If these patios are a joy to wander through, they are a pleasure to look down upon, too. From a balcony the serene simplicity of a patio's design reveals itself. The plants and their arrangements recede in importance and the paving dominates a viewer's attention. Patterns that weren't noticed at ground level become distinct.

Ordinary terracotta tiles are used alone in paving or with bands and bits of brightly glazed tiles. Colored gravels and earth-toned clays are used to define paths. Brick and cobble surfaces are common. Most distinctive of all are the black and white designs of water-worn pebbles the size of silver dollars, set on edge to depict images of lions, castles, and heraldic devices. The variety is unending. In one I found a panel of deep-toned azulejos in a design similar to that of a Persian rug—itself a representation of a Persian garden; beautiful imitation of beautiful imitations.

In some gardens, azulejos are the primary ornamentation. In flowerless patios

An arched alcove provides a choice theater for a wall-mounted display of plants behind a raised fount

they supply the only spark of color. In Seville, benches and fountains are fully sheathed with lustrous ceramics, as are walks, niches, and walls. Even the undersides of Spanish balconies are surfaced with colorful tile designs, to please the eyes of pedestrians (and perhaps serenaders?). Glazes of cobalt blue, ochre gold, and chrome yellow predominate, in handsome contrast with soft, weathered clay roof tiles and flowerpots.

Throughout Spain, tiles embedded in the stucco of buildings mark the names of streets, identify shops, and advertise wares. Azulejos are, in fact, almost a national form of expression: Barcelona boasts striking public ceramics by native artists Miro, Gaudi, and Picasso.

Captivated by their Spanish heritage, Californians of the early 1900s adopted azulejos, patios, and countless other conceits of Moorish architecture. The years between the opening of the Panama Canal and World War II saw the flowering of a passion for everything Iberian. In San Diego's Balboa Park, in Seal Beach and Pasadena, in Westwood and Palo Alto and Santa Barbara, architecture adopted Hispano-Moorish styles. These Valentines of that romantic infatuation enable us to enjoy the illusion of an Andalusian interlude—without ever leaving the Golden State.

OLD SANTA BARBARA GARDENS

ELIZABETH DE FOREST

WHEN I look back to the golden age of Santa Barbara gardens—that period from about 1900 until shortly after the Second World War—I see, as I muse over it in memory, that there is a progression here in garden-making which I find interesting to consider. Simply stated it is this: first came into this area the horticultural importations, the wealth of new plants from countries of like climates—from the Middle East, from Mediterranean lands, from Australia and South Africa—and later came an appreciation of the garden plans of those countries and how they could be adapted to Santa Barbara surroundings.

Newcomers to a new land bring with them the images of what their gardens were like at home. Nostalgia plays a part, as does the security provided by sameness. Those early residents, who arrived in the 1880s and '90s from New England and the Middle West to enjoy the pleasure of our winters, planted around their Victorian houses and shingled cottages the kind of gardens they had known in harsher climates; a sweep of green lawn surrounded by flower borders was just about as far as garden design went. They sat on their porches and verandas admiring their palms, their orange trees, their jasmine vines, and, above all, their geraniums that grew in profusion around them. Foreign to them were paved terraces open to the sky, patios for lounging in the sun, and tiled wall fountains.

During this time a rich treasure of exotics was being introduced into the region by a number of enthusiasts, some professionals like Joseph Sexton, who established the first nursery here in 1868, and some amateurs. Charles Eaton was one of the latter, moving here from Nice in 1888. He it was who persuaded his Italian botanist-horticulturist friend, Francisco Franceschi Fenzi, to settle here. It was Dr Franceschi Fenzi who founded the Southern California Acclimatizing Association that imported and tested so many of the trees and shrubs we grow here today. These men were collectors rather than garden designers; their gardens were full of new and rare plants, grown in the ground where each would have the best chance of surviving.

It was not until early in the 1900s, with the building of the house and garden for J. Waldron Gillespie, that the possibility was realized of using not only the plants but the garden plans from countries with a climate and topography akin to our own. It is my

Constantia, *the South African residence designed by Ambrose Cramer, Sr for Mr and Mrs Arthur Meeker. As landscape architect, Lockwood de Forest reflected in the garden scheme the Dutch influence apparent in the style of the house*

opinion that with the creation of El Fureidis (Mr Gillespie's "Pleasant Place"), future garden makers were inspired to look for ideas from other lands. And what an inspiration it was. Waldron Gillespie had owned a piece of property along Cold Springs Creek since 1890 and must have contemplated its adornment a long time, for about 1900 he took a gifted young architect, Bertram Goodhue, around the world with him to gather ideas for his future home. They spent a long time in Italy, aware of the similarity of the climate to that in Santa Barbara, and made an intensive study of the Renaissance villas and their gardens. They then pushed on to Persia where they became enthralled with the concept of the garden as a green oasis in a dry land: where the use of water in long canals, in tanks, in pools, in runnels, flanked by tall trees, did marvelous things to bright sunlight.

Bertram Goodhue wrote a short essay on their Persian experience and from it we know the impact the gardens of Shiraz and Isfahan had upon them: ". . . and after a moment one finds oneself in a veritable paradise, wherein great cypresses and plane trees cast their motionless shadows over cool walks paved with ancient marble, gorgeous intricacies of colored tile and square tanks of silent but invariably crystal clear water." And again, ". . . but the poetry is here and the mystery and above all else the art and craft of garden making no less perfect than that in Italy."

They returned to Santa Barbara and Goodhue designed El Fureidis. The house is a Roman villa, built around a central atrium; it sits on a broad terrace with a parterre of shallow pools for foreground on its south side. From this terrace, dramatically descending a steep hillside, Goodhue planned a narrow allée, lined with Italian cypresses, backed by palms and dense shrubbery. No green lawn here, only the

masonry of steps, walls, paths, and long rectangular pools of Persian proportions refracting shafts of bright sunlight. From the house terrace the eye is led down, down this long allée to a tea house pavilion at the far end. Thus did Mr Gillespie and Bertram Goodhue make tangible their Persian memories, and point a way that others would follow.

By 1906 Gillespie's house was complete and the grounds had merged into their canyon surroundings. Some ten years later, around 1917, Mrs Oakleigh Thorne, on property in the same general neighborhood, made a garden inspired by an Italian Renaissance villa. She designed it herself, even learning to use surveyors' instruments to determine accurately the levels of her terraces. The Casino Caprarola and gardens at the Farnese Palace near Rome must have greatly intrigued her, for it is the facade of Caprarola that inspired the design for the loggia on the old adobe building she remodeled on her new property. Edith Wharton's *Italian Villas and Their Gardens* was first published in 1905, and the two volumes of Charles Latham's *The Gardens of Italy* appeared the same year. She could have known both works. The Thornes were frequent travelers in Italy and knew Rome well; she would have visited many of the gardens described. She must have realized that at Santa Barbara, where the climate and terrain are so similar to those of Italy, she could make an Italian garden. Did she say to herself that if Waldron Gillespie could bring back ideas from Persia, she could do the same from Rome?

To be looked down on from her Caprarola loggia she planned a broad, strong, very formal vista. A curving architectural cascade descended the first slope, its waters reappearing at intervals in the pools below, which were set on a series of terraces. On each terrace a parterre was laid

The dramatic allée, seen from the tea house below, in the garden at El Fureidis, *designed by Bertram Goodhue for J. Waldron Gillespie*

out in geometric design, some of the beds filled with small colored stones in the Italian manner and others with flowering ground covers. Standard orange trees, clipped shrubs, and box edgings provided the accents. At the end of the vista a final pool mirrored the arches of a garden house. Olive trees, groups of Italian cypresses, and a high clipped hedge flanked the sides. It was a plan of great strength; its proportions were most carefully considered, and it proved that Italian garden design was admirably suited to the Santa Barbara landscape.

A fanciful Dutch effect included in Lockwood de Forest's design at Constantia.

Then in the late 1800s and early 1920s Santa Barbarans realized, largely through the architectural talents of George Washington Smith and James Osborne Craig, that they could turn to Spain for garden inspiration. Did not the region have a Spanish heritage? Had not Mediterranean plants been thriving here since the founding of the Mission? Trips to Spain and Mexico would show what could be done. The intimate enclosed space; the garden to be lived in, an extension of the house; the walled patio; the paved terrace shaded by an olive tree; the low hedges and symmetrical flower beds; the tiled fountain with its dripping water—all these features were eagerly adopted and incorporated into countless garden schemes.

George Washington Smith designed the garden for his own house and those of several clients. El Hogar, the home of Mrs Craig Heberton, was one of the most famous. Secluded by tall trees, the paths and beds laid out symmetrically; all straight lines emphasized by edgings of dwarf box; sunlight and shadow playing over an oblong sunken pool on the terrace; it was the inspiration for scores of other Santa Barbara gardens made in Spanish style.

Yet another source of exotic plants thriving happily in Santa Barbara is South Africa, where the climate matches our own. It is, therefore, not surprising that in 1930 architect Ambrose Cramer, Sr should design a South African house for his in-laws, Mr and Mrs Arthur Meeker. Constantia, Cecil Rhodes' house at Capetown, gave him his ideas (the Santa Barbara adapta-

El Hogar, *Mrs Craig Heberton's home, where both Spanish-style house and garden were designed by George Washington Smith*

tion bears the same name). It stands on a ridge with a superb view. My late husband, Lockwood de Forest, as landscape architect for the project, created a garden for it that not only used many South African plants, but reflected the Dutch influence inherent in that distant land. He designed a great pool—a sheet of water—mirroring the mountain barrier to the north; he emphasized the wide rectangular form of the pool with a double row of tall, standard, box-shaped trees, clipped and stiff in contrast to the rugged mountains. Tall camphor trees embraced both corners of the north side of the house, and the top of the hedge bordering the terrace was clipped to a form that repeated the curves of the house gable. On the west side he planned a

small formal Dutch garden, the beds laid out in scrolls and filled with South African succulent plants. While no South African garden may ever have looked like this one, he captured in his plan the Dutch tradition that the architecture recalled, so that the house and garden became one artistic entity.

I hope I have shown that over this thirty-year period garden making in Santa Barbara was greatly influenced by concepts from countries whose climates were similar to its own; that first came the plants, wonderful and strange, and then a wealth of new ideas in garden design. And after the plants became a part of the landscape and when the ideas were skillfully used, were the results so foreign after all?

THE COLOR GARDEN

HARLAND J. HAND

THE color motif of my El Cerrito, California, garden developed because of a practical problem with a path. I had made a dirt path that wound down the steep slope of the garden. But it was always full of weeds and the packed soil made them difficult to remove. To eliminate this problem, I made steps and stepping stones of concrete, doing them in place, directly on the soil. When the concrete was finished, I became intrigued by the color relationship between it and the surrounding plants. There seemed to be something special about the way the colors sharpened and gave drama to each other. To my eye, the concrete registered as a light color, while the contrasting color of the plants, for the most part, seemed dark. The significant thing was that the plants, though they actually were a middle tone, clearly registered as a dark color in contrast to the light color of the concrete.

The relationship of these dark and light colors reminded me of the gray granite glacial formations of the high Sierra. The area of the mountains near Silver Lake with its strong color contrasts between the light gray granite and the dark islands of conifers was one giant, dramatic, dark and light garden. I decided to use the strong dark and light contrast of that powerful landscape as the color motif of my garden.

I knew that light colors along a path would make for greater visibility at night, so I planted plants with light gray leaves near the sharpest curves. I discovered that, where I had placed these gray-leaved plants next to the light gray concrete, the two colors combined to make one shape. When I widened and narrowed the light shape of the path by placing gray-leaved plants next to it, I discovered a rhythmic pattern beginning to appear. I found that I could control the way my eye flowed over the garden by the way I varied these light shapes. So I began to add more and more concrete. I made paths through every area of the garden. If they led my eye too swiftly, I could vary the pace by narrowing them in some places and abruptly widening them in others. I eventually made such a network of light-colored paths that they isolated mounds of soil, plants, and native rock into islands of middle tone. Where these darker islands became too regular in size and shape, I made variations by running another path through them. For even greater variation I reversed the colors completely by tearing out some dark islands and replacing them with light-colored, level rooms with concrete slabs for a floor and concrete benches for furniture. The additional concrete strengthened and massed the light shapes so much that the whole garden appeared more and more dramatic. The islands of dark seemed to grow out of a bedrock of light-colored concrete slabs, benches, and paths.

I added concrete pools, placing them so that they appeared to flow into each other. This helped to give a suggestion of a riverbed and, through the exploitation of this idea, I established a flow of dark and light color throughout the entire garden. The more concrete I put in, the more the garden appeared to be a light-colored rock outcropping with islands of dark plants, much like that Sierra landscape.

I am constantly on the lookout for items that help widen and enrich the light-colored concrete areas. I am continuously searching for gray-leaved plants. Most such plants have special structures that make them appear gray. These structures give a texture to the leaf or stem surfaces that can further vary the color by producing tiny textural shadows that change with the season and time of day. The furry rabbit ears of *Stachys olympica* have dense soft hairs which give the leaves a very light, almost white color that, when seen next to the concrete, is quite unexpected. The white powdery covering of *Echeveria elegans* provides a delicate, pale gray-green that seems juicy in contrast to the hardness of the gray concrete. The leaves of some tansies are like tiny feathers. They are unusually soft and downy, giving a color that is actually an off-white. When planted next to the heavy concrete they make a contrasting combination that is nearly unbelievable. The short hairs on snow-in-summer (*Cerastium tomentosum*) make their leaves a dull greenish gray. I have found many plants that can be used to enhance or en-

large the light gray shapes of the concrete, but the above are my favorites.

White flowers give contrast to the light-colored areas. They provide highlights that push forward to enliven the grays and gray-greens. They are especially effective when the white-flowered plant itself has gray leaves. The small, airy, white flowers of snow-in-summer and the small white daisies of certain of the low-growing chrysanthemums are both ideal for providing subtle highlights within the light-colored shapes of the garden because both of them have gray leaves.

Other materials that act as light shapes or as part of a light shape are gravel (the coarse gray pebbles used as an aggregate for concrete), sculptures of birds and animals made of concrete or pottery, rocks (especially worn river rock), and driftwood.

The islands are made primarily of evergreen plants with some native rocks placed among them. Plants in leaf usually register as a middle tone which, in the color relationship of my garden, is dark. Most azaleas, rhododendrons, fuchsias, junipers, citrus, ferns, and camellias are middle tone. I use some deciduous shrubs and trees for their middle-toned leaves in summer and for their medium brown, airy branches in winter. These plants include lilacs, magnolias, roses, plums, prunes, apples, peaches, maples, and many others. Like the woody plants, most herbaceous ones also have foliage that is medium in tone. Agapanthus, hellebores, irises, lilies, arums, orchids, bergenias, and geraniums (pelargoniums) are some examples. Some very low rock garden plants that fit this category include thyme, achillea, armeria, violet, iberis, and some succulents. I also enjoy annual plants of this color range because they give quick color to a newly planted garden before perennials have time to mature. These annuals may include petunias, lobelias, verbenas, salpiglossis, marigolds, poppies, nicotiana, ageratum, violas, and pansies.

Whereas white flowers give contrast within the light shapes by acting as high lights, very dark plants give contrast to the middle-toned areas by suggesting deep shadows. Those plants that register as extremely dark are rare; however, some examples are purple-leaved plums, Irish yew, Hinoki false cypress (*Chamaecyparis obtusa*), *Agave victoriae-reginae*, and especially *Aeonium arboreum* 'Zwartkop' with its maroon-black leaves. Of course, the darkest color would be formed by the shadows on these dark plants. Some plants with strong architectural form, such as the conifers, also produce shadows of dark color, but shadows change during the day and so will not always give dark color where it is needed. To help make up for this illusiveness, I set life-sized figures of birds and animals, painted black, in places that need a bit of strong dark color for emphasis.

I try to group the plants within the middle-tone islands so that they work like a well-balanced flower arrangement. The tallest are off center, with middle-sized ones on the outside and low plants arranged around the edges so that they tie into the level of the concrete surfaces. This can allow the color to surround the viewer, especially in places where trees with overhanging branches are used.

Plant groupings within the islands also depend upon two practical considerations; one, the amount of shade in case there is a large tree; and two, the varying amounts of water because of sprinkler problems. Shade plants are grouped in the shade, bog plants in the drainage runs, and some scree plants or California natives in the areas missed by the sprinklers. By working the practical problems and color composition together, I have been able to

Many plants worked into dark and light shapes to provide fully orchestrated color

include thousands of interesting plants. They produce satisfying color relationships even in the most difficult problem areas.

To unify the color and to give a natural flow of color throughout the garden, I place some dark items in the light-colored areas and some light-colored things in the dark areas. Between and around the concrete structures I spot a few plants of the dark-leaved *Armeria juniperifolia* (white- or pink-flowered), *Veronica repens* (dark leaves and white flowers), *Iberis sempervirens* 'Snow Flake', *Achillea tomentosa*, and other low rock garden plants that have dark color but do not restrict the flow of traffic through the rooms and paths.

I mix some gray things into the dark islands to help tie them to the surrounding masses of light color. I use such plants as white roses, magnolia, agapanthus, and lilies. The white flowers provide a sharp contrast to the dark foliage within the islands. Gray artemisia, salvia, and oat grass are tall enough to hold their own when spotted within the islands. Gray driftwood pilings from San Francisco Bay are placed so that their light shapes soar out of the middle tone, carrying the light color up and above my head. I use vines such as clematis, pandorea, billardiera, wisteria, and climbing roses to soften the stark forms of the pilings. The white flowers and dark leaves of *Clematis* 'Henryi' against a gray driftwood piling are an astonishing combination.

The total effect of the dark and light design is planned to be one that not only leads the eye through the garden, but also moves out of the garden to the dark wooded ridges above and below, then on to the light gray buildings in the flatlands, to San Francisco Bay and the city beyond. Since the garden occupies a ridge, an enormous sky that fluctuates between darkness and light-ness envelops it. Strong dark and light seems to be the dominant color motif for the whole Bay Area.

FULL COLOR ORCHESTRATION

The most satisfying aspect of the dark and light motif of the garden is that it forms a base for fully orchestrated color. Any color that I want to use can be worked into it because every single color has its dark and light aspect. For example, yellow is a light color and works fine within the light areas. Other colors such as blue, violet, green, orange, and red are middle tone and work nicely within the dark islands. Pale colors (tints of the above) usually register as light. Shades (very dark colors) register from middle tone to near black. Each color can fit somewhere within the dark and light plan.

Besides fitting into the dominant color motif of the garden, each plant color has a special relationship with other colors. Colors do things to each other that are sometimes unexpected. For example, the yellow flowers of *Gazania uniflora* against its silvery leaves and the gray concrete make every color in this combination both brilliant and subtle. Because of the gray of the concrete, the yellow of the flowers is vibrant and because of the yellow the gray of the concrete takes on a strange blue-violet cast. A spot of purple violas nearby makes those same yellow flowers look like jewels in a silver mounting.

Another striking example of what a single hue can do is shown by the small rose 'Garnet'. Its dark red flowers and dark reddish green leaves against the light gray of pebbles and concrete make a combination that is bold yet deeply subtle. The eye will move toward this combination wherever it may be placed in the garden. This same rose makes blue ageratum shimmer in-

Garden room with view of San Francisco Bay

Muehlenbeckia axillaris *forms a nest for*
Echeveria elegans

Graptopetalum paraguayense *and*
Heterocentron elegans

tensely, and when I use it in a dark island with orange-red rhododendrons, magenta azaleas, and dark pink roses, it makes a deep, blended, glowing combination. If I use this same maroon-red rose with warm and cool reds, it produces a kind of red-on-red relationship with such depth of color that I stand fascinated by it. When orchid, pinks, and oranges are combined with the dark red of this rose, there is a feast of Persian color.

Within the middle tone of the dark islands, I experimented with all kinds of color relationships. To me, the most important idea that I discovered was that the closer the colors are in brightness and value (lightness and darkness), the more iridescent and glowing they all become and the less likely they are to cancel each other. This is especially true of cool colors. Blues, violets, and deep greens make a particularly rich combination within the middle tone of the islands. These are the peacock colors and are particularly useful both as background and foreground color.

COLOR IMPACT

There are two devices that I often use to develop a satisfying color impact; one is to use many plants with similar colors together; the other is to use small amounts of warm colors to bring out cool colors and small amounts of cool colors to bring out warm colors. To give impact to retiring colors that are often lost in a planting, I usually combine them with similarly colored flowers that are bold and rather vulgar in their impact. For example, I plant dull pinkish-flowered plants such as *Enkianthus campanulatus* or *Tamarix parviflora* (the spring-blooming tamarix) with the large-flowered pink and red reticulata camellias, pink rhododendrons, pink azaleas, and pink primroses. In this combina-

tion of similar warm colors, the small dull-pink flowers brighten considerably and in turn they soften the impact of the large flowers. To make the whole combination bright and rich, I add just a little cool color, a few violets and blue muscari are all that is needed.

Another special way of increasing the impact of small but richly colored flowers is to plant them near a bench or walkway where they can be viewed up close. The big vulgar-flowered plants can be subdued by planting them in more distant positions. Their boldness can attract the eye to areas that it might otherwise skip over.

Although flowers of nearly every color appear throughout my garden, each area is dominated by a special color combination wherein the abundance of one color unifies the others. For example, near the house is a quiet area with an abundance of white flowers throughout the entire year. Some white flowers that bloom in the spring are camellias, calla lilies, *Iberis* 'Snow Flake', *Magnolia soulangeana* 'Alba', primroses, and heathers. Following these come azalea 'Snow Bird', the flowering peach 'Iceland', white flowering broom, and *Wisteria floribunda* 'Longissima Alba' with the white *Clematis* 'Henryi' growing up the same pole and in bloom at the same time. In late spring and early summer, roses ('White Masterpiece', white polyanthus, and a white climber), white Japanese iris, abutilons, fuchsias, and late rhododendrons keep the area white. The roses continue through the rest of the year along with white hydrangea, *Gypsophila* 'Bristol Fairy', *Bouvardia* 'Albatross', white fuchsias, and many others. To help soften the whites, of course, there are gray concrete and gray-leaved plants. For subtlety and richness I add just a few very light colors such as 'The Fairy', a pale pink rose, cream-colored alyssum, and bright yellow *Achillea*

Gray-leaved plants and pale flowers emphasize light-colored areas of concrete

tomentosa. To brighten the whites I use dark-leaved plants and spots of dark red and dark blue. A 'Garnet' rose, deep magenta primroses, *Rochea coccinea,* gerberas, and others provide the spots of dark red. The spots of dark blue include agapanthus, *Felicia amelloides,* several campanulas, and *Sisyrinchium bellum,* among others. Because this area near the house is dominated and unified by an abundance of white, I call it the White Garden.

The Yellow Garden is one of warm colors with yellow dominating over oranges, golds, and warm reds. A few small, white-flowered plants are added for subtle highlights with a few spots of blue and violet to make the warm colors of this area glow like fire.

The Blue Garden (it has cool colors dominated by blue) was completed in the spring and in order to bring it into full color as soon as possible, I put annuals among the newly planted perennial plants which would eventually take over. I planted annual lobelia in dark blue, light blue, and mauve; petunias in purple, steel blue, dark blue, light blue, a few magenta, and three bright red ones; to this mixture I added blue ageratum; blue and violet verbena, with some blue violas and pansies for the more shaded parts. This planting was done in April, and in June there was a great show of billowing color. The whole combination glowed brilliantly even from a distance, especially after I added two fiery, orange-red gerberas.

TIME SEQUENCE COLOR

Some sections of the garden are planted so that different color combinations will dominate at different times during the year. To bring this about, I attempt to manipulate the color in order to produce a special kind of expression, like music, that is revealed in time sequences. The blue sequence starts in January with blue muscari, blue and violet primroses, blue Peruvian scilla, violets, and purple violas—all showing a little color. These bloom more and more profusely, especially the muscari, until they hit a peak in late March. Then the blues subside slightly and are gradually overwhelmed in late April and early May by a spectacle of reds, pinks, orchids, and yellows (azaleas and other rhododendrons mostly) with just enough blue and violet left to intensify them all. By late May the warm colors quiet down and the blues commence their main surge to dominate, beginning with blue-violet Siberian irises, then Japanese irises, with some blue agapanthuses just starting to flower. I have agapanthuses that are very tall, others that are shorter; some have heavy flowered heads and others airy ones. They are planted abundantly in clumps and drifts all through the garden and increase their flower production through June, becoming a crescendo of blue that has its climax in July and August. At this same time, blue-violet pleroma, blue *Solanum rantonnetii*, fuchsias in many shades of blue and violet, summer violets, several lavenders, campanulas, dark blue felicias, blue-violet and mauve *Tradescantia virginiana*, blue veronicas, blue-violet and mauve clematis, and many others are all blooming profusely, adding to the intensity of the blue which flows off in every direction, taking the eye through every vista of the garden. After this climax the blue subsides again, but this time it gently gives way to a saturation of greens.

The greens of my garden play a background theme with a climax in early fall. There are fewer flowers between September and February, so during this time the garden becomes a saturation of greens with a few spots of other colors to brighten and enrich them. The middle-tone greens that form most of the islands include green greens, rusty greens, blue greens, yellow greens, and others, all in rich variety of leaf and stem texture. The yellow greens of golden cypress, golden juniper, and tree ferns furnish the highlights. The dark, blackish greens of Irish yew, Hinoki cypress, rosemary, and some of the rhododendrons add the deepest shades.

During the late season, spots of red from roses intensify the greens, as do the pinks of fuchsias, roses, abutilons, and geraniums. Yellow flowers add bright highlights and, with the yellow greens, seem like beams of sunlight on a dull day. Blue and violet flowers inject a touch of mystery and richness to the tapestry of green. Plants with colored leaves such as purple-leaved plum, red phormium, and a rainbow of succulents continue a kind of subdued opalescence that does not end.

COLOR AND SPACE

During the late season, when flowering has subsided, I am most aware of the placement of color in the garden. At this time, it seems clearer to me just how color can distort the feeling of space. Warm colors seem to advance like a fire and cool colors seem to recede like the sky on a cold clear day. The warm color of the yellow garden, which is some distance from the house, seems close and makes the cool colors of the blue garden beyond seem so far away that to prevent its seeming to recede completely from the rest of the garden I had to plant the everblooming, salmon-pink rose 'Margo Koster' beyond it.

Another aspect of color that comes out of this advancing and receding is a kind of

Late in the year, succulents in many colors add a subdued but unending opalescence to the dominating background of greens

trompe l'oeil. For example, in order to give unity and rhythm to the garden, I place a color, such as yellow, in three different positions so that one yellow plant is close, the second is in the middle distance, and the third is in the background. If I stand so that the three yellow plants line up and appear to merge into one yellow shape, I will be slightly confused because I cannot quite figure the position of what now seems to be a single yellow shape. But if I move a few feet to one side, the single shape will again separate into three distinct shapes, each with a clear position in space. Purposefully arranging colors so that they alternately confuse and clarify spatial relationships is a device that can add an interest going beyond the mere presence of the items in the garden. This is one of those illusive things that can give a special magical vitality to a design.

Color relationships change constantly as

the viewer moves through the garden. Where a color is seen as the focus of attention from one position, from another position this same color is seen as part of the background for another color. This aspect can produce unexpected color relationships that add richness and unity to the entire garden. For example, one spring day while sitting on a bench at the top of the garden, I was surprised to discover that the colors from that view lined up like a rainbow (but not in that order); blue irises were closest, purple irises next, then magenta azaleas, red rhododendrons, then an orange-red azalea, orange aloes, and finally yellow alyssum in the far distance. This had not been planned, but it did unify several areas of the garden.

Pools provide endless color variation because the effects of water are ever-changing. The pools in my garden were conceived as having color that would reverse the space of the dark islands, that is, be a dark hole instead of a dark mound. Each one was to be a ring of light gray concrete around dark water, a kind of variation of the concrete slab. For the most part the pools do what I had planned. However, the extent of the color variation provided by the water goes beyond these ideas, because water reflects everything around it and changes color with the time of day and with the position of the viewer. Because of the organisms that grow in it, water can usually be seen as a dark color, but at times it becomes an intense light-colored surface, especially when it reflects the sky or light colors nearby. By its reflections, water pro-

vides echoing color that can rhythmically repeat any color that is around it. A solitary green fern is reflected in the water and so seems less isolated; or a clump of yellow alyssum is reflected in the water and the yellow becomes doubly abundant. A reflection can also increase the amount of a color to the point where the balance of the color relationship is destroyed.

Not only does light affect the reflections on water and thus change color relationships, but changing light affects the color in the whole garden. Morning light tends to cool all the colors, while afternoon light tends to warm them. The changing position of the sun moves the shadows around so that plant colors are bright and advancing one moment and dull and receding the next. Shadows can change a shape that is light-colored one moment into one that is middle tone the next.

Every single part of the color garden must be maintained because there is not a square inch that is without color. Dead flowers must be picked off, proportions controlled by pruning and by the removal or the installation of plants. Diseased plants have to be treated, weeds removed, and paths and rooms swept of garden debris. The colors can be dull and depressing one moment and, with a little cleaning, become bright and delightful a short while later.

I do not believe that full control of color in natural light can be achieved. However, it is fascinating to be able to understand what happens to color in the garden and to try to make the most of every circumstance.

GARDENING AT SEA WORLD

CHUCK KLINE

S EA World is part of the ambitious Mission Bay Recreational Park, a 4,200-acre marine-oriented recreational area built on a salt marsh at the edge of the San Diego River estuary. From its inception in 1963, Sea World's developers have held the landscape aspects of the project to be among its most important features.

Viewing the rolling mounded lawns, the fountains, and the huge variety of trees, shrubs, and flowering plants, one has difficulty imagining what this area looked like before it was developed. Wimmer and Yamada, first of a number of landscape architects to leave their mark on Sea World, faced a number of problems in turning this piece of land into an environment that would support a wide range of exotic plants. The intrusion of salt water from below (a permanent salt water level can be found from ten to thirty feet beneath any part of the park) and the salt carried in from the spindrift of the Pacific Ocean remain the major restrictions on plant growth. Added to this is a prevailing westerly wind, which continuously buffets any unprotected plants. Many nurserymen were doubtful that much could be done with this area, since previous plantings had largely failed to thrive.

First the sand and silt of the estuary were pumped out into designated land areas, leaving extensive waterways in between. The land areas then received large amounts of fill, which was mounded to provide sufficient topsoil for planting. The mounds also add visual interest to what had been a flat monotonous area, and they permit some privacy—an important feature in a park that receives more than 2.4 million visitors a year. Pleasantly winding walkways and diverse vistas of Mission Bay are other benefits of the mounding approach.

Changing the topography of the land has created problems of its own, one being excessive runoff. Since the park is open only in the daytime, automatic sprinklers have been set to water throughout the night, sprinkling each area twice at intervals to reduce runoff. The park cannot be allowed to go dry or the salt water will rise through capillary action to the level of the plants' roots.

Despite such problems, the benign climate of San Diego and the tempering effect of the ocean allow many kinds of plants to flourish. Frost is virtually unknown, and summer temperatures rarely go above the eighties.

Ducks in the bird area at Sea World

Every public garden has its own character and purpose. The basic concept of the landscaping at Sea World is to provide an atmosphere of beauty and peace to complement the marine shows, exhibits, and aquariums. But the idea of a laboratory for experimentation with seaside plantings has not been overlooked, and more than 2,000 kinds of plants are now grown here. The majority can be found in nurseries (though some may require searching for) or in local collections. One purpose of Sea World's landscaping is to show the public what mature specimens of these plants look like and how they can be used in the garden.

A heavily visited park usually must rely on fences to keep lawns and plantings in good shape, but the policy at Sea World has always been to have as few artificial barriers

Tropical effect at North Lagoon

as possible. Picnicking on the lawns and access to all plantings are permitted, even encouraged, as is the close, though careful, interaction with animals. When an animal (such as the flamingo) is likely to be harmed by human contact, its area is surrounded by a living fence of prickly holly (*Ilex*) or Natal plum (*Carissa macrocarpa*). Restrictive signs are kept to a minimum.

Sea World means different things to different people. Those who have limited time to visit may see it as a green subtropical garden and massed plantings of floribunda and multiflora roses. For others, many of whom have annual passes, there is time to enjoy the plant collections and the relaxed ambience of the grounds. Schools, universities, and garden societies make frequent use of the gardens for instructional purposes.

Mounded beds at Sea World

Visitors entering through the front gate are treated to the sight of a group of weeping acacias (*Acacia pendula* from New South Wales and Queensland, Australia), their silver-leaved branches forming a striking background for pink flamingos.

On some of the sunny mounds are magnificent stands of *Pinus torreyana* which have grown to thirty or forty feet from an initial height of five feet just ten years ago. Pines such as *P. thunbergiana, P. pinaster, P.* *radiata, P. canariensis, P. montezumae, P. muricata, P. densiflora* 'Umbraculifera', *P. massoniana, P. eldarica*, and many others have thrived on the larger mounds, showing no signs of salt burn. Grass is the main ground cover on most of these mounds, but many are embellished with plantings of dwarf cultivars of carissa, pyracantha, rosemary, ivy, and the prostrate junipers, especially *Juniperus conferta*.

These ground covers also are used on

Waterfall at North Lagoon

the mounds in the stadium areas, as are many varieties of gazania (including *Gazania* 'Moon Glow'), *Osteospermum fruticosum*, and *O.* 'African Queen'.

Massed color is difficult to achieve in mounded plantings because not only does the soil have a tendency to wash downhill, but every imperfect plant stands out because of the viewing angle. Among the most successful of these plantings at Sea World has been one incorporating the

many fine canna hybrids. In San Diego County, most cannas bloom throughout the year, their bold hues and strong foliage making magnificent sweeps of color.

Melaleuca quinquenervia, with drifts of *Pittosporum tobira* 'Variegata' and *Raphiolepis indica* 'Rosea', are the predominant plants in one section of the park. In this area also are a waterfall and a rock garden planted with species needing protection from the wind. Many ferns are luxuriating here, including, among others, adiantums, polystichums, aspleniums, pterises, dicksonias, cibotiums, alsophilas, and doodias. Begonias are beginning to settle in too, as are some real gems—*Tupeinocheilos* (from Queensland), for instance, though somewhat frozen one particularly cold winter, is growing back rapidly.

Among the special collections are carnivorous plants displayed with graphics explaining the different insect-trapping mechanisms. Other collections include bromeliads, the locally endemic Torrey pine mentioned above, many perennial herbs, and low Australian and New Zealand shrubs (e.g., a collection of hybrid New Zealand flax). Starting from a large planting of specimen-sized sago palms (*Cycas revoluta*), many other cycads have been added. And a collection of palms, including groupings of mature Mexican fan palms (*Washingtonia robusta*) and Senegal date palms (*Phoenix reclinata*), has been expanded recently with over forty species.

Selection and siting of plants has been a challenge in this difficult environment. Planning new plantings so that the more delicate plants are placed on the leeward side of the soil mounds has allowed the use of many, such as ferns and begonias, which otherwise could not be expected to grow well. In areas needing showy plants such as the potato vine (*Solanum rantonnetii*), which cannot be protected in this way, antitranspirants have been applied to the entire plant every two months with spectacular success. With this added protection, these plants now bloom throughout the entire year. And, for some of the most saline spots where even the hardiest hybrid Bermuda grasses such as 'Santa Ana' have failed, the recently introduced 'Adalayd', a cultivar of *Paspalum virgatum* from Australia, is doing well.

Because the subsoil is poor and saline, careful preparation of planting areas has been necessary. Large amounts of organic matter such as firbark or redwood leaf mold are worked into the soil in and below the root zone. Without such preparation, plant roots would not penetrate deeply enough to maintain growth or resist the onslaught of winter storms.

A good fertilizer also is important for lawns and shrubs on soil that lacks colloidal matter. The newer slow-release fertilizers have been found to work well, especially those derived from organic sources. With the constant leaching from heavy irrigation of sandy soil, applying these fertilizers according to the manufacturer's directions was found to be wasteful. Only half the recommended application now is given, but at more frequent intervals.

From experience the landscape department at Sea World has learned that chemical cure-alls are not what ensure a thriving garden in this difficult setting. Rather, it is careful planting, use of generous amounts of organic matter to provide humus, constant low-level feeding, continuous watering, and sufficient aeration and drainage that bring positive results.

We at Sea World strive to make our horticultural collections useful and enjoyable to visitors. With an ongoing labeling program, our goal is eventually to have all plants identified for the public. An active education department offers courses for local schools and interested groups, and tours are available for those wanting to know more about the plants and animals in the park. Recently the landscape department obtained a computer to store information on the plant collections, and it is the intention at Sea World to exchange plants and share data with other horticultural and botanical organizations.

A DESERT IN THE CITY

F. OWEN PEARCE

A DRAMATICALLY unusual landscape has been created during the past few years in a part of what was long called the Bancroft Farm, mostly in orchards, in Ygnacio Valley, now in the northeastern part of Walnut Creek, California.

Hubert Howe Bancroft, famed California historian and founder of the University of California's Bancroft Library, was the grandfather of Philip Bancroft Jr, the present owner. Hubert Bancroft purchased the property in 1885 when it was an extensive grain field dotted with valley oaks (*Quercus lobata*), many of which are still standing in all their statuesque glory. Several of these trees, with their broadly spreading, rounded forms and weeping lower branches, form magnificent framing and backgrounds for the house and for parts of the garden. The first Mr Bancroft planted fruit and walnut trees over the land, but in recent years encroaching residential developments and the consequent high assessments and taxes have changed the economy of land holdings in such locations. As a result, most of the Bancroft Farm has been sold and the orchards have given way to homes. The Bancrofts have retained about ten acres, and their home and gardens are in this area.

Ruth Bancroft, Philip's charming wife, is responsible for the development of the exotic garden. Her husband is the first to admit that he is too lazy to assume any responsibility for it. Lester Hawkins, partner in the Western Hills Nursery near Occidental, California, was called in at the beginning as landscape designer. The original design of the desert garden is his. He suggested the idea of the mounds and their locations and of the paths, the pool, and the shade house. He furnished eucalypts, the acacias, and other Australian plants, all of which are important elements of the garden.

Ruth Bancroft was interested in plants as a child, an interest that turned to cultivated plants as she matured. Raised in the higher reaches of the North Berkeley hills, she was enchanted with the wild flowers so plentiful at that time. She was a close neighbor of those two great horticulturists of the area—Sydney B. Mitchell, president of the California Horticultural Society for its first ten years and founder of its *Journal*; and Carl Salbach, dahlia and iris grower. These two had large gardens on adjacent properties, and through her close friendship with them she became an enthusiastic iris grower. She has continued to grow irises,

The dusky pink flowers of Aloe greenii *on long, gray, suede stems are sentries by the gravel path as it wanders toward the pool*

but she enlarged her interests to other plants as time passed. The present garden is the result.

After Ruth and Philip were married, the Ygnacio Valley farm became home, and about twenty-five years ago the house was redesigned and a garden was built around it. Theodore Osmundsen was the landscape architect for this garden, which featured a perennial border surrounding a sizable lawn on the south side of the house. The border is still growing in beautiful, neat order.

It is surprising to find that the lawns and borders, the great array of potted plants, mostly succulents, the lathhouse, and the five or six acres comprising the desert garden are, all of them, maintained by only two workers: Ruth herself, and her dedicated helper, John da Rosa. Maintenance is

here used in a very broad sense, for it includes not only the planting, weeding, and watering, the propagation and growing on of plants, but the continuous planning, creating, and layout of the plants and planting beds—and the care of the lawn. All the water for the garden comes from the Bancrofts' private well, but the desert garden is very sparsely watered.

The greatest of the interests in the garden is found in the growing of succulent plants, an all-inclusive term; and of other plants that do not depend on summer rains—plants found in the arid areas of the southwestern United States, Mexico, South America, Australia, and South Africa. Ruth became intensely interested in these drought-tolerant plants about eighteen years ago and began collecting them from many sources.

Notocactus leninghausii *in bud and flower*

The present extraordinary garden was started five years ago, in the spring preceding the freeze of December 1972. That freeze was marked by temperatures that went down to 12°F every night for almost a week, and for several days they never went above freezing in the daytime. Many plants were lost and the outlook was bleak and discouraging. However, Ruth's fascination with succulents remained, and the thought that had they been established for a longer period they might have survived the freeze persuaded her to replant those that could be obtained again. Visiting the garden now it is hard to believe that much could have been lost.

The first view of the desert garden from the entrance driveway, which borders it on the north, is nothing less than dramatic. An area of three or four acres simulates a desert landscape. As in a desert, plants or plant groups have spaces between them so that there is an overall sense of openness. In the desert plants are naturally separated because only the strongly rooted reach for and obtain the sparse rain water. This principle of openness is not completely adhered to in this garden, for there are sizable groups of close plantings; in such cases the groups are so related in size with other plants that the spaciousness is maintained.

One such group consists of a pool, planted with pond lilies surrounded by succulent plants. *Sedum* 'Peach Glory' gives a lovely spot of color on one side of the pool. The pool and its surrounding border form a color unit that is in harmony with the adjacent plants.

The whole scene seems dominated by

agaves—agaves of numerous species, sizes, and ages, all in different stages of growth. Some are developing flower stalks for this year's bloom and some retain last year's stalks, now brown and dry. A dried stalk foretells the death of that plant this year, and it will have to be removed by tractor and chain. The root and leaves will be sawed into manageable pieces and hauled off to the dump. This saddens Ruth, for it means that these dying plants will have to be removed shortly, leaving holes to be filled by other plants.

Every agave plant is worth studying—perhaps for the variations in thorniness of leaf edges and, most rewarding, for the varied leaf colorings. The flowering stalks of mature plants rise unbelievably rapidly to a height of twenty feet. Indications that a new stalk is forming can be seen in the more slender, smooth-margined leaves in the center of the plant.

The most noticeable large agave is *Agave ferox*, with leaves up to six or seven feet long and ten inches wide at the base. One specimen sheltered under a saran cloth covering in a court behind the garage, has leaves that, after rising four or five feet from the ground, droop over sharply so that the points almost touch the ground in a grand weeping effect. Other species of *Agave* to be seen are *A. univittata*, *A. victoriae-reginae*, and *A. franzosinii*.

After the first surprising impressions of the agave "plantation" have subsided, the many other desert-type plants—trees, shrubs, and ground covers—command attention, all harmoniously displayed against the brown crushed rock imported from nearby Mt. Diablo; it covers the entire desert area, including the commodious paths, which wind their way pleasantly through the plantings. The mounds were formed with imported soil before the crushed rock, which has an average thickness of two to three inches, was laid.

Conspicuously, Ruth's Folly stands out—a gracefully designed gazebo or lathhouse with two long wings and a square-domed center structure. Webster's Dictionary defines a folly as "any foolish and fruitless but expensive undertaking." Thus, kiddingly, this structure has been named by her husband and friends. Actually, foolish and fruitless it is not. Only technically might it be called a lathhouse, for its arched, timbered frame is covered with polyethylene rather than with laths. The purpose is the same—a growing house for potted plants that need some shelter from the sun in summer and from the cold in winter. The structure is set back from the entrance drive a short distance, and it is a completely harmonious adjunct to the garden.

From experience Ruth has learned the hard way about the effects of cold and heat on succulent plants, which are notoriously tender to such conditions. To meet this challenge, Ruth has areas in the garden protected by polyethylene-covered frameworks, sometimes for individual plants, and sometimes for an extensive group of plants. The covers are removed once the cold weather has ended, except for those plants that require protection from the hot summer sun.

Other noteworthy plants join the agaves in forming this delightful desert scene. Several specimens of *Parkinsonia aculeata* are subtly placed to show off as individual plants. A member of the legume family commonly known as the Mexican palo verde, parkinsonia is evidently happy in its habitat, for volunteer seedlings are profusely distributed around the shrubby parent plants. The desert willow (*Chilopsis linearis*), a member of the Bignoniaceae from dry washes in the California and Arizona deserts with lovely, almost orchid-like flowers, is represented by several flourishing specimens.

While exploring the garden observant

Shadehouse and garden entrance

eyes will notice many species of *Opuntia*, including *O. bigelovii* (teddy bear cactus), flowering stalks of the majestic *Yucca treculeana*, and several plants of the ubiquitous tamarisk from Europe and Asia which have become naturalized in many areas of the west. And to select particular species from numerous genera, we find *Aloe ferox*; several euphorbias, including *Euphorbia caput-medusae*, *E. coerulescens* and *E. myrsinites*; several eucalypts, including *Eucalyptus pendula*; and numerous small shrubs, including *Anthyllis barba-jovis*, *Coreopsis maritima*, *Hakea leucoptera*, *Cercidium floridum*, and *Grevillea* 'Canberra'. *Yucca elata* grows next to the pool.

The transition from the desert atmosphere to the house is accomplished by a screen of shrubs and trees, bordering which, on the desert side, is a large planting of irises. These border a half-hidden driveway on the west side of the house—the house being to the southeast of the desert area. The iris planting illustrates again the great task of caring for this garden. Each year one-third of the irises are taken up, the rhizomes are separated and replanted. This chore requires about six weeks of labor in the fall.

Finally we arrive at the lawn and perennial border, backed with shrubs and trees, on the south side of the house. The lawn is roughly semicircular, the house forming the base, with the border spreading around the lawn like a huge rainbow. There is a constant change of color in the border as the seasons change. Plants included in season are *Aurinia saxatilis*, *Primula malacoides*, *Helleborus orientalis*, and daffodils and tulips in quantity.

Ruth maintains a record of all the plants in her garden, and the complete list of names fills several notebooks.

THE MUSIC CONCOURSE, GOLDEN GATE PARK

ELIZABETH McCLINTOCK

GOLDEN GATE PARK'S first music concourse, dedicated July 4, 1888, was near the present-day tennis courts. After the close of the Mid-Winter Fair it was decided to move the music concourse to the Concert Valley of the fair site, opposite today's de Young Museum. Construction of the new bandstand was begun in 1899. At the time of its dedication September 9, 1900, it was called the Spreckels Temple of Music, honoring the generosity of Claus Spreckels, whose contribution of $75,000 made its construction possible. Designed by the brothers James and Merrit Reid in Italian Renaissance style and built of Colusa sandstone, it is still impressive. Its central arch, fifty-five feet wide and seventy feet high, is flanked on both sides by Corinthian columns. It faces an open area called at the time of its dedication the Great Court. According to the account of the dedication in the thirty-first annual report of the Board of Park Commissioners of San Francisco, for the year ending June 30, 1902, "The Great Court in front has been carefully turned, and a profusion of shrubbery and trees add picturesqueness to the scene." Among the trees, seating was provided for 20,000 people. On the day of the dedication there were 75,000 people "bending their heads to listen" and "this great crowd not only overtaxed this immense seating capacity, but the terraced grounds along the outer boundaries of the court were black with humanity."

Nothing more is said of the trees planted in the Great Court in the account of the dedication, but a contemporary photograph which features the bandstand gives an impression of a fairly uniform planting of trees facing it.

The trees in the concourse are still uniform, suggesting that they were planted about the same time. They are deciduous, so their appearance changes with the seasons, but a close look at the trees shows that their uniformity in height and shape is a result of pruning. During most of their years they have been pollarded once a year, their secondary branches cut back almost to the main trunk. This results in a dense head of long, slender new shoots that grow from the upper ends of the secondary branches, giving the tree a broad dome-shaped crown. Pollarding should not be confused with pleaching, another severe method of pruning closely planted trees or shrubs, in which the upper branches are sheared to encourage new branches to intertwine and form a high wall of foliage, a hedge, or an arbor.

Certain trees can stand more severe pruning than others and among those which can be successfully pollarded are London planes, elms, maples, willows, and black locusts. Pollarding has not been commonly practiced in America. It is more often seen in Europe where it is also carried out for utilitarian purposes, as on certain willows to obtain long slender twigs for basket-making.

Although pollarding does no harm to the trees, it drastically changes their appearance. Long, slender branches are produced each spring and these leaf out during the summer. The following winter when these branches are removed the cuts callus over, and when pollarding is done year after year the callused ends of the short secondary branches become enlarged and knobby. The resulting knobby enlargements are more prominent during the winter after the trees have lost their leaves, and the shortened secondary branches give these trees an appearance very different from those allowed to grow naturally.

Several kinds of trees in the music concourse can be picked out by their trunk and bark characteristics, but they are more easily distinguished and identified by their leaves. London planes and wych elms are most common, less so are English maples. Two black walnuts and a single little-leaved European linden are also to be seen. In addition there are two other elms and one or two other lindens. The London plane (*Platanus × acerifolia*), one of the trees most frequently planted in temperate regions, is so called because it is widely used in London streets and parks. Considered to be a hybrid between the Oriental plane (*Platanus orientalis*) from Asia Minor and the Ameri-

can plane (*P. occidentalis*) from the eastern United States, it has been grown in London for nearly 300 years. Early in the seventeenth century the two parent trees were introduced into England. About 1670 and thereafter, in and around London, plane trees different from the two earlier introductions were noticed for their vigor, hardiness, and intermediate characters. The vigorous new plane trees flourished in London and were eventually taken to other cities in Europe and America where they also thrived, showing tolerance for most soils, smoke, dust, and eventually smog, and of heat reflected from paving and buildings.

Leaves of London planes are usually five to seven inches long, six to eight inches wide and have three to seven lobes. Their texture is unusually thick and leathery and they do not disintegrate readily after falling. They have a leaf stalk with a swollen base that encloses the young bud—a useful means of recognition. The small flowers of the London plane, as well as those of other planes, are grouped into rounded clusters about an inch wide. These hang in twos and threes on long stalks, another unusual feature.

In the United States the three native planes are called sycamores. However, the name sycamore is used in England and Scotland for a maple (*Acer pseudoplatanus*) introduced there from central Europe.

Leaves of elms are always more or less lopsided. At their bases where the blade joins the leaf stalk their two halves are unequal, one half being somewhat longer than the other. On leaves of the wych elm the longer half almost always overlaps the adjacent leaf stalk. Leaves of the wych elm are two to four inches long, one to two inches wide, and have irregularly toothed margins. Elms have small flowers in spring before the leaves appear and these

Pollarded trees in the Music Concourse

are followed by quarter-inch-long papery winged seeds which are blown about by the wind.

The wych elm, also called Scotch elm (*Ulmus glabra*), is native to the British Isles where its wood, considered stronger and more easily worked than that of other elms, has been used for furniture and other purposes. In Great Britain as well as in the United States it has often been planted because it thrives in cities despite smoke, dust and smog, and poor soil. The word "wych" as used in the British Isles originally meant pliant or supple but it was often used in the past for any elm tree.

English maple (*Acer campestre*) is the only maple native to the British Isles where it is often seen in hedgerows and along road-sides, as well as in open fields. For this reason it is sometimes also called hedge maple or field maple. Because it seeds so freely it is seldom planted. It has hard, smooth-textured wood which in the past has been used for carved bowls, spoons, and other utensils. Leaves of most maples are lobed and always in twos, opposite each other on the stems. Those of English maple are usually three-lobed and about two inches long. Flowers of maples are always small and inconspicuous and are followed by winged seeds. The winged seeds are paired, made up of two equal halves in contrast to the winged seeds of elms which are not paired. Maple seeds with their wings are also carried about by the wind.

The two black walnuts (*Juglans nigra*)

are to be seen on the west side of the music concourse. A native of the eastern and central United States, the black walnut is best known for its timber; its nuts, though flavorful, have a very hard shell. Because it is one of the world's most valuable timber trees it has become rare in the wild. A handsome tree, it has long been planted as an ornament in the United States and Europe. It may be recognized, and distinguished from all other trees in the concourse, by its compound leaves which are made up of a number of leaflets arranged along a central rachis.

A small-leaved European linden (*Tilia cordata*) is on the east side of the concourse in the front row of trees closest to the music stand. It is the common linden of northern Europe but is not as frequently planted as some other lindens. Its leaves are heart-shaped, about two to three inches long and the margins are saw-toothed. A remarkable feature of all lindens is the attachment of their small flowers and fruits to rectangular papery structures called bracts. When the fruits are mature the bracts become detached from the tree and are carried on the wind, taking the seeds with them.

PART THREE

PLANTS FOR WESTERN GARDENS

MEDITERRANEANS FOR THE GARDEN

LESTER HAWKINS

To begin with, let us imagine a walk planted on both sides with a deep border of Mediterranean plants. Many of the plants are famous for the fragrance of their foliage and among them are rue, wormwood, hyssop, lavender, sage, and other herbs. Most are almost equally well known for the distinctive color of their foliage, which varies from almost pure white through shades of blue and gray to deep green, with an added few that are golden or purple or red. Also pleasing is the texture of the leaves, which can be fine and heather-like, as in santolinas and thymes; lacy, as in some artemisias; or deeply woolly as in *Phlomis fruticosa*. And then, of course, there are the flowers. Almost all year something is in bloom in mild gardens along the West Coast and, at some seasons, the spectacle rivals that of the English perennial border. Unlike the latter, however, this garden is basically evergreen—as befits our climate, for we certainly do not want our plants to hide underground just when the rest of nature is flourishing.

If I were to use the old classifications inherited from England and the eastern United States, we would have to say that what I have been describing is indeed part perennial border and also part herb garden and even partly a shrubbery. But we can ignore these formulas as old-fashioned, absurd, or, at least, not applicable to us. In colder climates the perennial border lies dormant all winter like the rest of nature and comes into its own only in high summer and fall. In winter and early spring—prime seasons for us on the Pacific Coast—it is nothing.

Again, many of our plants are traditionally known as herbs. The Royal Horticultural Society's *Dictionary of Gardening* describes an herb garden as "a separate ornamental garden, often of formal design and based on early knot gardens or parterres in which herbs were grown in Tudor or Elizabethan times. These were usually edged with shrubby box, lavender, lavender cotton, winter savory, hyssop, and so on, which were kept closely trimmed." What an idea. Here are plants that in nature like to spill, spread over rocks, form marvelous natural domes, or grow into and twine around other plants, all of which is half their charm. Therefore we must erase this image of the herb garden, since we certainly have no intention of mutilating these plants to fit some geometrical or architectural fancy.

And, of course, the old formulas for

Right: Euphorbia acanthothamnos, *lavenders, and brooms on the island of Euboea, Greece. Above (top):* Euphorbia acanthothamnos. *Bottom:* Lavandula stoechas '*Atlas*'

shrubbery and herbaceous borders do not apply. Since our garden is largely evergreen and consists almost entirely of Mediterranean plants with the horticultural characters we want, the plants may be herbaceous, subshrubby or entirely woody, without distinction.

However, enough of what is not. Let us return to our path through charming, colorful, and fragrant plants from the sunny hills bordering the great inland sea. Of the many thousands of flowering plants in this region, we have selected for our purposes those that have obvious attractions of form or flower or foliage or fragrance (and sometimes all four) and that are also good garden subjects in more practical ways. (They are dense and suppress weeds, or they are at least compact, not tall and rangy, and they do not become pests by reseeding or running at the root.)

But let us start again and try to describe

our walk. On either side in the foreground are low, somewhat spreading plants such as *Lithodora diffusa*, *Genista lydia*, *Anthemis cupaniana*, middle-sized plants of *Dianthus*, *Erinacea pungens*, and the larger acantholimons with perhaps a few tufts of *Iris unguicularis*. Since these plants like to grow among and sometimes spread over rocks, there will also be a few flattish stones among them. Behind these, for the most part, will be somewhat taller plants (al-though only for the most part; we shall follow no rigid scheme of low, medium, and high, but shall consider only that the lower ones do, after all, have to be seen.) These are dwarf forms of *Lavandula angustifolia* (*L. officinalis*), *Origanum dictamnus*, *Dianthus superbus*, *Onosma frutescens*, and *Hypericum olympicum*. From this point we ascend through plants of the height of *Euphorbia rigida* and *Hyssopus officinalis* to the taller *Rosmarinus* and *Artemisia arborescens* to a background (if there is space) of larger shrubs and small trees.

I have included plants often thought of as rock garden subjects, but I have carefully omitted alpines proper and tiny buns that would soon be overrun by more rampant neighbors. High alpines require the special conditions that only a rock garden can supply, and they are never seen in nature around the shores of the Mediterranean with the other plants—the lowlanders and year-round performers—on my list.

CONSTRUCTION AND CARE

All the plants we shall consider are easy enough to grow, but they do require drainage. The shores of the Mediterranean are for the most part rocky. If the soil in your garden is heavy and apt to become waterlogged, it is wise to mound up the areas to be planted to the height of a foot or so. Crushed rock should first be worked into the substratum with, perhaps, gypsum, and the mounding should be done with light topsoil or a sand, firbark, and topsoil mix. Make certain that water runs off readily on all sides. The mounding, incidentally, serves aesthetic as well as practical ends by raising the foreground plants to a level where they can be more easily seen and from which they can drape downward onto the path instead of horizontally across it.

Our Mediterranean garden requires only the simplest care. All but the foreground plants have excellent weed-smothering properties, and the plants should be allowed to grow together as they would in nature for this purpose. The practice of separating all plants with a neat border of bare cultivated soil has never been to my taste. A far better rule, I think, is never to cultivate (which brings up weed seeds). If the charming natural flow of plants threatens to become an unsightly tangle (there is a fine borderline between the one and the other) the condition is best cured by pruning.

All the plants described here are drought resistant and will grow in the coastal areas of California with little or no irrigation. In warmer areas deep watering once a month is usually sufficient. We should remember that, while the climate of the Mediterranean is much like California's, most of the areas from which these plants come receive a scattering of summer rain and have a somewhat less prolonged dry season than our own. This may account for the fact that virtually all the plants described have good garden tolerance, that is, they will take regular irrigation provided drainage is adequate.

The kind of path I have been trying to describe can serve a variety of functions within a larger landscape. I first used its prototype as a substitute for an herbaceous border on a dry hillside otherwise planted with California native shrubs. In this case, every plant had to provide color, either from flowers or foliage. The herbal fragrance proved to be an added bonus; I had not given it a thought. It was only later that I began to ask myself if this weren't the answer to one of our gardening problems. The brilliant silver of some artemisias under our clear skies and the smell of lavenders in our dry air can, after all, be very special features in our gardens.

In the descriptions that follow I shall try to list what I have found to be the best plants and the best forms of them for the Mediterranean garden. Selecting the most appropriate of these and combining them into a path that is restful or exciting, quietly charming or impressive, is, of course, part of the art of gardening for which there is no recipe (and for which I hope we

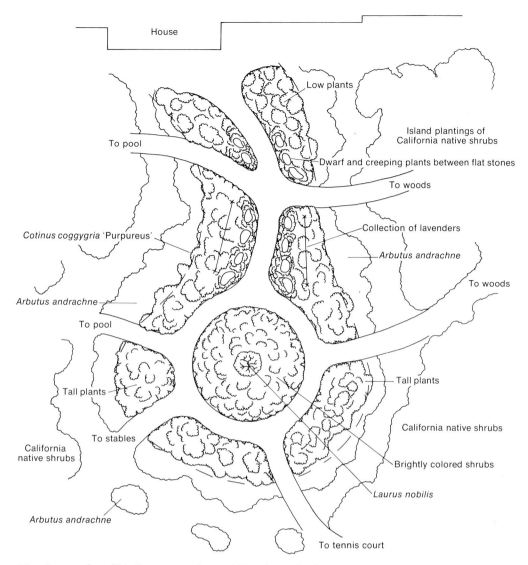

Labels in figure:
House
Low plants
Island plantings of California native shrubs
To pool
Dwarf and creeping plants between flat stones
To woods
Cotinus coggygria 'Purpureus'
Collection of lavenders
Arbutus andrachne
To woods
Arbutus andrachne
To pool
Tall plants
Tall plants
California native shrubs
To stables
Brightly colored shrubs
California native shrubs
Laurus nobilis
Arbutus andrachne
To tennis court

Plan for a garden of Mediterranean plants within a larger landscape design

wouldn't want one). We do, however, have the example of nature and our freedom to experiment (and if one attempt fails, to transplant and transplant again).

LOW PLANTS

There are almost too many candidates for the foreground of our path. The hills around the Mediterranean are usually low brushland (maquis) or stony wastes (ga-rigue) that still manage to harbor a large number of desirable and low-growing garden subjects (*Erinacea pungens*, for example, or *Genista horrida*). If we raise our sights to the surrounding mountains and include those alpines of the right breadth and stature that will do well in ordinary garden conditions at low elevations, we shall at least double the number of possibilities. Here I can describe only a few that I have found to be accommodating and durable all-season performers for Pacific Coast gardens.

Of the sizable number of mat-forming achilleas, I have found the best for our purpose to be *Achillea umbellata*, with deeply lobed white felted leaves, *A. ageratifolia*, with very finely toothed, almost entire narrow gray-green leaves, and *A. clavennae* (*A. argentea*), with deeply toothed silvery leaves. All three plants creep around rocks without ever becoming unduly invasive; all remain perfect silver or gray cushions throughout winter; and all are reasonably resistant to the effects of heat and drought. Their flowers, which are of far less importance than their foliage, are white daisies on short stems, very showy for a brief period in spring. *Achillea tomentosa* makes a low, ferny green mat with yellow flowers, somewhat like a miniature of our common yarrow, *A. millefolium*. It is attractive, but I have found that it takes neither heat nor drought nor winter wet as well as the first three on our list. *A. rupestris*, from southern Italy, is praised by Farrer as the most beautiful in flower of all the low achilleas; it has green entire leaves and masses of white daisies on six-inch stems, but Farrer notes that it also suffers from the effects of dampness in winter.

Many aethionemas make excellent pathside plants. All have an abundance of pink flowers in spring, and tiny, bluish evergreen leaves on spreading plants that tend to be somewhat woody at the base. By far the best of these that I have seen is *Aethionema grandiflorum* from Lebanon, which has flowers of sparkling bright pink, much larger than the more deeply colored but somewhat dingy *A.* 'Warley Rose'.

Alyssum murale (*A. argenteum*) is an upright, silvery, thinly clothed shrub to about eighteen inches, with umbels of yellow flowers. It is a little high for the foreground but I include it here because it seems so well placed growing out from a rock next to a path. The hills and mountains around the Mediterranean are rich in alyssums, most of which form small tufts for the rock garden, but others would be more useful for our border if we had them: *Alyssoides cretica* (*Alyssum creticum*), for example, has the habit and flowers of the well-known *Aurinia saxatilis* (*Alyssum saxatile*), but is an astounding silvery-scaly plant.

Anthemis cupaniana is one of the best pathside plants of all, the perfect foil for a background of lavenders and euphorbias. Here I should quote Farrer:

Anthemis cupaniana is a treasure from Italy, perfectly hardy and of the greatest value, though not by any means small or dainty. It forms a vast decumbent mass often a yard or more across and perhaps six inches deep, of fat shoots embedded in masses of neat, ferny foliage, rather plump and gray and pleasantly aromatic. From these . . . springs an unceasing profusion of large and brilliant showy Marguerites carried well aloft, some six inches or more above the mass. This beauty seems indifferent to sun or shade, heavy soil or light.

Anthemis nobilis, chamomile, on the other hand, is an invasive pest that should never be planted unless in an area with solid masonry borders, but there are a number of equally ferny, better-behaved mats from Crete, Sicily, and other sunny places, some of them silvery, that need to be brought into cultivation.

Arenaria montana is not, as its name suggests, a high alpine: it is really from the foothills and lower mountains of Spain. In time it forms a large, prostrate, evergreen mat covered solidly, like snow, with pure white flowers for a long period in spring. One great advantage in growing plants of this kind along paths instead of in the rock garden is that here they can be given room to spread to a yard across without injury to delicate and diminutive neighbors.

Plants of the ordinary *Armeria maritima* from seacoasts almost throughout the northern hemisphere, including the Mediterranean, make perfectly foolproof low tufts of grassy foliage that are always pleasing, with pink flowers appearing for long periods. Better, however, is *Armeria leucocephala* (*A. corsica*), a somewhat smaller plant with brick-red flowers.

Artemisias, unfortunately, will have to be omitted from our foreground. All the low-growing ones I know of are deciduous, and most are not from the Mediterranean.

Asteriscus maritimus (*Odontospermum maritimum*) is a most attractive, silky-woolly dwarf shrub with neat, upstanding grayish leaves and large yellow daisies surrounded by leafy bracts. This plant grows not only near the sea but also in dry places inland on both the African and European sides of the Mediterranean. A similar, but much larger and more tender shrub is *Asteriscus sericeus* from the Canaries.

Ballota pseudodictamnus, from Crete, is a charming and peculiar white-woolly evergreen perennial to two feet, narrowly upright in habit. I list it among the foreground plants because it should stand alone, isolated from other plants of its height. The leaves of this deeply felted subshrub are attractively veined and somewhat scalloped and cupped, like shallow seashells, and the tiny flowers, borne in the leaf axils, are surrounded with woolly chartreuse bracts.

Campanulas, of course, abound in the Mediterranean. Everywhere there are bellflowers resembling *Campanula rupestris*, or variants of *C. glomerata*, or, often, twining through lavenders, frail plants of the *C. rotundifolia* kind. *Campanula isophylla* is a native of sea cliffs near Genoa, and *C. portenschlagiana* grows among rocks around the Adriatic. Beside our path is a good place to grow these showy plants that are too large and a little too ordinary for the rock garden (which should be reserved for *C. raineri*, *C. zoysii*, *C. morettiana*, and other rarities). They are valuable, also, for providing flowers when the season for most of our low plants is over.

Chrysanthemum atlanticum, from the Atlas Mountains, seems perfectly happy at low elevations. It is another mat of ferny foliage with wide-spreading masses of white daisies, but is altogether smaller than *Anthemis cupaniana*.

Convolvulus sabaticus (*C. mauritanicus*), from North Africa, sends out large violet-blue flowers at ground level all summer; a single plant will grow to five feet across. *Convolvulus boissieri* (*C. nitidus*) from middle elevations in the Spanish Sierra Nevada is supposed to be even better, with silvery foliage and rose-tinged white flowers, but has, so far, not succeeded here, perhaps because of our excessive winter rains.

Daphnes are found here and there in small localities all across the northern Mediterranean countries. We have found *Daphne cneorum*, and some cultivars, and *D. collina* perfectly faithful plants in full sun and given little water. Sometimes one will die from no discernible cause, but, if there are two or more plants in the garden, there is no great cause for concern. As Farrer once noted, you can cosset a daphne and give it every ideal condition only to find it will not grow for you, and then discover that your neighbor has simply planted one out in ordinary soil among his bedding plants, and it is thriving. Therefore, there seems no reason not to plant one or two of these loveliest of low shrubs along our path. For its fragrance alone it is worth a place. It is perhaps worth noting that, on the island of Euboea, I saw a wide low shrub, a mass of interlaced branches that I now know to have been *Daphne jasminea*, one of the most beautiful of all daphnes. There it was, thriving in a twenty-five-inch rainfall area with long, hot, dry summers.

Perhaps one day we shall succeed in acquiring and growing a plant of it.

Pinks are not only excellent flowering plants for our purpose, but they also provide low mats of blue or silvery foliage the year around. The best of these I have found to be *Dianthus gratianopolitanus* (*D. caesius*) and *D. plumarius* and their hybrids with their very blue foliage and large deep pink flowers smelling of cloves. Unfortunately, neither is strictly Mediterranean; the center of the best dianthus seems to be Central Europe and the Balkans (and, of course, the higher mountains). Those I saw in the Mediterranean hills were tall, rangy plants, only one of which, *Dianthus fruticosus*, shrubby, with a picturesque gnarled trunk, seemed worth introducing.

Dorycnium hirsutum is a charming, very white, and very woolly spreading pea shrub that mounds up to a height of about eight inches and will, in time, grow a yard across. White flowers flushed with pink appear here and there in this soft mass of foliage over a long period.

Erinacea pungens is perhaps the best of a number of spiny low hedgehogs that have survived the ravages of goats and drought on hot rocky hillsides (the others include *Poterium spinosum* and *Genista horrida*). The spines of *Erinacea* (it is a monotypic genus) are dense and a shining silvery green. The flowers are large, violet blue, and papillionaceous, but their most attractive feature is the large, fluffy, and silvery calyces among which they are set. The plant is slow growing, but a number of them placed in a clump will hasten the time when they can be enjoyed.

MORE MEDITERRANEANS
FOR THE GARDEN

LESTER HAWKINS

ONE highly satisfactory way of arranging plants in a garden is by geographical areas. This is not always possible, of course, but where it is and space allows, it can create an interest that in many ways transcends a planting in which size, form, leaf texture, and color are the only considerations, and geography is largely left out of account. For one thing it is a way of paying tribute to some of the great floristic regions of the world. A few proteas and leucospermums planted together clearly indicate a sampling of the much larger number of these marvelous plants in which the Cape flora is so rich. Also, the association allows us, as a single plant could never do, a glimpse of a distant place; this ability to transport, to transplant from one region to another, is after all, one of the great, almost miraculous, rewards horticulture has to offer. And there is a final advantage that is more dependable and difficult to define, but that is nonetheless real; and that is the help that natural associations can give us in our efforts to create better gardens. Roy Elliott once spoke of some highly sensitive plantings that nonetheless reminded him of outdoor upholstery. It is my conviction that in gardening, as in other art forms, there is a difference between the merely decorative (or ornamental, as we often say) and the more profound, and that the key to the latter lies in the success with which it points back to and subsumes one or another aspect of nature.

For us on the West Coast, the most important areas of the world are quite obviously those with a Mediterranean climate. The largest of these and the one most comparable with our own is, of course, the Mediterranean Basin itself. In the preceding chapter I began to describe my idea of a garden of Mediterraneans, and here we resume our list, alphabetically arranged, of good garden plants for this purpose that are not, like brooms and rock roses, mentioned in their own chapters.

Erodiums abound around the Mediterranean and the most frequently planted of them, *Erodium chamaedryoides*, comes from Corsica and the Balearic Islands. The less commonly grown *E. corsicum*, which forms somewhat larger, silvery mats with the veined rose-pink flowers characteristic of the genus, is, however, better for our purposes, and some forms of *E. absinthoides* are said to have the best flowers of the genus.

Erysimum kotschyanum and *E. pulchellum* (*E. rupestre*) form wide-spreading low mats totally covered with vividly yellow and orange wallflowers in spring. They are, perhaps, the brightest of carpeting plants.

Euphorbias are among the most important of all plants for our border, and the taller ones will be described later. Among the low ones are some of the greatest value for giving our path its Mediterranean look: They are *Euphorbia myrsinites* (and its miniature counterpart, *E. capitulata*), *E. robbiae*, and *E. acanthothamnos*. The first is a smaller version of *E. rigida* with prostrate stems about a foot long. The whole plant, stems and leaves, is blue-gray and instead of flowers, bright yellow bracts shine out on cloudy days in late winter and early spring. *Euphorbia robbiae* is a dark green plant with densely set, round leaves, a perfect foil for the light green bracts in spring. This plant, incidentally, is excellent for dry shade as well as for a sunny spot on our walk. *E. acanthothamnos* is another hedgehog that loves to creep over rocks and cover them with brilliant chartreuse-yellow bracts set among masses of tiny spines.

Hippocrepis comosa is a prostrate leguminous subshrub with tiny leaves divided into a dozen or so minute leaflets, looking much like an astragalus. The foliage is dark blue-green, an ideal foil for the small bright yellow pea flowers that appear in the leaf axils. While nothing special, this plant makes a useful and colorful mat on the ground; also it is very tough and endures long droughts with, apparently, little distress.

Hypericum coris, *H. olympicum*, and *H. empetrifolium* all come from warm dry hillsides in Greece and Asia Minor. *H. coris* is a small shrub of less than a foot, with tiny leaves and the usual yellow St. John's wort flowers about three-quarters of an inch across, rising well above the foliage. *H. olympicum* is somewhat larger, although not much, with flowers up to two inches across. A particularly beautiful variant with pale

yellow flowers, *H. empetrifolium*, is drought resistant, has yellow-green, small, heath-like leaves and small flowers with prominent stamens. Both prostrate and upright forms can be seen in the hills near Athens.

Iberis sempervirens is very commonly grown, although few of its cultivators realize what a tough and drought-resistant plant they have. The shrub, as usually seen, is about a foot high and two feet across. It is dependably evergreen and covered with white flowers for a long period in spring. *I. sempervirens* 'Snowflake' is a still more floriferous cultivar. *I. semperflorens* is a similar shrub of twice the size. It comes from Sicily and southern Italy and blooms continuously, as its name suggests, from November to April.

Lavandula is another of the great genera for our path, but here we shall list only the few somewhat low-growing plants of it. Most of these are forms of English lavender and are of garden origin. 'Munstead Dwarf' and 'Hidcote' are both compact plants, although their flowering stems rise nearly two feet. 'Munstead Dwarf' has the bluer flowers of the two. There is said to be a much smaller cultivar called 'Nana' with flowering stems only six inches or so above the foliage, but plants under this name are apt to prove of almost any size. From reputable suppliers, plants of the cultivars 'Baby White' and 'Baby Blue' have proved reliably dwarf. *Lavandula lanata* is an attractive dwarf, gray, woolly plant, but its flower spikes, when they appear, are disappointingly long and small-flowered.

Lithodora diffusa (*Lithospermum diffusum*) 'Heavenly Blue' and 'Grace Ward' are widely planted in California. These prostrate shrubs, perhaps the showiest of all the borages, with sheets of brilliant blue flowers rivaling the best of our ceanothus, are natives of stony hillsides in Spain, southern France, and North Africa. In nature they

Mediterranean plants at Western Hills Nursery. Left: Euphorbia biglandulosa *(*E. rigida*) in January. Below:* Phlomis fruticosa, Lavandula stoechas, *and* cistus

grow among other shrubs and sometimes climb into them. If we follow this cue and plant them in front of somewhat taller shrubs and allow them to climb into their lower branches, we shall produce a charming effect. A healthy plant will grow three or four feet across, and we should allow room for it to do so. If the less commonly grown white-flowered plant can be obtained, it makes a striking contrast with the blue. Like *Daphne cneorum*, *Lithodora diffusa* grows in deep pockets of leaf mold on a limestone base. I have found it perfectly happy with a neutral soil at the base, but it prefers peaty to sandy soils. Given this condition, it is very drought-resistant. Two other wide-spreading lithospermums should be introduced to California gardens, *Buglossoides purpureocoeruleum* (*Lithospermum purpureocoeruleum*) and *Moltkia suffruticosa* (*Lithospermum graminifolium*), both of which produce sweeping mats and masses of blue flowers in the wild.

The onosmas are another group of plants, all singularly beautiful, some of which are high alpines for the rock garden and others somewhat larger lowlanders (though still dwarf) and ideal for edging our path. One of the best of these is *Onosma frutescens* from hillsides throughout Greece with long hanging bells with incurved openings that shade from gold at their tips to violet at their base. *O. fruticosa* from Crete is also shrubby and has white to yellow flowers in large heads of a dozen or more of these unique hanging flowers.

Origanums, the dittanies and marjorams, are important foreground plants. They all send out tufts of evergreen leaves from short creeping rootstocks and make excellent, non-invasive ground covers. The dittanies have gray, often woolly foliage and in summer (sometimes very late summer) send up branching flower stems with hanging panicles of labiate flowers,

usually pink, surrounded by pink or purplish bracts, the whole looking somewhat like hops. The most commonly grown is the dittany of Crete, *Origanum dictamnus*, a subshrub whose flowering stems rise to about a foot and carry a few rounded, gray, woolly leaves and cylindrical spikes of nodding hop-like flowers, pink surrounded with rosy bracts, which remain attractive for a long time. Perhaps even more beautiful are the two forms of *O.* × *hybridum* (*O. sipyleum* × *O. dictamnus*). One of these sends up a branched stem from which hang eight or nine heads of pink-purple hop-like flowers. This is a most graceful and airy plant. Another form of *O.* × *hybridum*, which blooms in very late summer even in the driest locations, sends out flopping lateral stems, up to eighteen inches long, in large numbers, creating, for a time, quite a sizable mound of dark pink flowers.

Origanum laevigatum, gray but not woolly as its name indicates, also blooms in late summer and fall. It makes a smaller clump with flower stems twelve inches long that arch gracefully and are, therefore, only half that high. *Origanum rotundifolium* from Turkey is a most picturesque prostrate, round-leaved plant at the end of whose branches in summer appear panicles of large light green bracts—looking more like hops than any. The rare and desirable form of this plant with striking pink bracts may well be a hybrid of *O. rotundifolium* and *O. pulchellum*. There are many others, including the beautiful, very woolly *O. tournefortii* from the Greek island of Amorgos, and all are eminently suited to our Pacific Coast climate and worth cultivating. The wild marjoram, *O. vulgare*, is notable for its yellow-leaved forms, which make perhaps the most effective of all golden ground covers. When the mat of roundish ovate leaves sends up leafy flower stalks, it rises to a foot high; throughout the rest of the year, however, it is flat and very golden, especially in the spring.

Paronychias are odd and wonderful carpeting plants, the best of which put forth masses of silvery, papery bracts that glisten in the sun and last well into summer. *Paronychia capitata*, *P. kapela*, and *P. argentea* are three that thrive in the hottest locations and are excellent for the spaces between rocks or at the base of the smaller lavenders.

Putoria calabrica is a dwarf evergreen shrub with smallish glabrous leaves and pink trumpet-shaped flowers carried over a long period. It comes from the hills of Spain and Greece and is remarkably heat- and drought-resistant.

Some santolinas have green (very green) and others white leaves. They make neat, almost heather-like mounds for a time, but after flowering are apt to get leggy in a horizontal direction. There is a dwarf form—'Weston'—of *Santolina chamaecyparissus*, the species with short, stubby, white leaves, that requires less pruning to keep its original, elegant shape. Other santolinas are described below under medium and tall plants.

Saponaria ocymoides hangs in great masses over rocks and cliffs in southern Europe and its sheets of pink flowers appear over a long period—much longer than most plants of its type. There are far more elegant saponarias for the rock garden, but we should not despise this lowly plant which flowers for such a time just because it is so easy to cultivate.

Saturejas, the savories, are all wiry little shrubs, extremely aromatic, with tiny leaves and white to rose flowers larger than those of the thymes, to which they are closely related. The most common species is *Satureja montana*, one of the sources of the cooking herb; it has given rise to plants with variegated leaves and to especially de-

sirable plants that make domes a foot or so wide rising to six inches that are sometimes listed as *S. pygmaea*. *S. parnassica* and *S. spinosa* are both spiny—more hedgehogs—from poor garigue country in Greece. There are half a dozen others, all rather alike. In nature you see an occasional plant with deeper-colored flowers, but, so far as I know, no one has bothered to collect them. Since saturejas have the look of creeping thymes, but grow somewhat taller, are mounding rather than spreading, and are not—unlike thymes—apt to become invasive pests. They are of capital importance for our path. Certainly no other plants recall the Mediterranean more vividly.

Of the white-felted senecios of southern Europe, *Senecio cineraria* in its various forms is by far the best. However, I find its large leaves out of scale with the rest of our plantings, while its flopping habit dictates a foreground position. It is, perhaps, better suited to bedding schemes and the making of white gardens, if one goes in for that sort of thing.

Stachys byzantina (*S. lanata*) is not a Mediterranean native but a citizen of the Caucasus and Iran. *Stachys corsica*, however, makes a low, shining green mat with small spikes of pink flowers.

Tanacetum haradjanii (*Chrysanthemum haradjanii*) from Turkey makes an unusually ferny, low white mat—perhaps the whitest and best of all. Its white flowers are nothing, but, as a colored foliage plant to associate with the golden origanum or the yellow or purple variegated sages, it is unsurpassed. For the confusion of the gardener, this low plant is often sold as *Chrysanthemum ptarmicaeflorum*, a three-foot Canary Island native with similar foliage.

The genus *Thymus* contains many plants necessary for our border, but its nomenclature is in such confusion that I am hesitant to write about them for fear I may be describing plants with mistaken identities. The genus is often thought to be strictly Mediterranean, but this is not so; it has members all over northern Europe and extending even to Greenland, Siberia, and Japan. If we are to find the plants that will do well for us, we must know their origin in nature. During our recent great drought, many thymes in gardens suffered severely or died, a minor disaster that could have been averted by planting those, like *Thymus capitatus*, that we know come from hot stony Mediterranean hillsides. Basically, thymes are of two types, the spreading, mat-forming ones and those that make small shrubs, almost always less than a foot high. Many of the former are known by gardeners as variants of *Thymus serpyllum*. However, *T. serpyllum* is, as I understand it, a northern species, abundant in Sweden and similar localities, while the name is used to cover at least seven species and innumerable hybrids derived from them. If my reading of the confusing literature is correct, most mat-forming thymes come from areas with either year-round rainfall or considerable summer moisture. (The Atlantic cliffs of Portugal, the western slopes of the British Isles, and parts of the Crimean Peninsula all have areas densely covered with mats of thyme.) I did see a few scattered carpets of thyme on the Athos peninsula in Greece, but these I considered to be southern outliers of species more abundant in the Balkans. It is probably for these and similar geographical reasons that the attractive-sounding thyme carpet of English books is so unsatisfactory for warm California hillsides. The plants often look good in spring, but, as the season progresses, they show the effects of heat and drought. If they are irrigated lavishly to bring them back to health, they respond by spreading widely in all directions

and become invasive pests. A notable exception is the mossy *Thymus caespititius* (*T. micans, T. azoricus*) from the Azores. While scarcely a Mediterranean, this lovely plant does not object to heat and spreads only moderately when watered. There is another mat-forming thyme from Cyprus, *T. integer*, which should be introduced in the hope that it will be more suitable for our climate.

The better plants for our border are not the mats, but the small shrubby thymes from known Mediterranean localities, all of which have tiny wiry stems, small leaves, and flowers varying from white to purple. One of the best of these is *Thymus capitatus*, Greek thyme, a somewhat sparse, hairy shrub to ten inches high with rose flowers and whitish foliage. *Thymus ciliatus* is a spreading subshrub, almost low enough (less than six inches) to qualify as mat-forming. It has narrow leaves half an inch long, purple flowers, and comes from Morocco and Algeria. *T. cilicicus* from Asia Minor is similar with mauve flowers. *Thymus herba-barona*, the familiar caraway thyme, is a diminutive shrub with rose-colored flowers from Corsica and Sardinia. *Thymus mastichina*, from the Iberian Peninsula and North Africa, is a little white-flowered erect bush, and *T. nitidus* is a sprawling, picturesque little plant with unusually tiny leaves from the island of Marittimo, near Sicily. Finally, there is the herb thyme, *Thymus vulgaris*, which is a widespread Mediterranean native. It is a sprawling bush to about eight inches with the tiny leaves and wiry branches typical of thymes and with lilac flowers. Closely related is *T. hyemalis* from Spain, with shorter leaves and purple flowers.

In coming to the end of the low-growing plants, I know I have omitted many worthy subjects, the lovely, silvery *Geranium argenteum* for example, but our list must be kept to reasonable length and durable serviceability has been as much a criterion as beauty. There are still other candidates, known from descriptions, that would be ideal if only they were obtainable.

Medium and Tall Plants

And now we come to the larger plants that make up the better part of our border. Since we are aiming at year-round effect, I shall limit myself to evergreen perennials and shrubs. In practice, of course, this limitation need not apply; having established a basic evergreen scheme we can, if we wish, add a few deciduous plants, or biennials like the giant mulleins, or bulbs, adding greatly to the warm season effect without sacrificing cool season interest.

Anthyllis barba-jovis is a tall, upright, extremely narrow and very silvery pea shrub with finely pinnate leaves (there are up to nineteen leaflets to a stalk) and crowded heads of pale yellow flowers. At its best, it is a most handsome, glistening, silvery shrub. It is, however, usually at its best only in its upper half; the lower branches, having lost their vigor, show considerable dieback. It follows that the shrub should be placed behind other plants of about four feet and at the very back of the border, where it makes a handsome accent with just the right Mediterranean appeal.

Artemisias are widespread around the Mediterranean and most are well worth planting for the color or laciness of their foliage or for their fragrance on warm days. Even their flowers, which rise on tall thin stalks and are usually the same color as the foliage, I find attractive, although they are, naturally, not showy; for a time the plants change their form and become a mass of narrow, leafy, filigreed spires. *Artemisia arborescens* is perhaps the best of the genus; it is certainly the most monumental,

forming wide bushes three feet high and four or five feet across. The foliage is light blue-gray; Graham Thomas says that it is "the most silky and lacy of all gray foliage plants." *A. abrotanum* is the herb southernwood, famous for its sweet fragrance. It has feathery, sage-green foliage and forms clumps two feet high, which rise to four feet when in flower. *A. absinthium* is at its best in the cultivar 'Lambrook Silver' with almost pure white, deeply lobed leaflets with scalloped edges like a maidenhair fern; it grows to about two feet, above which for a time rise the airy flowers that have been likened to tiny yellow bobbles. *A. nutans* is a small, narrow, lacy white shrub from the Canaries, a description (so poor are words) that equally applies to *A. canescens*, which is more strictly Mediterranean. Both of these are a foot and a half high and could be used in the foreground. Of the same height but more substantial is *A. vallesiaca*. There are, of course, artemisias from other parts of the world, including our own Pacific slopes, that would do as well along our path. Our object here, again, is not to be purist but only to limit the format of our descriptions, to cut a somewhat narrow swathe through the seemingly limitless number of potential garden subjects of almost any type that the world's flora has to offer.

Atriplex halimus is a large silvery bush to about eight feet with ovate leaves about two and a half inches long. It is a very drought- and salt-resistant plant, a native of the sea coasts of southern Europe. It is whiter and less apt to lose many of its leaves in winter than our native *A. breweri*.

Bupleurum fruticosum is an odd shrub, one of the few woody members of the Umbelliferae (there are also some in Australia). It has bluish, more or less rounded leaves two to three and a half inches long and three-quarters to one and a half inches

*Left: euphorbias and cistus in the ruins at Mistra,
Greece. Top right:* Centranthus ruber *in a wall on
the Athos peninsula. Bottom right:* Artemisia *sp.*

wide, and small yellow flowers, in umbels typical of the family, three to four inches across. At its best, it is a beautiful plant, the yellow flowers shining among glaucous leaves. It is extremely drought resistant and its flowers appear in late summer, a feature singularly in its favor.

I would like to put in a good word for *Centranthus ruber*, which has escaped to become a weed in parts of California. If you consider how drought resistant it is and how long it flowers, and if you have seen it festooning old walls in Greece, you must hold it in esteem. The flower color varies, however, from white, through clear pink to dingy reddish purple. The flower spikes are deciduous, but the base of the plant forms an evergreen mass a foot or so high.

Cheiranthus semperflorens is a tall (to three feet) evergreen perennial, shrubby at the base, that puts on a magnificent display of purple wallflowers for a long period in early summer. It is a native of Morocco and the Canaries. More strictly from the Canaries and therefore somewhat outside our range is another beautiful evergreen wallflower, *C. scoparius*, which makes a compact mound of foliage two feet high and three feet across from which rise in season numerous spikes of flowers, also purple.

Convolvulus cneorum is undoubtedly too well known in Pacific Coast gardens to need description here. It is an indispensable Mediterranean and perhaps the best of all low, silvery, evergreen shrubs with a bonus of white morning glories over a long season.

Coronilla glauca is a blue evergreen bush to about seven or eight feet with rich yellow leguminous flowers in two-inch clusters. Few shrubs present a more overall blue effect than this. *C. valentina* is a somewhat lower evergreen shrub with smaller and more numerous leaflets but with even larger flower clusters.

Euphorbia rigida (*E. biglandulosa*) is one of the most beautiful of all glaucous plants with bright blue-green branches to about two feet set with rigid pointed leaves of exactly the same color. The extraordinarily cheerful, bright yellow bracts begin appearing at the end of the branches by Christmas; in January and February they make the brightest spot in the entire garden.

Euphorbia characias is a variable plant that clothes whole hillsides in the Mediterranean. The handsome, tall (to four feet) subspecies *wulfenii* (*E. veneta*) has broad, almost feathery spikes of yellowish green flowers with brown centers. Its leaves are longer and more lax than those of *E. rigida*. The intrepid English gardener Margery Fish selected a brighter cultivar called 'Lambrook Yellow', which is said to be an improvement on this already beautiful and statuesque plant. *E. dendroides*, a shrub to seven or eight feet, deserves a special place in our border. This is a much-branched plant that, given room, will form an enormous, hemispherical dome and every branch tip will support a rosette of light green bracts. A good way to accommodate this plant is to place it among expendable plants—some extra rock roses, for example—which can be removed as the giant euphorbia grows and spreads.

Helichrysum angustifolium is a delicate, pure white perennial or soft woody shrub with an upright habit to three feet, narrow, pointed, curry-scented leaves, and the usual knobby, papery, yellow flowers of the genus. *H. sanguineum* is a lower plant, also with narrow leaves but more thickly clothed; its flowers, however, are surrounded by handsome crimson bracts.

Hyssopus officinalis is one of those herbs that is also a good evergreen, flowering garden perennial. It is a deep green, narrowly upright plant to two feet with terminal spikes of white, blue, or red flowers in whorls.

With *Lavandula* we come close to the heart of the matter. When you tramp around the Mediterranean hills you see more lavenders, phlomises, euphorbias, rock roses, and brooms than perhaps all other conspicuous plants put together. The lavenders are basically of two types, those like *Lavandula angustifolia* and *L. lanata* whose foliage bulk is quite low but which send up masses of tall (up to three feet) straight, naked stems crowned with the usual cylindrical heads of flowers, and those like *L. stoechas* and *L. dentata* in which the leafy parts of the shrub are higher but the flower stalks shorter. *L. stoechas* is a compact-growing gray-green shrub that I find the most handsome of all for year-round effect. It is sometimes called French and sometimes Spanish lavender. Actually, it grows over wide areas around the Mediterranean and is the most common lavender met with in Greece. As you would expect from a plant with such a wide distribution, it has many variants. In one of its many attractive forms it is a low bush of only about eighteen inches, very glaucous and woolly with heads of remarkably blue flowers set down close to the body of the plant. A similar but somewhat larger plant used to be known as *L. pedunculata*, but this is now recognized as a subspecies of *L. stoechas*. Many years ago we raised a plant from seed of *L. stoechas* collected in Morocco that has the largest bracts of any lavender I have ever seen; we have propagated this plant and given it the cultivar name 'Atlas'. It differs from the forms of *L. stoechas* described above not only by its larger bracts but also by its longer flower stalks; the leaves are larger than those of other plants we have of *L. stoechas* and the plant is less compact. There is no doubt that many more distinct variants of *L. stoechas* could be found in na-

ture if someone would take the trouble to ferret them out. A fernier, looser bush is *Lavandula dentata*, sometimes also called French lavender; it is a glabrous dark green shrub with the usual heads of lavender flowers, but without showy bracts.

The many plants known as English lavender are now thought to be hybrids between *L. angustifolia* and *L. latifolia*, both of which were brought into cultivation in England from the Mediterranean centuries ago. The present cultivars range from the dwarfs already discussed to large plants such as 'Grappenhall' and Victor Reiter's splendid selection, 'Provence', and from white-flowered forms to pink and deep purple, and there are various combinations ('Nana Alba' or 'Twickel Purple'). It should not be necessary to persuade any Pacific Coast gardener to grow lavenders; their virtues are obvious and a garden without them is a garden with an absence.

Phlomis fruticosa is ideal rising behind bushes of *Lavandula stoechas*. Its golden-yellow labiate flowers in large whorls arise in spikes; in flowering season the shrub is six feet high and perhaps as showy as it is possible for a shrub to be. When later the seed heads are trimmed off (mechanically, with a hedge-trimmer, of course) we are left with a gray-felted shrub of about three feet with handsome large leaves. Because it admits of this treatment, *P. fruticosa* is the best of the genus. *P. viscosa* is also a handsome shrub, gray again, but with smaller leaves and flowers. It is still showy, but it blooms on shorter stalks throughout the body of the plant, leaving us with no way of getting rid of brown seed heads quickly. *Phlomis samia* makes great mats of large, hairy, heart-shaped leaves at ground level and from these rise flowering stems to three feet, also with large whorls of creamy yellow flowers. Here, too, the hedge shears can be used. And there are phlomises with large pink flowers; those from the Mediterranean include *Phlomis purpurea*, *P. italica*, and *P. pungens*. All have the great soft-felted leaves of others of the genus and all are worth a place. If there is room for one only, *Phlomis fruticosa* it must be.

We should use only upright rosemaries. The prostrate plants spread too far; they are excellent for draping over walls and banks, but take more space than they are worth along our path. Taller rosemaries give us a choice of white flowers, pinkish ('Majorca Pink'), blues ('Severn Sea', 'Tuscan Blue') and of different textures, including the fine-leaved *Rosmarinus angustifolia*. An extremely good form of middle height, with deep blue flowers, is available as *R. officinalis* 'Collingwood Ingram'.

Ruta graveolens, especially in its cultivar 'Jackman's Blue', is the bluest of all leafy plants. A perennial to two and a half or three feet, it is dependably evergreen. The light yellow flowers, which appear in small terminal corymbs throughout summer, are not unpleasant. This is the herb rue, and the leaves, when brushed, give off an odd and pungent—some say acrid—smell.

Apart from the common sage, the Mediterranean has few evergreen shrubby salvias to offer in comparison with the numbers of California natives or those of Mexico. *Salvia dichroa* 'Magnifica' from the Atlas Mountains is a spectacular perennial, but its stems are deciduous.

The santolinas are richly aromatic plants, widely grown for their feathery foliage and (with a little help) mounding habit. The most commonly grown is *Santolina chamaecyparissus*, whose dwarf cultivar we have already considered for our fore-ground. Plants of this species are prized for their whiteness and for the thick masses of tiny leaves. Equally white but with somewhat longer, more thread-like leaves is *Santolina neapolitana*. *S. pinnata*, with tiny pinnate leaves (the segments are only about one-eighth inch long) and *S. virens* with entire, very narrow leaves are both intensely green plants, as green as grass. All these shrubs will in time mound up to about two feet in height. All, unfortunately, need to be trimmed annually after flowering or masses of dead flower stems will appear among the leaves and the plants grow lank and floppy.

Such is the basic material for our Mediterranean walk. It goes without saying that we can add to this list in various ways. We can, for example, include some deciduous shrubs and perennials from the Mediterranean or even some Californian and Mexican salvias without destroying its total effect or its overall Mediterranean character. For our background, if we wish to be elegant, we can choose from a wide variety of more substantial and taller woody plants from the Mediterranean—*Arbutus andrachne*, *Laurus nobilis*, *Vitex agnus-castus*, *Viburnum tinus*, *Tamarix pentandra*, *Cotinus coggygria*, and many others. However, this is not necessary. The border plan in the preceding chapter shows a planting on a hillside of California native shrubs which would, after a couple of years, be virtually self-maintaining. The path shown was in answer to a request for a limited area of flowers and herbs where people with little free time could enjoy some rewarding gardening. What I have outlined here is one answer to this request.

VIREYAS RETURN

MARGARET ADAMS

NATIVE to mountainous jungles of the Malay-Indonesian archipelago, vireya rhododendrons have been almost lost to plant lovers since World War I. From the 1800s until recent times, the supply of vireyas, also called Malaysians and Malesians, has been interrupted by war, theft, economic hard times, and politics—not to mention the perils of collecting them where climate and terrain are inhospitable. But the dark ages for vireyas may well be over.

Since 1960, botanists and plantsmen have collected, hybridized, and grown some 300 species and their hybrids. Despite the disasters that have plagued even these recent propagation efforts, vireyas are now available commercially to home gardeners. As container plants that winter indoors on a sunny windowsill or as landscape plants in areas as mild as southern California, vireyas are horticultural jewels. They are well suited to lowered thermostats in today's homes and the small spaces allocated for gardens in modern subdivisions.

Vireyas bring qualities found nowhere else in the genus *Rhododendron*. Golden yellows and vibrant oranges lead an array of brilliant colors—pure pinks and fire-engine reds to pure whites. Some with white flowers produce intense fragrances that entice pollinators in the wild and pervade the home with scents seldom enjoyed beyond a tropical mountainside. Flowers, tubular or bell-shaped, are unusually long-lasting and plants are generally ever-blooming. They have lepidote foliage and are drought tolerant. In most cases they do not readily hybridize with hardier Asiatic rhododendrons.

Their beauty alone is worth the plant explorers' struggles through uncharted, snake-infested jungles that harbor black-water fever and malaria. The natives of these lands, not always welcoming, have customs unfamiliar to westerners, such as drying their dead relatives and arranging them around their huts. After a long and perilous history that threatened obscurity to vireya rhododendrons, these pioneers can feel proud of their victories. They preserve a tradition begun by Victorian horticulturists in England with the discovery of *Rhododendron malayanum* in 1823 by an official of the East India Company, Dr William Jack.

Vireyas rose to prominence in England with the work of the James Veitch nursery and its collector, Thomas Lobb. From a handful of species—*Rhododendron malaya-num*, *R. jasminiflorum*, *R. brookeanum*, *R. javanicum*, *R. multicolor*, *R. javanicum* var. *teysmanii*, and *R. lobbii*, Veitch produced over 200 hybrids by 1897. Victorian gentlemen filled their conservatories and cool greenhouses with the glowing pink flowers of 'Princess Royal', and the snowy blossoms of 'Princess Alexandra', an offspring of 'Princess Royal', and the white, pink-centered flowers of *R. jasminiflorum*. But competition from hardier rhododendrons discovered in western China and the Himalayas pushed aside the exquisite vireyas that were thought to be exclusively greenhouse plants.

The hardships of World War I made the keeping of greenhouses and conservatories a luxury even for the well-to-do, and many large gardens were abandoned. The result was the loss of all but ten or twelve of the Victorian hybrids in Great Britain. Remnants of the nineteenth-century work remembered today are 'Ne Plus Ultra', a true Christmas red; 'Triumphant', the reverse cross of 'Ne Plus Ultra' between 'Dutchess of Edinburgh' and *Rhododendron javanicum*; 'Princess Alexandra'; 'Red Prince'; 'Sybil', a clear pink that resulted from the joint work of Veitch and Lionel de Rothschild; 'Taylori', a pure pink; 'Sir George Holford'; 'Souvenir of J. H. Mangles'; *R. brookeanum* var. *gracile*, fluorescent coral-orange; 'Pink Seedling'; and 'Pink Delight'. But vireyas were much too beautiful to be forgotten forever. In the late 1930s, the director of the Singapore Botanical Gardens, R. E. Holttum, believed vireyas were suited to the hot, humid climate of his city and began collecting them from Malaysia. War again interfered. When the Japanese invaded Malaysia at the outbreak of World War II, Holttum's pursuit of vireyas ended and all of his hybrids were lost.

Interest revived in the early 1950s, perhaps as a result of westerners being drawn into the Malaysian forests in the name of war. Botanical expeditions followed. The German Hermann Sleumer, who had studied vireya rhododendrons systematically for many years, undertook an expedition in 1961, of which the American Rhododendron Society was a sponsor. He introduced hundreds of new species that set the base for the current popularity of vireyas. The National Arboretum in Washington, D.C., had the foresight to acquire some of the British plants in the early 1950s. These were propagated, and in 1961 plants were made available in limited numbers. Some came to the Strybing Arboretum in San Francisco, and these, with Sleumer's plants, and others from friends of the arboretum in Australia and Great Britain, were used to develop hybrids suitable for the San Francisco Bay Area. Progress at Strybing was such that by 1969 plants could be sent to several interested California growers. It was as well that this was done, for in a few years most of the plants at Strybing Arboretum were destroyed.

Most of the vireyas were planted on a normally frost-free hillside in the arboretum. On a night in December 1972, the temperature unexpectedly dropped to 23°F. and remained below 32°F. for some time. The plants on the hill were lost; only those in greenhouses were saved. Many lost heart and interest in vireyas waned, but at Strybing Arboretum the collection was rebuilt. Many of those who had received plants from the arboretum in 1969 were able to send cuttings or young plants back again. Several amateur rhododendron enthusiasts in the San Francisco Bay Area helped, and eventually hybridization of vireyas began again at Strybing Arboretum.

Once again material for propagation

Above: a lightly fragrant vireya rhododendron raised by Carl Deul. Left: 'Dr. Sleumer', a rhododendron named for the botanist who introduced many vireyas

flowed from the arboretum to those anxious to experiment with vireyas. In southern California, where the climate seems more suitable for vireyas than for most other rhododendrons, enthusiasts in the Southern California Chapter of the American Rhododendron Society had help and advice on growing them from the Strybing staff and many of them have since made their own contribution to the study and hybridization of vireyas.

In 1976 the collection of vireyas at Strybing was hit again—not by the weather, but by a strike of city employees. During the difficulties that ensued several vireyas were lost through theft and vandalism.

Despite these troubles vireyas are finding their way into commerce and they now seem destined to remain. Among those available is a hybrid with flowers of orange and yellow that resulted from a cross between *Rhododendron christianae*, with small, red-yellow flowers, and *R. laetum*, which has the richest and purest yellow flowers of any in the genus *Rhododendron*. There is another with flowers of similar color, raised from a cross between *R. christianae* and *R. macgregoriae*, which may prove to be hardier than most. 'Red Prince' is one of the surviving Victorian hybrids. It has deep pink flowers and unusually compact foliage. Crosses between *R. lochiae* and *R. javanicum* have given a compact plant with bright red flowers that is especially suitable for use in hanging baskets. 'Princess Alexandra', with snow-white flowers, was raised a hundred or so years ago from 'Princess Royal' and *R. jasminiflorum*. 'Sybil' has pink flowers and is another of the survivors from the past. More are being developed.

Their natural habitats give us guidance in cultivating vireyas. Some vireyas are epiphytic and are found in the mossy boughs of trees; others are terrestrial in the savannas and grasslands of New Guinea, Java,

Borneo, Sumatra, and other islands of the Malay-Indonesian archipelago. In their tropical homes, they experience little seasonal variation in temperature and daylight, but the monsoons bring intense rainstorms and long dry periods. With this in mind the best treatment for vireyas in cultivation will be easy to recognize. Commercial growers in the West suggest the following methods.

To grow vireyas as houseplants, use containers that can be easily transported. Keep them in a sunny southern windowsill or in a well-lighted room during winter months and move them outdoors after danger of frost is past. Return them to the house when fall temperatures begin to drop to the low 40s. Vireyas are excellent for patios and porches. In southern California heat waves occasionally cause sharp humidity drops and growers there may need to use pots larger than usual to help keep the soil moist.

As bedding plants in landscapes for mild winter areas, such as southern California, vireyas are best on the north and east sides of the house. If your region is subject to hot, dry, summer winds, shelter the plants with windbreaks. Screens of tall plants able to withstand wind will retain moist air near the vireyas. Should you plant on the south and west sides of the house, protect the plants from late morning and afternoon sun with filtered shade from trees, laths, or shade cloth.

Vireyas are generally best in raised beds two feet wide and fifteen inches deep, or in large pots and tubs. The growing medium should be a soil-free mix that is acidic and porous. A loose, well-aerated medium that allows quick drainage can be mixed from equal parts of screened five-eighths-inch bark—redwood, hemlock, or fir (this is sold as orchid bark); coarse peat moss (greenhouse grind); and coarse perlite. Do

Above: the hybrid 'Red Prince'. Left: a fine garden shrub, offspring of Rhododendron christianae *and* R. macgregoriae

not use packaged orchid mixes, bromeliad mixes, Supersoil, or azalea planter mixes, and avoid finely ground peat.

Ideal light conditions are direct sun from sunrise until 11 a.m. and filtered sunlight thereafter. Fluorescent lights can supplement natural light indoors. If humidity is high and your climate is generally cool, vireyas can tolerate more direct sunlight. The closer you are to the equator, the more need you may have for sunlight-filtering devices. A 60 percent shaded lath cover, or 55 percent polypropylene shade cloth, can be used where light is not filtered by trees.

Never allow vireyas to freeze; however, they will tolerate short periods down to 30° F., some even to 25° F. They can stand summer temperatures of 105° F. or more, with proper humidity. Ideally, average temperatures should vary overall 10° to 20° F. from summer to winter with an average daytime temperature of 70° F. and an average nighttime temperature of 45° F. On the other hand, some experienced growers report that when grown as houseplants, vireyas perform better if they are in rooms where the greatest variation in temperature—night to day—is allowed.

Vireyas perform well outdoors in areas designated in *Sunset Western Garden Book* as climate zones 21, 23, and 24. They need protection from occasional freezes in zones 16, 17, and 20. They perform best in cool greenhouses where relative humidity can be kept above 20 percent and where they have protection from temperatures below 30° F. in zones 18 and 19. Vireyas have been grown outdoors in zones 18 and 19, but low humidity restricts their performance there.

Keep plants on the dry side but increase watering during major flowering periods, usually between October and March, and while plants are very young. Avoid a continually soggy mix. Water thoroughly and then withhold water until the medium is light and dry again. Water early in the day and do not mist houseplants often as moisture in static air encourages mildew. Fertilize several times in spring and early summer and shortly after flower buds first appear with a half-strength, or weaker, solution of fish fertilizer or liquid fertilizer such as Rapid-Gro or Peters. Dilute the fertilizer even more if foliage shows signs of damage. (Southern California Chapter of the American Rhododendron Society has developed a special formulation for vireyas that overcomes the alkaline water conditions peculiar to that region. This fertilizer is available to chapter members.)

Prune and pinch young plants to encourage bushy growth. From the time the plants are a few inches high until they are two and a half years old, pinch out any single apical buds as they begin to elongate. Buds begin to form nine months ahead of flowering so you may prevent blooming if you delay pinching. To prune plants older than four years, establish a routine of cutting out a third of the plant each year. Cut branches that have flowered back to the lowest healthy rosette of leaves.

Mulching the surface of the soil, outdoors or in pots, retains moisture and keeps roots cool. Use the longest needles of spruce, cedar, or pine trees—avoid the short, fine ones—or use coarse bark.

While vireyas seem safe at last in the United States, they are now threatened with extinction in their native habitat. In removing the trees, timber harvesters are destroying 280 kinds of rhododendrons in Indonesia and Malaysia as they move across broad tracts of tropical forest. Great increases in population in tropical countries are creating demands for food production that accelerate destruction of the forests. The U.S. National Academy of Science pointed out in July 1980 that all tropical forests will be destroyed within the next fifty years at the present rate of exploitation. Perhaps the lowered thermostats and reduced yard space of American homes, along with intelligent propagation and hybridizing, will insure a place for vireyas. They are too lovely ever to be lost again.

WESTERN IRISES

ROY DAVIDSON

GRASSLANDS and open woods of the Pacific slope are graced with an unusual number of irises, about twenty species in all. All lack the beards of the usual garden irises, yet are quite recognizable as being related; all have garden potential; and all are easy once the slight variability in requirements is understood and provided. Of these, all but three belong to a group of irises termed Californicae Apogon. Two belong to the Longipetalae Apogon; and the last is a member of the Evansia or crested group of the genus.

The crested species, *Iris tenuis*, is of special interest in that its nearest kin are found in Japan and eastern North America. It is a soft-leaved, deciduous plant growing to about one foot, spreading widely from surface stolons to form colonies rather than the clumps usual to irises. Deeply forked stems bear two or three graceful, white blossoms, etched lightly in raisin purple and marked with golden guidelines. In nature it is found only in a small area off the southwest drainages from Oregon's Mt. Hood beneath vine-maple, *Acer circinatum*. In the garden it has the happy quality of reflowering in late summer and autumn; it prefers a light, woodsy soil.

Of the two Longipetalae (if they really

are two), *Iris longipetala* itself is confined to the greater San Francisco Bay Area, from Monterey to Sonoma County. Where once great areas of hillside and meadow were blue with their March and April flowers, the great cities now sprawl. The second is *I. missouriensis*, an intermountain species, common from Canada almost into Mexico and in all western states to the Rocky Mountains, plus South Dakota. There are, however, several non-montane colonies, both in northern and in southern California (as on Mt. Pinos). These two are exceedingly alike, so much so that one Mendocino colony has long been controversially identified. All representatives are light-colored (whitish to palest blue), with an all-over veined design of blue or purple and pastel blue, or deeper, inner segments (the true petals, or standards). The main difference between the two is that *I. longipetala* is able to commence growth with the first fall rains and to continue growing in its mild habitat through the winter months; thus to flower early, seed early, and go entirely dormant from May to October. When it has been transplanted into a colder situation, it behaves and looks precisely like *I. missouriensis*. Both can give exquisite pure white forms, and the intermountain one occa-

'Del Rey' a modern hybrid of Pacific Coast native irises

sionally may produce flowers so heavily veined that little or none of the ground color is evident. This was the "prairie blue flag" of wagon train emigrants.

In cultivation the Longipetalae need full sun and will tolerate heavy soil that may be wet during the winter and the growing season in spring; but if they are to be happy and to remain with the gardener, they must bake completely in the months following formation of the seed capsules.

It is certainly within the Californicae that the major interest in western American irises lies; indeed, there is sufficient variety among their wildflower forms to have incited the collector's interest. Why then need the hybridizer have meddled? To see his innovations is to provide the obvious answers; they are not only beautiful, but

they display improvements in both plant habit and garden constitution, to say nothing of appearing in an array of colors exquisite and unknown in the wildflower antecedents, and rivaling the rainbow of variations so well known in iris literature.

In nature they have a distribution from southern California into southwestern Washington and are possibly best represented in Oregon, where no less than five species are known. Of these, *Iris innominata* is the most prized, particularly in its pure golden colors, and it has been extensively used by perceptive plant breeders, more so than any other single species.

Iris douglasiana is probably the species most familiar to Californians as it is constant within the narrow maritime fogbelt of land from mid-Oregon southwards; along the Big Sur, and in its infrequent dune appearances in Santa Barbara County, it has found life possible only farther up the slopes. There it grows in light woodland areas more than on the open headlands, as it does farther north. It is a strapping, big thing easily recognized by its broad, long leaf and its multiple-flowered stalk. Flowers are usually in the blue-purple range and, as in most blue-flowered plants, albinism gives occasional colorless individuals, lovely as carrara. One such is in the nursery trade under the name 'Agnes James'.

The two species mentioned above constitute the basic blood-lines of most of the garden strains, although it is difficult to say with any assurance just what any garden-grown seedling may derive from, as all the Californicae are interfertile. In recent years other species have been intentionally used, and *Iris munzii*, from the sheltered foothills of the southern Sierra, has been tapped for its potential of purer blue pigment and for its sturdiness. Grayish-leaved and as robust as *I. douglasiana*, it has all its lovely flowers at the summit of the stalk, rather than providing some on side branches. Its horticultural shortcomings appear to be an intolerance of summer water and a similar dislike of freezing in winter.

Another Oregon species, and one occurring only in yellow, is *Iris bracteata*, named for the numerous short, bract-like leaves that act as a sheath to the few full-length ones. This has sneaked into the breeding of garden strains and has given lovely flowers, although the rather straggling plant habit and dislike of summer water are drawbacks.

Iris tenax is from the valleys of northwestern Oregon and southwestern Washington and is tolerant of a variety of conditions including cold and wet. It is to be found in a great many colors, even pale yellow; usually it is orchid to lilac, but all sorts of pretty pastels, deep purple, blue, and red-violet, also blended and patterned combinations, and of course pure white, are to be found by those who search. It is the one species of Californicae that is deciduous, or nearly so, in cold weather, and this tendency is linked with a need for cold; like tulips and lilacs, it is not for the balmier climes. The influence of *I. tenax* in hybrids is noted in generally unbranched, sturdy, erect flower stalks, whereas those hybrids without it flop on the ground in rain and heavy dew.

Those who drive the byways of northern California may have noted plants of as many as four other species of the Californicae group, all of them without branched stems and usually with only two flowers. Near the coast a purple one with a very long tube of purple connecting the petals of the flower to the ovary is *Iris macrosiphon*. It has grayish, narrow leaves, grows in a variety of terrains and seems most intolerant of any water in summer. In some areas this long-tubed iris occurs exclusively in pale yellow, and elsewhere in lovely blends of copper and peach, where the two intermix. Although its deep navy and pure parma coloring, especially, have attracted notice, its reluctance to accommodate the gardener allows it to remain essentially untamed, although its natural hybrids with *Iris purdyi*, the redwood iris, would seem to belie any reluctance whatsoever.

Iris purdyi in its pure form is (or was; it is nearly extinct) a large, buff-yellow, flat flower, marked mahogany in a lightly veined pattern of great intrigue. It, too, seems reluctant in gardens, although its aforementioned hybrids, which are replacing it as the areas are opened to more light by logging operations, are seemingly easy. But they are almost invariably an insipid orchid color with none of the special charm of either parent.

Further north and inland, *Iris tenuissima*,

Iris 'Montara', another hybrid, showing the range of flower color

the Shasta iris, is a pale yellow, long-tubed species with bright green leaves. Further on, in Oregon, is to be found its shorter counterpart, *Iris chrysophylla*, which not infrequently meets and mixes with *I. tenax*, to give pretty but perplexing hybrids. Neither of these pallid, long-tubed irises is of great appeal individually because of the narrowness of the floral parts, imparting a spidery look; in a large clump, however, this achieves a lovely, star-like effect that is quite charming and a relief from the solid conventional look of all the others.

Somewhat similar and differing technically is *Iris fernaldii*, the pale yellow Santa Cruz iris, found between Monterey and San Francisco Bay (sometimes pale purple or orchid, which could indicate an old acquaintance with *Iris macrosiphon* or *I. douglasiana*). In Sonoma County is to be found a very wild mixture where *I. macrosiphon* and *I. fernaldii* meet. None of the resulting natural hybrids is of the quality a discriminating flower lover would want to perpetuate—disappointingly so.

The Sierra iris, *Iris hartwegii*, is quite another thing, differing from all other California natives (except *Iris munzii*) in the extremely short tube uniting petals to the ovary beneath. This is an exceptionally variable iris found in rather dry foothills, and it, too, is difficult to acclimate to garden conditions. Typically it is yellow—that is, from ivory to buttercup, usually fading to cream, and no less than four subspecies have been designated, the southernmost (San Bernardino County) being purplish, not yellow at all.

Of the hybridizer's offerings, first to be known was a series that strongly resembled *Iris douglasiana* (if not purely of the species). The full history of the hybrids is another story, which is global in dimension. Seeds of these western American irises found their way to Britain and Australia, and in both places proved admirably suited. Two seemed exceptional, and when the two, *I. innominata* and *I. douglasiana*, were grown together and allowed to intermix, the results of hybridization proved far more beautiful than anything of their sort to that time. Seed was forthwith sent back to native shores, and our own gardeners continued the research and exploitation. *Iris innominata* is clearly the strongest influence in all known garden strains; in fact, most of what goes for *Iris innominata* in cultivation is, in reality, of hybrid nature, although giving a splendid impersonation of the species. Vigor and tolerance are not, however, strong attributes of that iris when removed from its native Siskiyou Mountains, and thus these qualities must come from another. *Iris douglasiana* contributes secondly, and when the resulting hybrids (very fertile) are crossed back to *I. innominata*, a good innominata lookalike results. The species is found in both yellow and purple color forms as well as in colonies where the two meet, producing fascinating and lovely variations.

A distinct strain of these native irises bred for winter tolerance has resulted in the Rosedown Strain in the Pacific Northwest, from a concentration of *Iris tenax* crossed with *I. innominata* with perhaps traces of other species, since all are interfertile and the bees do not discriminate. While we may idealistically deplore such bastardization, it must be admitted that, as our coniferous forests are cut for lumber, their constant associates, the irises, must either perish or survive by evolving, as did the hybrid in the aftermath of *Iris purdyi*. But with foresight the gardener may provide himself, and the future as well, with irises even more beautiful than those nature gave him originally.

HARDY GERANIUMS

DENNIS THOMPSON

WHEN cornered I describe myself as an ecosystematic gardener. I want to live in a landscape, not the intensive-care ward of a plant hospital. Neither do I want my garden to be a prison where I must do bed checks nightly to be certain that someone isn't assaulting someone else. I assume plants are like children; there are going to be some squabbles, most of which they will work out themselves. If they can't work it out, eventually they will be separated. My garden has been fertilized with some exotic compost, but it is inhabited by hardy plants, and the genus *Geranium* offers some of the best.

When geraniums are mentioned, most people think of pelargoniums. Unfortunately, the misuse and overuse of pelargoniums has marred the reputation of the subtler, hardier plants of the genus *Geranium*. To separate geraniums from pelargoniums, members of the genus *Geranium* are commonly referred to as hardy geraniums. Hardy geraniums form clumps or mats from a few inches to several feet in height and spread. Some make plants that are dense at the base with leaves that may be deciduous or evergreen. Flowers are borne on the stems singly or in small groups. They are found in both

Geranium macrorrhizum *'Ingwersen's Variety'*

hemispheres from the arctic regions to the tropics.

The plants considered here are for the average garden. They prefer rich loam, but most are tolerant of less fertile soil and casual attention. I divide hardy geraniums into four categories by their garden habits: the homebodies, the ramblers, the wanderers, and the guests.

Homebodies are moved into the garden and are immediately comfortable. They thrive for years with only occasional lifting and without great increase in size or numbers. This group includes *Geranium platy-petalum*; *G. cinereum*; *G. renardii*; *G. pratense* 'Kashmir White', 'Kashmir Purple', and 'Plenum Violaceum'; *G. phaeum (G. puncta-tum), G. sylvaticum,* and *G. macrorrhizum.*

My ramblers tumble and sprawl. They are Christopher Lloyd's "weavers" that twine among companion plants. Not only do they form thick carpets on their own, but they thread their way into companion plants from which their flowers often surprisingly appear. They are valuable used with low, early spring shrubs and with foliage plants for extra summer and autumn color. Ramblers include *Geranium himalayense, G. sanguineum, G. wallichianum,* and *G. wlassovianum.* The mingling does not overpower the companion plants. In shade or tight proximity other geraniums may also act in this way.

Wanderers are the free spirits. As with most non-conformists, they are apt to create concern among the extremely ordered. They remain in the garden in spots of their own choosing. Bringing these plants into a tidy landscape is akin to inviting a horde of teenagers for dinner. Often beguiling and dainty in appearance, they prove surprisingly prolific. But they are easily pulled when they land in a restricted area, and they serve as a mulching ground cover in hidden corners. Favorites from this group include *Geranium robertianum, G. endressii, G. sessiliflorum* 'Nigrum', *G. carolinianum, G.* 'Claridge Druce', *G. nodosum,* and *G. procurrens.*

Guests are those that do not remain long. With these I break all my rules, swallow my pride, and bring them back whenever I can find stock. This miffy group includes *Geranium psilostemon (G. armenum), G. traversii, G. maderense,* and *G. anemonifolium.*

Besides these four groupings, there are also the West Coast natives which are con-

Geranium sanguineum *var.* lancastriense

spicuously absent from most geranium lists. Some are omitted for good reason; others simply are not known. Four should receive attention: *Geranium oreganum, G. erianthum, G. fremontii,* and Canadian plants of *G. viscosissimum.*

Garden-worthy Geraniums

Geranium cinereum is a compact plant, six inches tall and less than twice that wide. The leaves are refined, five- to seven-lobed, gray, and often hairy. However, in *G. cinereum* var. *subcaulescens* and the cultivar 'Ballerina', they are glabrous. The showy flowers are pinkish magenta with a shocking black eye. *G. cinereum subcaulescens* is noted for its flowers of vibrant magenta-carmine. 'Ballerina', raised by Alan Bloom, is said to be a hybrid between *G. cinereum* and *G. cinereum subcaulescens,* producing a mauve flower with royal purple veins.

Geranium endressii provides a long show of medium-sized pink flowers. The leaves resemble those of buttercups. Plants range from one to two feet tall and two to three feet wide. Of its cultivars, 'A. T. Johnson' has luminescent, silvery pink flowers, and 'Wargrave Pink', with rose flowers that stand above gray maple-like leaves, is noted for its aggressive spreading habit. George Schenk points out that it will tolerate mowing. Another cultivar, 'Rose Claire', similar in appearance to 'Wargrave Pink', has flowers rose-striped on white. 'Claridge Druce' is a hybrid with *G. versicolor*, a weedy British native. The hybrid, which is vigorous and noted for smothering weeds, has gray-green leaves and rose flowers. 'Russell Pritchard', considered to be a hybrid between *G. endressii* and *G. traversii*, a New Zealand native, has inherited some of the tenderness of its New Zealand parent. It is one of the most floriferous of the genus; the pale pink flowers stand above a mat of gray-green leaves. Unfortunately, neither the hybrid nor its parent is happy with Seattle winters. *Geranium traversii* 'Elegans' has rich pink rather than the more typical white flowers. The foliage is silvery and elegant.

Geranium himalayense (*G. grandiflorum*, *G. meeboldii*) is under two feet tall and sprawling, spreading slowly by rhizomes. Its leaves are finely cut, and the blue-violet flowers as large as two inches across hover like butterflies above the foliage. Plants once known as *G. grandiflorum* 'Alpinum' (or 'Gravetye') have flowers with red centers, making the violet-blue petals look even darker. It is thought to be a natural hybrid between *G. himalayense* and *G. procurrens*, a sympatric species of the Himalaya. *G. procurrens* has a reputation for rampaging through the garden. Christopher Lloyd warns: "Unless you have a death wish for anything smaller in your garden than a six-foot shrub, avoid the beguiling *Geranium procurrens*, whose purple, blackcurrant-eyed flowers so much enliven the autumn scene." Thus far it has been somewhat touchy with us, but certainly not a problem. In England it is particularly lovely draping dry walls.

Geranium macrorrhizum, often listed as a ground cover, has clammy, aromatic light green leaves. Pungent might better describe the leaves than aromatic; to some they are pleasant smelling, to others antiseptic or decay-sweet. The plant is one by two feet, generally with rose petals inside red calyces. The flowers are held sideways like those of the closely allied, petite *G. dalmaticum*. Flowers of 'Ingwersen's Variety' are soft pink, and of 'Bevan's Variety' crimson-purple, but my favorite is 'Album', with clear white petals inside red calyces. A closely related plant, grown in the San Francisco area and called *Geranium balkanum*, has larger, distinctly less pungent and more fragrant leaves. The flowers are rich maroon-rose.

Geranium maderense is really too tender to survive most Seattle winters. Native to Madeira, it was named in 1969 by Britain's geranium authority, Dr Peter Yeo of Cambridge University. The plant stands dramatically tall, above waist height, with very

Geranium endressii

Geranium psilostemon

large elegantly fringed leaves and large pink flowers borne in loose clusters. Also tender and as lovely, but on a much smaller scale, is a plant called *G. anemonifolium*. I first saw this plant in Watsonville, California. The grower had waited several years in vain for it to bloom before realizing that the leafy runners she was nipping off to prevent the plant from spreading were in fact the flower stems. The flowers are under an inch across, bright salmon with golden-orange anthers.

Geranium nodosum is eighteen inches tall; glossy green leaves form tussocks, and small pale lilac flowers appear continuously throughout the summer. It thrives in deep shade and has naturalized in Britain.

Geranium phaeum has small, curious, black-purple flowers. The common name of mourning widow alludes to this color. The cultivar 'Album' is showier in the garden and there are several color intermediates. Similar plants called, perhaps incorrectly, *G. punctatum*, have great value as ground cover for their bold, notched leaves and maroon blotch at the base of each notch. This group also tolerates shade.

Geranium platypetalum, from the Caucasus and Turkey, has spectacular two-inch violet-blue flowers and bold foliage to two feet. Our plant is grown from seed collected by McPhail and Watson in its native habitat. The plant remains under a foot tall, and the blue flowers are striped an intense red-purple over a white eye.

Geranium pratense occurs over a wide range in Europe and Asia and is one of the longest in cultivation. Many European plants seed rather freely, although the two-foot stems of violet-blue flowers are usually welcome. The double-flowered cultivars 'Plenum Album', 'Plenum Caeruleum', and 'Plenum Violaceum' remain in place. The last is the most pleasant. Other cultivars are 'Striatum' or 'Bicolor', striped white or splotched blue, and 'Mrs Kendall Clark', rose-gray with delicate white veins. The support of sturdy companions often improves the appearance of European plants; the Asian plants are considerably shorter and less in need of assistance. 'Kashmir White' (*G. rectum album*) has cool white petals with pale blue veins, and 'Kashmir Purple' (commonly mislabeled *G. bergianum*) has deep lilac flowers. Both of these are only a foot tall, as is the hybrid with *G. himalayense*, 'Johnson's Blue'. 'Johnson's Blue' is a finely cut and densely leaved plant; its lavender-blue flowers have dark veins and continue for months.

The annual disappearance from my

Geranium cinereum 'Ballerina'

garden of *Geranium psilostemon* is a source of great woe. It is vigorous, to three feet tall and wide, and its brilliant black-eyed carmine flowers light up a border. Also known (but incorrectly) as *G. armenum*, this species is not fond of cool, wet winters.

Geranium pylzowianum is a lovely plant with gold and green mottled leaves that darken during the season. The early effect is like sunlight through the foliage of deciduous trees in the spring. Plants may reach two feet in height, with flowers larger and brighter than *G. sanguineum*. *G. stapfianum* 'Roseum' is dwarfer, more refined, but with similar foliage and dark rose flowers. Both spread readily.

Geranium renardii is stately, sage green, and one to two feet tall and wide. The leaves are rugose, bold, and striking. The flower color is gray, rather like the roses 'Gray Pearl' and 'Angel Face'. Although some people may like that color, I'll concede only that the gray-purple striping on the dingy mauve-white petals is interesting if observed closely. The leaves are more than enough reason to grow the plant anyway.

Geranium sanguineum is native to Europe and western Asia and good in all its culti-

vars. Plants are densely clothed in finely cut leaves and grow to about a foot tall and two to two and a half feet wide. (In shade or among other plants it may stretch beyond three feet). The flowers are usually dusky magenta and an inch across. Plants of the cultivar 'Prostratum' and *G. sanguineum* var. *lancastriense*, from the Isle of Whalney in Lancashire, are usually under nine inches tall. 'Glenluce' from A. T. Johnson has clear pink flowers, and 'Jubilee' from Jack Drake has large pink flowers, but is somewhat temperamental. Seedlings produce a rainbow of intermediates.

Geranium sylvaticum is two feet tall and slightly less wide. It resembles *G. pratense* with broader leaf lobes. Flowers are usually light blue and cupped, but there are plants with white flowers, and they make more show. Among the cultivars, 'Mayflower' has violet-blue flowers, and 'Roseum' and 'Wanneri' have pink.

Plants of *Geranium wallichianum* are a foot tall and sprawl three feet wide. The flowers are an inch across, slate blue with white eyes, opening over a long season. 'Buxton's Variety' is nemophila blue, but most plants distributed under the name are seedlings and may vary.

Graham Stuart Thomas suggests combining *Geranium wlassovianum* with plants having copper and gray foliage. Its flowers are violet and an inch wide on two-foot stems. The leaves are dark green and velvety.

Annuals often are omitted by growers of perennial plants, but there are some superior annual and short-term perennial geraniums that perpetuate themselves by self-seeding. *Geranium robertianum* (herb Robert) has been used for centuries for medical complaints. Eleanour Sinclair Rohde cites *The Feate of Gardening*, the earliest English treatise on gardening, for her statement: "Herb Robert was one of the plants used for edging before the ugly box edgings." Plants are variable, starting as small, tight clumps that may stretch to almost two feet. One particularly vigorous plant I received with flowers larger than normal made itself at home among the roses and peonies, growing three feet tall. The cultivar 'Album' is charming, with white flowers and red sepals on red stems. When the plants outlive their usefulness they can, like forget-me-nots, simply be pulled out.

Geranium sessiliflorum 'Nigrum' falls into the same category. The leaves are dark bronze and create interesting patterns when growing through cracks in stone or concrete. Plants are about four inches tall and nine inches wide, but can be starved to smaller stature. The flowers, which are white and insignificant, are rarely seen, but evidence of their existence keeps popping up. I particularly like to have a few extra to stuff into dark brown bonsai pots or onto lava for display on the dining table. (Herb Robert also works well.) In shade, the plants seem to wane and disappear.

The native Western geraniums need drainage as sharp as possible to do well in Seattle. *Geranium bicknellii* is a decumbent, wispy native annual that wandered into the school garden from the wilds and for the last five years has followed me around without getting in the way. It produces a few pink blooms all summer and in autumn the leaves turn yellow and red before disappearing.

Geranium oreganum extends from southern Washington through northern California. It seems to be most at home on steep slopes under high shrubs or mingling with grasses. The plants, about a foot or slightly more tall and twice as wide, are ramblers or weavers in the wild. The flowers, up to two inches across, have pink to rose-purple petals with hairs along their bases. The coarse foliage shows a close relationship to the larger plant, *G. viscosissimum. G. viscosissimum* is the largest of our wild geraniums, sometimes reaching three feet in height. The flowers, often small in relation to the plant, are anemic rose-purple. The exceptions are some smaller Canadian plants with flowers of strong red-purple.

Geranium richardsonii, from dry areas east of the Cascades and in the Rockies, may range from a few inches to two feet in height. The inch-wide flowers are white with pale salmon-pink striping, or in areas where the range overlaps *G. viscosissimum*, pale lavender or lilac. The leaves of *G. richardsonii* are generally more like those of *G. oreganum* than *G. viscosissimum*.

Geranium erianthum ranges through British Columbia and Alaska into Asia. The leaves are much dissected, almost fringed, dark green, and pubescent. The flowering stems are stout and about a foot tall, with one-inch flowers of rose-purple to violet. Although much admired, this plant appears rarely in cultivation.

This is by no means all of the hardy geraniums—just a selection of my personal favorites. Reginald Farrer summed up the genus in these words: "Geraniums . . . from the weeds and glories of the tropics to the weeds and glories of the Alps."

ALSTROEMERIAS:
COLORFUL PERENNIALS
FOR SUMMER-DRY CLIMATES

S. L. GULMON & H. A. MOONEY

I T is a mystery to us why alstroemerias are not much more common in western gardens. Though sometimes accorded their own family, they are closely related to *Amaryllis*, which is noted for impressively showy flowers. Hardly a poor relation, the genus *Alstroemeria* includes species whose flowers are unsurpassed, if not unrivalled, in the plant kingdom for beauty of form and variety of color and pattern. Since drought in recent years has heightened awareness of the high water use of many commonly grown garden flowers, we hasten to add that some of the most striking members of this South American genus can be grown with natural rainfall even in California.

There are about sixty species of alstroemerias, all herbaceous perennials that arise as aerial shoots from underground rhizomes. The leaves on the single stems are twisted at the petiole, giving, in some plants, an attractive pinwheel effect. Alstroemerias are found naturally only in South America, but there they occupy an extremely broad climatic range, which includes the Brazilian tropics, the cool, wet lake region of southern Chile, the cold, high altitudes of the Andean cordillera,

and some of the driest areas in the Atacama desert where plants are found.

The largest number of species, and the most spectacular flowers, occur in the summer-dry, Mediterranean climate of central Chile. Because of the cold ocean currents off both coasts, the climates of Chile and the west coast of North America are similar at equivalent latitudes. The peak of *Alstroemeria* distribution in Chile corresponds to the region between Santa Cruz, California, and the mid-Baja California peninsula.

Alstroemerias were first described in 1714 by the French clergyman and botanist, Father Louis Éconches Feuillée, during his travels in central Chile. He described three plants and allied them with the daylilies (the genus *Hemerocallis*). One of these we now know as *Alstroemeria pelegrina*, which was cultivated in the Royal Gardens at Kew by 1753 and became the type species when Linnaeus named the genus.

Feuillée also described a plant called *ligtu* in Chile, but apparently had to leave the area before seed was available. By the time Linnaeus published the second edition of his *Species Plantarum* (1762) another somewhat different alstroemeria had entered Europe, and Linnaeus simply assumed that Feuillée's description was inaccurate and called the latter *Alstroemeria ligtu*. Linnaeus' son subsequently confused *A. ligtu* with a scented species from Brazil with which it had no affinity at all. Uncertainty over *A. ligtu* and its hybrids remains to this day, though Father Feuillée has been vindicated by more recent taxonomic work.

The first known hybrids of *Alstroemeria* were raised by Louis Van Houtte of Ghent, Belgium, between 1870 and 1890. They have been variously described as hybrids between *A. hookeri* and *A. chilensis* or *A. hookeri* and *A. haemantha*. *Alstroemeria chilensis*, though frequently mentioned by growers, is a confused name. Taxonomists do not include it in their treatments, and one writer says of *A. chilensis* that he lost it "because it crossed so readily with *A. haemantha* and the ligtu hybrids that its progeny are all mongrels." In 1927 a group of plants called ligtu hybrids arose from gratuitous garden crosses between *A. ligtu* and *A. haemantha*.

One of the most important events in alstroemeria history occurred in the 1930s with the appearance of 'Walter Fleming', a beautiful, long-blooming hybrid between *Alstroemeria violacea* and either *A. haemantha* or *A. aurantiaca*. When the Hollander Jan Goemans rediscovered this hybrid in the 1950s, he was so inspired that he spent the next ten years developing the now famous Parigo hybrids. These are grown exclusively as cut flowers by Goemans' Parigo Horticultural Company in Great Britain and its licensed growers. Goemans will not divulge the parentage of these hybrids (which are sterile) except to say it includes *A. aurantiaca*. Dutch breeders, including Van Staaveren and Van Der Zwer, have also been developing a range of hybrids for the cut flower industry, but 'Walter Flem-

ing' still constitutes the bulk of their production.

This encapsulated history points up the importance of reliable, soundly documented information, which is still sadly lacking on the genus *Alstroemeria*. Most breeders are unsure of the parentage of their hybrids or the availability of species. Most seeds from garden catalogs are hybrids. Because of uncertainty regarding the origin of plants, cultural practices are developed by trial and error rather than through knowledge of the environments to which the plants are adapted.

On a recent trip to Chile, we saw several of the best-known alstroemerias in their native habitats. We hope the following brief descriptions of these plants as they grow naturally will give some insight into their cultural requirements and the role they can play in gardens.

Most northerly was *Alstroemeria violacea*, which grows in the fog forest at Fray Jorge on the edge of the Atacama Desert (latitude is equivalent to the northern Baja California peninsula). This region gets only about three inches of rainfall a year, but a rich vegetation of trees and shrubs is supported by the almost daily fogs that sweep over the high bluffs from the sea. *A. violacea* grows in open clearings among shrubs of *Adesmia*, *Porlieria*, and *Encelia* in loose sandy and rocky soil. Its flowers are pink to lilac in color with deep maroon and yellow markings on the upper petals.

Since Fray Jorge is a national park, we could not dig up the roots of *Alstroemeria violacea*, but we did excavate *A. pulchra*, growing farther south near Papudo (corresponding climatically to San Diego). Starting at a depth of six inches, the fleshy roots went straight down in deep clay soil. This growth habit is indicative of the difficulty in vegetative propagation. Though growing in a heavy soil, *A. pulchra* occurred

Above: Alstroemeria pelegrina; *left:*
Alstroemeria pulchra *var.* maxima

Alstroemeria *ligtu hybrids naturalized in the University of California Botanical Garden, Berkeley*

on very steep slopes. We invariably saw al-stroemerias in well-drained soil, and this is important to successful culture.

In describing the plant we know as *Al-stroemeria pelegrina*, Father Feuillée said that because of its beauty it deserved a place in the gardens of the Incas. Seeds of it were sent to Linnaeus from Spain by his friend Alstroemer, after whom the genus was named, and it is reported that Lin-naeus so valued the acquisition that he kept the seedling plants in his bedroom through the harsh Swedish winter. We ob-served *A. pelegrina* along the immediate coast at latitudes equivalent to San Diego

and south. Little rain falls in this region, and, as in the case of *A. violacea*, the plants are sustained by frequent coastal fogs. The fragile finger-shaped tubers are nestled in crevices or among cracked stones where condensed moisture is trapped and or-ganic debris collects. This habit suggests that *A. pelegrina*, which is tender to frost, would be the most adaptable of the alstroe-merias to pot culture.

Like *Alstroemeria pelegrina*, *A. haemantha* was cultivated in Europe by the beginning of the nineteenth century. The brilliant red-orange clusters of flowers are arrest-ing against the steep grassy hillsides and stream banks where these plants are usually found. Hardier than *A. violacea* and *A. pelegrina*, *A. haemantha* occurs at latitudes 32° to 38° (Ensenada to San Francisco). In cultivation, *A. haemantha* has been largely replaced by its hybrid progeny, but it is difficult to imagine an improvement on the original.

All of these alstroemerias produce vegetative shoots during the winter, flower in spring or early summer, and go dormant during the summer dry season. This growth cycle, in combination with extremely deep roots, enables them to grow in dry habitats. Concomitantly, the thick, fleshy rhizomes are extremely susceptible to rot if moist soil coincides with warm weather.

Where winter temperatures frequently drop below freezing, and rain falls during summer, *Alstroemeria aurantiaca* may be a good choice. Its Chilean range extends south to the latitudinal equivalent of Portland, Oregon. Hardly a newcomer, *A. aurantiaca* was first cultivated in Europe in 1831 and received an Award of Merit from the Royal Horticultural Society in 1893. It bears bright yellow to deep orange flowers streaked with red all summer and grows vigorously to the point of being somewhat invasive. *A. aurantiaca* can be grown in summer-dry climates as well as in cooler, moister areas.

The ligtu hybrids are another group with a similarly broad climatic tolerance. Despite uncertainty about the origin of any cultivar that admits in its name to ligtu parentage, these hybrids are a well recognized group frequently mentioned in descriptions of alstroemerias. In 1939 a selection of hybrids between *Alstroemeria ligtu* and *A. ligtu* 'Pulchra' was imported from England by the University of California Botanical Garden in Berkeley to exhibit at the Golden Gate International Exposition. These have naturalized in the garden and flower throughout the summer. Although *A. ligtu* is red-orange with yellow markings, much like *A. haemantha*, the hybrids include a wide range of flower colors, which have been variously described as cream, cantaloupe, soft shell pink, deep watermelon, pale lilac, and flame.

Propagation from root stock is difficult in alstroemerias because the roots are extremely fragile, they grow deep in the soil, and each cluster must have a bud apex for subsequent growth to occur. However, plants often flower the first year from seed sown in the fall or early spring. Freshly harvested seed germinates readily, but older seed takes six weeks or longer. Germination may be improved by keeping the sown seeds at 75° to 80° F. for a month and then transferring them to a cooler place. The young plants should be protected from frost during the first winter.

Unfortunately, opportunities to see alstroemerias in flower or obtain more information about them are rare. In southern California Leo Song, head of plant propagation at California State University at Fullerton, grows a number of alstroemerias, including most of those mentioned here. In Sumner, Washington, Donald Duncan has been growing alstroemerias for many years, and his articles on them have appeared in *Plant Life*, the journal of the American Plant Life Society.

Scented flowers of Hosta plantaginea

A treasured miniature from Japan, Hosta venusta *'Suzuki Thumbnail'*

Hosta undulata *var.* univittata

THE HOSTAS OF HORTICULTURE

ROY DAVIDSON

THERE are no more striking herbaceous plants than the hostas, and scarcely any quite so easy, so adaptable—nor quite so indestructible. Few other hardy subjects can impart such an air of elegant luxuriance to the temperate garden scene. They are effective in large containers as well as in the garden proper, and they are prized by decorators for indoor effects. In Victorian times they were grown extensively as conservatory subjects.

Hostas come in all sizes from neat penwipers to rhubarbs, in greens from pale lettuce to deep sea, in blues fogged with cool powder like a plum, and in yellow. Many have an uncanny variegation of white or pale yellow-green, often tri-colored. Textures may be waxen, matte, or crystalline, and plants may be airily grass-like or bold, like elephant ears. Although it is mainly for foliage effect they are grown, the flowers can be telling. For the most part they are colored as lilacs, from pale milky amethyst to violet. Some are sparkling white. A few lists entice buyers with offerings of plants with pink and blue flowers, but catalog writers are known for their hyperbole.

Graham Stuart Thomas, one of Britain's most trusted plantsmen, has written: "Some plants make work while others save our time by covering the ground so densely that no cultivation is needed, and few do this so well as the hostas." Roots will penetrate dense clays and even succeed in sand if they are well watered and fertilized, although, as woodland plants in nature, they are probably happiest in humus-filled loamy soils. Such luxuriant leaves indicate a love of cool shade.

We must all know someone who disdains any plant that is not of evergreen habit; could these be true gardeners? If there is anything in the entire garden more refreshing than crisp hosta foliage, I have yet to find it. In spring the spears emerge in subtle coloring—some early, others much later—the leaf blades slowly unrolling like banners, some gaudy, some plain, some pleated, and others puckered in seersucker fashion. Then come airy flower spikes perfectly understating the opulence of the leaves. At year's end when yellowing leaves catch the fire of autumn sun, the garden takes on a mellow golden light. For winter there are hellebores among the hostas. The two kinds of foliage are the perfect mask for maturing daffodil leaves as spring unfolds into summer.

Everyone who writes of plantain lilies (as we Americans have called them) unfailingly mentions durability and longevity. Certainly some of the old garden hostas that do not make seed are unbelievably old. Adversity they can deal with, although they may become somewhat depauperate. Leaves may be subject to bleaching and even to burning in intense light. Pruinose and wax-textured kinds suffer least from sunshine. In the shelter of a warm and humid wind-free glade leaf development is so encouraged that familiar sorts appear even more luxuriant. Observation of the spreading rootstocks tells us something of the growth rate and how frequently the crown may need attention to replanting, thinning, or division for increase. Some few are very slow, forming a fleshy tuber-like crown, while others run off in all directions on short stolons to form a splendid ground cover; fortunately these are the smaller ones. A real advantage is the ease with which hostas may be moved at almost any time of year without suffering permanent damage.

At the time the first hostas were being brought into European horticulture there was no universal system of nomenclature and names became attached to them without regard for their origins in eastern Asia. Since their boldness endeared them to the large estate owners, it was those giant hostas that gained greatest favor. Smaller hostas went unsung for as long as two centuries, but are now finding champions.

One of the complications to nomenclature among hostas stems from their natural variation. Plants with colorful and contorted foliage arise from time to time, and it is the nature of mankind to pay attention to them. Orientals overlooked none of them, passing them down to further generations of admirers. Each botanist in turn has taken a fling at an orderly system of names, but the results have been incomplete and unsatisfactory. Even among the

old standard hostas familiar in cultivation for a century or more there is uncertainty surrounding names. "The gardener must . . . pardon the botanist who hesitates to identify his plantainlilies," wrote W. T. Stearn, the eminent British authority who worked out the horticultural monograph for the ones grown in Britain, citing both obvious and obscure complications. Not only do the majority of hostas resemble one another, but they are given to bud-sporting to a most unusual degree, and all of them are seemingly capable of interbreeding, not only in the wild, but as cultivated bedfellows. From a technical viewpoint, Stern pointed out, cytotaxonomic study is hampered by the large number—about sixty—and very small size of their chromosomes.

Of the confusion in names, the plant commonly grown as *Hosta japonica* is a fine example. It is also known as *Hosta lancifolia*, *H. calliantha*, *H. rhodeifolia*, and (by one authority) *H. albo-marginata*. Recently, a translation of the Japanese treatment of nomenclature has enabled us to remove much of the confusion.

The Royal Horticultural Society's Wisley Garden staff mounted an exhibit at the 1968 Chelsea flower show to demonstrate the great variation in garden hostas and to help establish names for them. The popularity of hostas soared, and in 1970 the American Hosta Society was formed to coordinate the efforts of enthusiasts in applying a universal system of names. It also encouraged exchange of plants and their evaluation. The results were mixed; while getting at the root of the identification problem, members were also disseminating many new plants, some of them from species new to cultivation outside Japan. Happily, there was some record of most of these new plants, and many of them have proven distinct, especially among forms

Yellow-leaved form of Hosta sieboldiana

Hosta *'Frances R. Williams'*

Hosta undulata

Yellow-margined Hosta fortunei *with* Peltiphyllum peltatum

and hybrids of the small to medium-sized plants. It is these smaller plants that have generated most of the recent interest.

From what has been said about hosta names it follows that choosing plants for the garden is fraught with uncertainty. Visiting the nursery where they grow is the best way of ensuring that plants bought are the ones wanted. Good photographs, which show such details as the stance of the leaves, their color and shape—details not easily put into words—are a great help in identification. One specialist grower of hostas offers a set of photographs for sale from which plants can be ordered. Of the better known hostas, those listed give a fair representation of the many available. For names I have relied upon the system of L. H. Bailey, to which most horticultural forms relate.

PROPAGATION

In addition to selection among wild populations and perpetuation of the results of mutations and hybridization as sources of new and superior garden plants, there is a fourth method: induced polyploidy.

As with other plants, the usual method of achieving polyploidy is through treatment with colchicine. The Long Island nursery of Viette has treated thousands of plants, yet to my knowledge none has been introduced from the work. *Hosta tokudama* has yielded three tetraploids, plants of which were sent me from Dr Hirao's garden in Zushi, near Yokohama. They are similar, but one is more vigorous, and I am sure it will be acceptable as an improved blue-leaved plant of medium to large size. In addition to the mutation inclination, hostas often have been observed as forming seed by apomixis, avoiding the sexual process and allowing seeds to be produced without cross-fertilization. Plants from this seed duplicate the parent. But seed is not the usual way to perpetuate the finest garden selections. Division of rootstock must be resorted to.

A Japanese gardener told me how he increases slow-growing plants. When the plant has formed a good rosette of leaves and is about to put up a flower stalk, he cuts the whole thing off at the base. Soon afterwards several buds, or "eyes," appear about the wound, and after a season of growth the rootstock can be divided with an eye to each portion. I was not told what to do with the cut-off portion, but accidentally discovered a possible answer. One of the very slowest plants in my collection is *Hosta tardiflora*; quite by accident I broke off a rosette, and since this is such attractive foliage I put it into a glass of water in a room at about 70° F., never suspecting it would take root, but it did, and by autumn it had grown strong enough to flower. The rootstock meanwhile had budded as my Japanese friend had said it would, and I now repeat this each year with that one. Another method, one I have not tried, is by root cuttings. I heard of an accidentally severed surface root left in place that produced a small crown of leaves.

Hosta crispula. Similar to *H. decorata*, but has larger leaves with undulating margins and more pointed tips; striking in clumps.

H. decorata. White-margined, blunted leaves and tall stalks of purple urn-shaped flowers in August; imported as 'Thomas Hogg', and there are others similar.

H. fortunei. A group of hybrids with ornamental leaves in a variety of patterns, all generally large, vigorous, and handsome; fascinating to collectors, but there are many confusing latinized names. *H. elata* is sometimes known as *H. fortunei gigantea.*

H. lancifolia (*H. japonica*). Lance-shaped leaves of rich green; lilac flowers freely given on vigorous plants in summer. There is a white-flowered form and others with variegated leaves, one of which is the cultivar 'Louisa'.

H. nakaiana (*H. nakaimo minor*). Small heart-shaped leaves and graceful stalks of light violet flowers. It is a parent of several splendid hybrids of medium size. There are others, such as *H. venusta*, which are similar, but of interest to collectors.

H. plantaginea. Olive green heart-shaped heat resistant leaves; scented white flowers in August. The cultivars 'Honeybells' with mauve flowers and 'Royal Standard' with near-white flowers are hybrids of it.

H. rectifolia. Tall and erect leafstalks with lance-shaped blades and tall, handsome violet flowers in late summer; usually listed as *H.* 'Tall Boy'.

H. sieboldiana. Large bluish or green heart-shaped leaves; stems of lavender flowers in early summer. There are yellow-leaved forms of *H. sieboldiana*, and variegated forms, the best known of which is 'Frances R. Williams'.

H. "tardiana." A race of hybrids between *H. tardiflora* and *H. sieboldiana* with small glaucous leaves and fine pale pinkish flowers. The cultivar 'Dorset Blue' from England promises to be one of the remarkable new hybrids. Still scarce, it may nevertheless lend itself to the technique of tissue culture to become widely available in the near future.

H. tardiflora. A most distinct plant, cultivated for eighty years or more but unknown in the wild; small shining lance-shaped leaves and purple flowers in autumn.

H. tokudama (*H. glauca*). Blue leaves puckered like seersucker; short stalks of whitish flowers.

H. undulata. Leaves variegated, white and two or three shades of green, and contorted. It is known as the wavy-leaf plantain lily; lilac flowers are unimportant. There is also *H. undulata* 'Univittata', which has less white variegation.

H. ventricosa (*H. caerulea*). Large rich green leaves; inflated violet flowers in summer; unmistakable.

TREE FERNS

BARBARA JOE HOSHIZAKI

ACROSS from the Conservatory in San Francisco's Golden Gate Park is a little forest of Tasmanian tree ferns, *Dicksonia antarctica*, and other Australian tree ferns, their stout trunks and plumes of stiff fronds so distinct from the surrounding trees as to be impossible to overlook. My own "forest" of tree ferns, very small by comparison, gives me great pleasure and has for many years. I especially enjoy watching the play of light and shadow on the trunks and canopy as the sun sets.

Most of my tree ferns were set out from two-and-one-half-inch pots, some about twenty-five years ago. One is from spores I collected. A few, not necessarily the oldest, are now as high as the roof of my two-story house. Under ideal conditions they seem to grow about ten inches a year in the Los Angeles area.

Tree ferns can thrive in the mild areas along the Pacific Coast, with particularly luxuriant growth where mist and fog prevail. Many of these plants are native to moist, misty mountains in a vegetation zone appropriately called cloud forest. Dense stands may form continuous overhead canopies, sheltering an array of plants on the forest floor and supporting various epiphytes on their trunks. Though I have seen tree ferns above and below the slopes of cloud forest, they are seldom as abundant or magnificently developed as in their favorite location. (A few species have adapted to some unlikely habitats. A New Zealand species survives in climates where snow may settle in the crowns; an African species grows in seasonally dry grassland; some Central American species thrive only in highland bogs.)

Tree ferns have been used for many purposes by native peoples who share their habitats. The Maoris of New Zealand still use the trunks for many of their arts and crafts. Polynesians extracted starch from the pith for food during times of famine, though in times of plenty it was fed to pigs. They also used the trunks to line roads and to construct the roofs and door frames of their long houses. Fiddleheads of some tree ferns and fully developed fronds of others have been used as food, and the hair on the buds of the Hawaiian tree fern was used as pillow stuffing, even in California, to which it was exported before cotton was plentiful.

Twenty years ago, it seems, there were more tree ferns in the local nurseries. Today only two are commonly sold: the Australian tree fern, *Sphaeropteris cooperi* (*Alsophila australis* and *A. cooperi* in the trade), and the Tasmanian *Dicksonia antarctica*.

Like most fern fanciers, I collect any that come my way, but I find I have more of the common ones. There was a period when I planted tree ferns whenever I could get them and wherever I had room. Later I became more critical of their arrangement and wanted to create a setting with ferns scattered here and there in a natural way. I began to fret over tree ferns that looked as though I had intended to line them up but missed. From where I sat at the dinner table their placement looked wrong to me, though no one else seemed bothered by it. Today the differences in their sizes and angles of growth are such that the nearly-lined-up look I objected to is obliterated.

There is a handsome formal planting of tree ferns at Longwood Garden in Pennsylvania's Kennett Square. Within a large enclosure, stately rows of ferns flank a long rectangular pool. The tall slender trunks of the Australian tree fern rise above a row of spreading Mexican tree ferns, *Cibotium schiedei*. I cannot help wondering if they ever had to replace a plant that dared to disturb this elegant symmetry.

When I started to landscape in earnest I was impatient to have my tree ferns tall enough to fill in the spaces intended for them. I planted the fastest growing, the Australians, where they would eventually hide the neighbors' television antennae. That they have done—in some cases overdone, with crowns now well above the chimneys. Unlike those of most trees, the crowns of tree ferns cannot be headed back without dire results. The tip of the tree fern trunk is analogous to the apical or terminal bud of a stem. The distinctive form of the usual tree fern is due to the absence of any lateral or side buds that could grow into branches. As is also true of most palms, the loss of the apical bud results in the death of the plant.

The fastest growing plants tend to shed more heavily. The old fronds and even some middle-aged ones hang down wearily from an otherwise beautiful crown. Some people call these limply hanging fronds "skirts," but this euphemism leaves me unreconciled to their messiness. Unfortunately, however, my pole pruner is too short to reach the highest of these derelicts; and for the fronds I can reach for removal I must prepare for the shower of chaff that descends. (A youngster once told me that he collects this chaff for sale to his friends as "itch powder.")

None of the commonly cultivated tree ferns is more copious in the formation of spores than the Australian tree fern. With the help of a magnifying glass of about eight power, clusters of spore cases may be seen on the undersides of fertile fronds. On fronds of other species clusters of spore cases may be enclosed in small membraneous spheres, cups, or boxes. Without a hand lens, the shedding spores are evident in the fine dust that covers the walks and surrounding foliage, especially during the summer months. Despite their profusion, these spores, although viable, generally do not grow, the outdoor climate of southern California being much too arid. In Florida spores produce volunteers in the open garden.

Recent years have brought new kinds of Australian tree ferns. Dwarf plants are being offered in the trade, but the specimens I have seen were not mature so I do not know how large they will become. There is also a cultivar, *Sphaeropteris cooperi* 'Brentwood', an exceedingly robust plant that produces a more massive trunk and denser foliage than other Australian tree ferns. A grower in Florida tells me that plants of the cultivar 'Brentwood' are more resistant to the fungus rhizoctonia (though this fungus rarely infests Australian tree ferns in California).

Tasmanian dicksonias have not given me the problems that Australian tree ferns

A group of tree ferns at Lotusland, near Santa Barbara, designed by Bill Paylen

Tree fern fronds gathered for food near Goroko, New Guinea

Vase made in New Zealand from a tree fern trunk

have. They are slower growing and have tested my patience sometimes. But they require little care and keep to the scale appropriate for small gardens such as mine. Then too, their leaves do not age as rapidly, nor do they bend into sharp awkward positions when old. These are the hardiest of our commonly cultivated tree ferns and survive short periods at temperatures below freezing.

Of the other tree ferns that have come and mostly gone in the trade, most are slow growers and not commercial favorites. I miss the abundance of the Hawaiian tree fern, *Cibotium glaucum*, but I do not regret that the harvesting and importing of bare tree fern trunks, once indiscriminate, is now restricted. Future generations may see the magnificence of mountain slopes again entirely covered with tree ferns.

The regal Mexican tree fern, *Cibotium schiedei*, was popular in Victorian times. It hardly forms a trunk, but its fronds are large and numerous. They easily may ascend to five feet, then flow over to touch the ground. The folds of soft foliage provide good hiding places, and I must confess that behind these folds I have concealed garden debris, such as discarded Australian tree fern fronds. A well-grown Mexican tree fern is a large and beautiful plant, but one rarely sees them in the trade.

The silver tree fern, *Alsophila tricolor* (*Cyathea dealbata*), when mature, has silvery undersides and stalks, while the black tree fern, *Sphaeropteris medullaris* (*Cyathea medullaris*), has a black trunk. Neither is available from local growers these days.

Sadleria cyatheoides, the fern seen growing on lava rock in Hawaii, continues to move in and out of the trade. Its narrow fronds are sparingly divided and it tends to form offshoots at its base. A form bearing redder immature fronds is circulating among fern growers. Unlike other tree ferns mentioned, sadlerias are sensitive to transplanting and I use the utmost care in moving them. There is a scattering of other tree ferns from Mexico and the Pacific area circulating among fern collectors. Some are slow growing or difficult in cultivation, while newer introductions still need to be assessed.

In arid southern California tree ferns develop only a scant layer of aerial roots, except for 'Brentwood', whose massive trunk is due mainly to its many aerial roots. In more humid climates, aerial roots grow in abundance and envelop the trunk. Tree ferns with a thick mantle of aerial roots provide a natural rooting medium for epiphytes. Commerce has not overlooked this, and many tree ferns are cut and the trunks fashioned into planters.

The stubs left by old fronds of Tasmanian dicksonias make ideal crannies for other plants. (The stubs of Australian tree ferns eventually dry out and shed.) I have tillandsias, small orchids, and other epiphytes on the trunks. A pad of sphagnum moss helps new residents get a footing and a length of transparent nylon fishing line holds them in place.

I have also planted creeping ferns around the bases of my tree ferns. Some of these now clothe the lower trunks, particularly those with aerial roots. These creeping ferns will eventually meet the orchids and tillandsias at eye level. I can wait. If there is one thing that growing tree ferns teaches the gardener it is patience; that and a vast appreciation for these attractive and quite fascinating plants.

ORNAMENTAL GRASSES

PAMELA HARPER

DURING the last five years there has been a surge of interest in ornamental grasses. The landscape architects Oehme, van Sweden & Associates of Washington, D.C., have had a lot to do with this. They have demonstrated how beautiful grasses can be, not only in private gardens but in such conspicuous public places as the park-like area around the Federal Reserve Building in Washington. Some of the thousands of visitors to the nation's capital will certainly have gone home with new ideas for their own gardens. A frustrating search for the plants may have followed, but the situation is improving, though demand still often exceeds supply. Making a choice among over a hundred listed grasses might now be the problem. Many are new to me, especially the prairie grasses. One little gem among these is mosquito grass, with tiny pink and white combs of flowers held obliquely to the stalks and seeming to hover; a curiosity for the rock garden. Other than this I'll confine myself to familiar grasses, using the term loosely to include a few sedges, reeds, and rushes.

Many annual and tender perennial grasses are grown for their inflorescences, to be admired on the plant or dried in bouquets. Seed catalogs illustrate quite a lot,

with such evocative names as animated oats, cloud grass, golden top, bridal veil, and ornamental corn. Quaking grass, *Briza maxima*, has been grown by generations of gardeners for its panicles of pendant lockets quivering on wire-fine stalks. This is an annual, and so is the scaled-down *B. minor*, but *B. media*—also known as trembling grass, shakers, and doddering dickies—is a hardy perennial, about eighteen inches high, deciduous, but almost evergreen in mild areas. At the front of a flower border its trembling fat spikelets, green fading to beige, add a light touch to the brighter colors.

Fountain grass well describes the four-foot flowering clumps of *Pennisetum setaceum* (*P. ruppelii*), variable in color but rosy pink in the preferred form, sometimes grown as an annual. Where frost is infrequent it is perennial, as in California, where it is frequently planted, but clumps may rot in winter in wet soil. No sun seems too hot for this drought-resistant grass, but wind can leave it battered. It is a pest if plumes are not cut before the seeds fall, but the dark-flowered, dark-leaved *P. setaceum* 'Cupreum' is said not to set seed, although this needs to be confirmed in California. Excessive self-seeding seldom occurs in

Upper left: Bowles' golden sedge, Carex elata; *lower left:* Miscanthus sinensis *'Variegatus' with* Rudbeckia fulgida; *right:* Miscanthus sinensis *'Zebrinus'*

colder areas, where the dead plumes of this and the hardier, but less colorful, *P. alopecuroides* are left for winter interest.

BAMBOOS

I could say much about bamboos, and little of it polite. Several proverbs apply: "give them an inch and they'll take a yard," "once bitten, twice shy." Bamboos must have caused more friction between neighbors than any other plants because the taller ones seem so suitable for boundary screens; unfortunately, stoloniferous bamboos recognize no boundaries, and most of the clump-forming kinds are rather tender. If I did feel inclined to try a hair of the dog, it would be with *Chusquea culeou* or *Arundinaria viridistriata. Chusquea culeou* is Chilean, and Chilean plants are noted for two things: their beauty, and their poor adaptability to other climates. So it would be a gamble, but one worth taking in mild climates where it could be given moderately moist, fertile soil and shelter from wind. Plume-like stems of slender, two-inch, deep green leaves comprise the dense, ferny, slightly vase-shaped, exceptionally graceful non-invasive clumps, seldom more than eight feet high though capable of twice as much. Unlike most bamboos, the canes are solid and the leaves do not wilt when stems are cut. Mature canes are clad to the base with short leafy branches, but first-year canes are bare, dark green, and punctuated with conspicuous white sheaths from the nodes.

The other bamboo that tempts me from time to time is hardier but less restrained, and I've seen it escape too often to put my trust in bottomless tubs or flue pipes sunk in the ground, let alone the old tires sometimes entrusted with the job of containing it. *Arundinaria viridistriata* seldom grows as much as waist high. An earlier species name, *A. auricoma* (having golden hair) was apt, because the effect is of a vividly yellow plant, and young leaves are velvety. Look closer and you find that the spear-shaped mature leaves vary: yellow; pale green; yellow flushed green; green flushed yellow; or yellow with green pencil-striping. Raised containers, or beds surrounded by paving set on concrete slab, will keep it in its allotted spot. The color is brightest in full sun, which may, however, scorch or curl the leaves, especially if the soil is dry. Each gardener must experiment to find the best place. Hard frost kills the leaves, but they stay on the plant—shantung-colored and with a silky sheen when struck by the low rays of the sun.

For those averse to yellow foliage, there's a white and green counterpart in *Arundianaria variegata*. For more about bamboos,

turn to *Sunset New Western Garden Book*, where thirty-six are described.

Pampas grass, *Cortaderia selloana*, is too imposing to be a good mixer and most fittingly stands alone in grass or paving. Where hardy it is easy to grow, even below high tide line on the beach. In California care must be taken in planting pampas grass to be sure that *C. selloana* is used and not *C. jubata*, which is an invasive pest throughout the state. For gardeners deprived of this because winter lows fall regularly below 10° F., there is an equally impressive substitute in *Erianthus ravennae*. Less bushy but loftier plumes, rearing up ten feet or more, have the spun-glass lucency of a squirrel's tail against the light. The foxy brown winter color is also appealing—all in all an under-appreciated plant for fertile, moist, but well-drained soil, hardy well below zero, though with the risk that the flowering plumes may be damaged by early autumn frost.

My resolve never again to grow pampas grass, after cutting myself on the saw-edged leaves while trying to hack a clump apart, weakened at sight of the cultivar 'Gold Band' combined with gray artemisia and blue agapanthus, the prettiest association seen during a three-week gardens tour. The name misleads, it is striped, not banded. I bought it, it died, and its place has been filled by *Miscanthus sinensis* 'Zebrinus', which really is gold-banded. There are hundreds of plants with vertical striping but very few with horizontal bars, which go "against the grain" so to speak. In the moist (even wet) soil preferred by these plants, 'Zebrinus' stands shoulder high, topped through autumn and winter with feathery plumes. *M. sinensis* 'Strictus', called porcupine grass, is similar but shorter, narrower, and more upright. At least a dozen other cultivars are obtainable, of which 'Gracillimus', a four-foot fountain

Grasses in a landscape designed by Oehme, van Sweden and Associates. Included are Calamogrostis epigejos,
Miscanthus sinensis *'Gracillimus',* Pennisetum alopecuroides

of narrow ribbons, and white-striped 'Variegatus' are easiest to find and among the best.

When to divide or transplant grasses depends on where you live. Transplanting should, ideally, be followed by the longest possible period without excessive cold, heat, drought, wind, or rain, but the ideal must sometimes yield to expediency. In prying off a chunk of 'Zebrinus' I broke a fork and nearly my back, so anyone much over forty years of age might do well to tackle the job whenever they happen to have around a strong man with saw, mattock, and axe. If in doubt about the plant's survival leave part of the clump where it is as insurance.

REEDS

Two impressive grasses of somewhat similar appearance are the giant reeds, *Phragmites australis* (*P. communis*) and *Arundo donax*, wetland plants invaluable for beautifying low-lying wasteland, as phragmites does along stretches of East Coast interstates. Both have Jekyll-and-Hyde characteristics, being extremely invasive in wet soils but quite likely to die in dry ones. Of several cultivars, only *Arundo donax* 'Versicolor' seems to be available; this is reminiscent of sweetcorn but with each leaf striped in cream and green broadly margined with white. It is cold-tender (more so than other plants of the species), vagrant, and the leaves may scorch in dry climates, but effort to overcome these shortcomings is well worthwhile for this showiest of all variegated grasses.

If a plant is attractive, fairly easy to grow, and not too difficult to propagate, it is well on the road to popularity, but not necessarily universal popularity. Having met those requirements, a less obvious factor comes into play, one I became aware of when, on moving from England to the southeastern

United States, I found that yellow foliage had lost some of its appeal; the psychological effect is different under sunny skies. On the East Coast many grasses, wild and cultivated, are most appealing in autumn and early winter. As the year explodes in a climax of brilliance from the trees, the dead stems and leaves of deciduous grasses have the same tawny gleam as the sunlit coat of a golden retriever, while the plumed or hazy inflorescences assume a radiance in the Indian-summer sunshine unexcelled by any other plant. Deciduous grasses favored by Oehme, van Sweden and Associates for this effect include the three-foot vertical clumps of *Calamagrostis* ('Karl Foerster' is a particularly fine cultivar), arching *Pennisetum alopecuroides*, and *Miscanthus sinensis* 'Gracillimus' with its slender weeping leaves and feather-duster plumes. By combining these with evergreens such as yuccas and mugo pine, foreground ground covers such as epimediums and bergenias, and perennials that stay long in bloom and remain attractive when dead, especially *Sedum* 'Autumn Joy' and *Rudbeckia fulgida*, a picture is created that changes with the seasons and never lacks interest. Sometimes the grasses are massed, sometimes well spaced among rocks and gravel. The grasses remain effective through most of winter and are never more appreciated than when rising above a sparkling carpet of snow.

But what of regions where summers are dry, winters mild, and rainy autumn heralds not a winding down but a resurgence of growth? Might green better suit the mood of this new growing season? In any event, dead brown grasses are seen at their best where autumn is sunny and comparatively dry; under persistently gray skies they may look drab and rain bedraggled. There are evergreen sedges from New Zealand (*Carex buchananii* is one) that are always brown or copper-colored; might

Top: Molinia caerulea *'Variegata' with*
Allium tuberosum, Achillea taygetea,
and marigold; left: Hakonechloa macra;
above: Carex morrowii *'Aurea-Variegata'*

these be in keeping where brown is the characteristic color of the summer landscape, or would they seem to have died of drought? I'd need to live there to know. These coppery sedges are uncommon and names are confused: *Carex buchananii* should be V-shaped, but a grass of weeping habit (equally desirable) sometimes bears this name.

Most of the reeds and rushes and some of the sedges need or prefer marshy soil or shallow water, and so do a few of the grasses, but those mentioned next will also grow in soil only moderately moist. *Acorus gramineus* 'Variegatus' makes gappy foot-high clumps of sword-shaped leaves grouped in narrow fans. Roughly half the quarter-inch width of each leaf is green, the other half cream; it looks more at home in a manicured setting than a naturalistic one and never better than when growing through pebbles in a pot.

Umbrella plant, *Cyperus alternifolius*, makes a good pot plant for those who find it hard to gauge the right amount of water. Over-watering is almost impossible, and under-watering can be guarded against by standing the pot in a water-filled outer container. In summer, or year round in warm climates, it can be plunged in a garden pool or grown in a moist border. An elderly lady told me she got new plants by cutting off the "umbrellas" and putting them upside down in shallow water (hers were in the bird bath). I was skeptical, but tried it, and found she was right. It is killed at 20° F., as are most of its kin but not, unfortunately, that beautiful but pestiferous weed, *Cyperus esculentus* or nut grass, seed of which is sometimes offered for sale; avoid it like the plague.

VARIEGATION

Bowles' golden sedge might be found under *Carex stricta* 'Aurea', *C. riparia* 'Bowles',

or *C. elata* 'Bowles' Golden'—they are all the same thing, and a lovely thing it is, with slender, flexed leaves about two feet long, seemingly pure golden yellow though actually thinly margined green. The color is brightest in full sun, and wet soil alongside a pond or stream is the perfect spot for it. It isn't a beginner's plant, being often difficult to establish. Don't confuse it with Bowles' golden grass, *Milium effusum* 'Aureum', a graceful yellow-leaved wood millet, easily grown from seed, and a cheerful plant for heavy, moist soil in partial shade.

Three rather similar, winter-dormant wetland grasses grown for their striped ribbonlike arching leaves are: *Glyceria maxima* (*G. aquatica*) 'Variegata', or manna grass, about four feet high with leaves striped cream; *Phalaris arundinacea* var. *picta*, ribbon grass or gardeners' garters, of similar height with leaves striped white; and the taller *Spartina pectinata* 'Aureomarginata' with leaves striped yellow. Assessed solely on appearance, my own first choice would be glyceria, which is at its best in mud or shallow water. Spartina would be the one for brackish marshes. Phalaris, besides being beautiful, is exceptionally hardy (to about −30° F.) and will grow in quite dry soil. All three are determined colonizers, phalaris less so in dry soil but it still needs watching. *P. arundinacea* 'Feesey's Form' is said to be superior and non-invasive, and 'Dwarf's Garters' is a shorter, twelve-inch, variegated cultivar; neither seems yet to be available in the United States.

GRAY AND BLUE

Now a group grown mainly for the appeal of their living leaves, though most also have attractive flowers. Trying not to play dog-in-the-manger, I'll put the blue ones first. On acid seashore sand in Virginia these are among my failures; humid heat and high rainfall is probably what upsets them, as it does a lot of gray-leaved plants.

Most gardeners know blue fescue, usually sold as *Festuca glauca*. *Hortus Third* calls it *F. ovina* var. *glauca*. In his recent book, *Ornamental Grasses*, Roger Grounds calls it *F. caesia*. Kurt Bluemel, Inc.,* a nursery with a long list of grasses, calls it *F. cinerea* 'Superba' and lists also the cultivar 'Blausilber'. Under whatever name, blue fescue makes pattable cushions of soft, needle-fine blades six to eight inches high, not good for massing because the tuffets maintain their individual rounded shape and weeds insinuate themselves into the gaps. Crowded clumps may rot, and even well spaced ones get shabby if not divided every year or two. *F. amethystina* is a similar but taller plant of eighteen inches or so.

Of similar color, but taller and of firmer outline, *Helictotrichon sempervirens* (*Avena sempervirens*) seems to demand a formal setting—perhaps a single plant in paving, or a group of three well-spaced clumps growing through a ground cover of pebbles. Slender spiky leaves grow upright at the center of the clump, those at the edges are arching. When topped with stalks of loosely clustered grayish flowers the plants reach four feet in height. Sandy soil in sun is said to be their preference. Metallic blue and broader bladed, plants of *Elymus arenarius* are of more relaxed mien—rather untidy in fact. Though it was lauded by no less a personage than Gertrude Jekyll, I'd hesitate to admit to my garden a plant of such uncurbable exuberance. It is a seashore plant, sometimes used for stabilizing dunes, but the handsomest planting I've seen was in wet, heavy clay—which only shows that you can't always go by the book.

The only blue thing about *Molinia caeru-*

*2543 Hess Road, Fallston, Md. 21047. I have found a good selection of grasses also at Andre Viette Farm and Nursery, Rte. 1, Box 16, Fishersville, Va. 22939.

lea 'Variegata' is the name. The flowers are sometimes purplish and purple moor grass is one popular name. There is a gentleness about this plant, the leaves limply arching, the creamy striping merging with cream stalks holding aloft slightly arching sprays of brownish or purplish flowers to a height of two feet or so. It is clump forming, blends with almost everything, does well in sun or part shade, and adapts to most soils not excessively wet, dry, or alkaline. It is hardy at −10° F., but the leaves turn brown with the first frosts.

YELLOW

Hakonechloa, from Japan, is a winner. Plants of *Hakonechloa macra*, with green leaves, are not being sold, though they are in cultivation. Three cultivar names appear in literature but all the plants I've seen have been the same. White Flower Farm* claims to have introduced it to the United States, and they give it the name *H. macra* 'Albo-aurea Variegata'. It is the same plant as *H. macra* 'Aureola' of English gardens. Moist, humus-rich, acid soil suits it best, with shade from direct sun where summers are hot. Slowly spreading clumps combine dramatic color with delicate texture and graceful form. They look yellow, but each slender tapering blade is pencilled with green and sometimes flushed pink or bronze. It is flowerless so far, and there seems to be doubt about whether it belongs with the grasses or the bamboos. *Alopecurus pratensis* 'Aureo-variegatus' has similarly brilliant coloring on a denser, more upright plant, scarcely eighteen inches high with cylindrical clusters of flowers held well above the foliage. Grow this in full sun or part shade, in fertile, well-drained soil. Clumps spread moderately

*Litchfield, Ct. 06759

fast, but an infestation need not be feared.

Variegated bulbous oat grass, *Arrhenatherum elatius* 'Bulbosum Variegatum', is easily recognizable, if you dig a bit up, by the chain of maize-shaped basal nodes, each capable of making a new plant. This is one of the prettiest grasses, with clean white striping and dainty flowers. In my garden it tries to go summer-dormant, doesn't quite manage it, and hangs about looking shabby. It smartens itself up for a couple of months in autumn and then goes dormant with the coming of cold weather. It may behave differently in other climates.

PROBLEMS

Finally—though not because the topic is exhausted; I've barely scratched the surface—two current favorites. Attempts to unravel the tangled names of these two somewhat similar sedges have met with only partial success. They resemble each other in size and habit: in moist leaf mold and partial shade fist-sized divisions have made dense clumps eighteen inches in diameter after three years. Each slender leaf is over a foot in length, but because they arch or spread sideways the height of the clumps is little more than eight inches. The tough, once-pleated leaves look glossy and smooth, and they feel that way if you run your fingers from base to tip, but rubbed the other way they are raspy toward the tip. So much for similarities; now the names and differences. From sundry names thrown into the pot by catalogs, articles, reference books (no two of which quite agree, nor do their descriptions precisely match the plants before my eyes), and learned friends, I have picked the two I think most likely, with other names under which they might be found in parentheses. Both plants are from Japan.

Carex morrowii 'Aurea-variegata', or 'Aureo-variegata', or 'Variegata Aurea' (*C. morrowii* var. *expallida*, *C. morrowii* 'Variegata', *C. morrowii* 'Evergold') has leaves one-quarter inch wide. Sometimes the striation is a bit more complicated, but most of the leaves are deep cream in the middle with a fairly narrow dark green edge. The overall effect is a showy creamy yellow in combed clumps from which fallen leaves are easily raked. In my garden this plant does extremely well if given deep, moist soil and some shade from afternoon sun. It is an undamaged evergreen down to 20° F., is shabby at lower temperatures, and perishes at about zero. It is not uncommon, and all seem agreed that it belongs to the species *C. morrowii*.

EASILY GROWN NORTHWEST NATIVES
FOR ROCK GARDENS

JOSEPH A. WITT & JEAN G. WITT

ORTHWEST natives, suited naturally to a climate with winter rainfall and summer drought, adapt readily to gardens in the Seattle area, and a surprising number will thrive in our gravelly soils with minimal care. These are not the difficult high alpines nor the hard-to-please drylanders from eastern Washington, but species largely from lowland or intermediate elevations west of the Cascades—in other words, plants requiring little or no special treatment that can be expected to survive and thrive for the average gardener. Without benefit of really green thumbs, and with only the soil and rocks left us by the last continental glaciation, we have in the course of twenty-five years built up a small collection of attractive and undemanding natives for both sun and shade. Here are a few of them:

Allium cernuum, the nodding onion, is native over wide areas of North America besides the Northwest. Its pendant clusters of starry pale pink bells on eight- to ten-inch stems come late enough in the summer to avoid being overpowered by showier foreign bulbs. The gravelly glacial till of our small east-facing rockery, with some addition of compost, seems to be quite to their liking, although in the wild they would certainly occupy a less shady location.

White-flowered *Erythronium oregonum*, dogtooth violet or fawn lily, along with rose pink *E. revolutum* and several others unidentified, share with dwarf rhododendrons and various cyclamens a west-facing bed against the house which barely qualifies as a rock garden by virtue of being slightly crowned and furnished with some chunks of garnet schist. The soil was enriched with compost and rotten wood before the rhododendrons were planted and this has sufficed for the bulbs as well. Originally this area was shaded from the full force of the afternoon sun by a large madroña tree, and we feared the plantings would suffer from too much heat after the demise of the tree, but so far this has not been the case. The erythroniums send up their handsome mottled leaves through the cyclamen foliage before it dies down in the spring, with one or more elegant recurved flowers on six- to twelve-inch stems. A cover of bark mulch holds in moisture and, together with the almost solid mosaic of cyclamen leaves, keeps the area weed free as well as providing a substrate in which both erythroniums and cyclamen self sow.

Penstemon fruticosus *'Charming'*

Brodiaea coronaria, harvest brodiaea or blue dicks, from the coastal bluffs and rocky coastlines of Vancouver Island and the San Juan Islands, came to us as commercial bulbs and is very much larger flowered and more prolific than the wild form. The few starter bulbs have rapidly increased to a large clump now in need of dividing. They bloom enthusiastically in full sun with good drainage at the top of the front rock garden slope, quite at home in the lean soil.

Ten or more years ago a few bulbs of *Camassia quamash*, common camas, from the Nisqually Prairies, went into temporary quarters in a vacant niche at the upper edge of the sunny rockery slope, where they proceeded to bloom and seed so satisfactorily that we have never bothered to move them to the damper location they presumably would prefer. However, as with the native violet from the prairies, *Viola adunca*, in our garden the flowers are light blue instead of the rich dark blue that they show in the wild—apparently due to the difference in soil. This could perhaps be corrected with fertilizer, but we haven't really tried, and they receive only the all-purpose fertilizer that we put on the garden as a whole.

Fritillaria lanceolata, mission bell or rice root, is among those bulbs (mostly exotic) that we grow in pots and are lifted and dried out in summer. Our plants bear only one- or two-inch long brown and green diffusely checkered bells on their ten-inch long stems, though we've seen up to four flowers on plants in some locations in central Washington and know of places in western Washington where the color of the bells pales out to a mottled greenish yellow. Protected from disturbance by the pot, the bulbs have produced prodigious numbers of the rice-grain bulblets that give this genus one of its common names, rice root. We

will plant some of the bulblets out in our driest, sunniest location; perhaps they will yield more flowers.

Among the shade-loving perennials with which we have been successful, *Cornus canadensis*, Canada dogwood, is perhaps our favorite, and one of the few to which we have made concessions in bed preparation. In one shady corner we built up a special garden using old stumps instead of rocks, and adding large amounts of rotted wood and compost to the rather sandy soil. Though slow to establish at first, the little dogwood now romps happily over the decaying logs in the company of *Vaccinium vitis-idaea* and *Ledum glandulosum*.

Tellima grandiflora, fringecup, might be considered weedy since it seeds everywhere, but we're fond of its spikes of fringed, greenish flowers which turn rosy with age. It grows without any care whatever, irrespective of soil, and plants that come up in an inconvenient place can always be pulled out or moved. *Tiarella trifoliata*, foam flower or lace flower, another member of the saxifrage family, with sprays of dainty white flowers and somewhat maple-like leaves, has been the victim of dry shade and really should be moved to the edge of the bog garden where conditions would more nearly match the streamsides along which it grows in the wild. *Heuchera cylindrica*, alum root, with leaves similar in shape to those of its relative, coral bells, but with spikes of greenish or cream-colored flowers, has done well in a sunny position.

Dicentra formosa, the western bleeding-heart, has been in our garden for more than thirty years—descendants of plants collected from a vacant lot long since blacktopped for shopping center parking—and is surely among the most permanent of natives for the garden. Over the years we have discarded the pale, few-flowered

Erythronium oregonum *(fawn lily)*

Adiantum pedatum *(maidenhair fern) at Colonial Creek, Northern Cascade Mountains*

seedlings in favor of those with fuller clusters and deeper rose color. Their pale pink rhizomatous stems meander through the damper, compost-enriched parts of the shady rock garden, but can also take full sun. The slightly bluish, much dissected leaves tend to disappear by late summer so they need to be associated with plants that retain their leaves. The white-flowered selected form 'Sweetheart' grows in a friend's garden with even more abandon—she values it as a foil for her extensive collection of small, early-flowering irises.

Another friend blessed with rich damp lake-bottom soil grew *Aquilegia formosa*, the western wild columbine, with no special effort. It seeded prolifically and even hybridized with her garden columbines. Memory of her display keeps us trying, but so far we have been successful only with one of its relatives from the southwest, *A. triternata*, which seems to be able to take poor soil and a hot location.

Native ferns are among the most attractive, long-lived, and satisfactory garden subjects, although many of the easiest are too large for most rock gardens. Deer fern, *Blechnum spicant*, dug as sods in the wild, was scarcely disturbed by moving and sends up its inrolled fertile fronds over dark green rosettes of sterile fronds every year in dry shade under the red huckleberry, *Vaccinium parvifolium*. Sword fern, *Polystichum munitum*, sprouts by the steps where the back path drops through the shady rockery—these cannot be more than short-term rock garden subjects since the handsome evergreen fronds eventually will reach three or four feet in length. Lady fern, *Athyrium filix-femina*, appears unbidden in the bog garden, and though their lacy pale green fronds lend a light touch among the iris leaves, they are weeded out as really being too large and prolific. *Adiantum pedatum*, the native maidenhair fern,

which came from a damp location in the wild, has proved to be much tougher and more tolerant than its delicate appearance suggests. It has endured twenty years in a relatively dry and shady spot at the foot of the rockery and new plants have appeared in the bare niches under the steps. It even survived a litter of kittens whose idea of fun was to jump into the midst of the clump until only the stumps of the stems remained; but new fronds appeared after the kittens went off to new homes.

Geum triflorum, aptly called fairy lanterns from the shape of its triads of nodding dusty rose flowers, is a prairie and mountain plant for full sun. It takes its other common names, prairie smoke and old-man-with-a-beard, from the tufts of seeds that follow the flowers. The clumps of ferny cut-leaved foliage put up their eight-to ten-inch stalks of flowers in late spring. The pinkish plumed seed heads are equally decorative.

The small shrub, *Dryas octopetala*, white mountain avens, has spread in a leisurely fashion, flat to the ground, across the sunny end of our shady rock garden. The dry gravelly soil, filled with rocks, rather closely resembles its mountain habitat. Wild-rose-like white flowers filled with yellow stamens are raised on short scapes over small dark evergreen leaves with inrolled edges and white undersides. The stems tend to root as they spread, and this plant is therefore easy to acquire from pieces already rooted.

Sedum spathulifolium, broadleaved stonecrop, widespread on cliffs from British Columbia to California, is entirely content with a slight slope in the rock garden and thrives in even the poorest, driest soil. Its mats of succulent silver-dusted gray-green rosettes color up like little red roses in exposed situations, and are especially welcome to offset the drabness of winter. A great many leaf colors have been reported, including silvery lime-green from shady crevices, and ice-green edged in lavender or mauve. Almost any rosette will have a few roots at the base of its stem, if pulled off carefully, so that superior plants are easily transferred to the garden. Small spikes of clear starry yellow flowers are an added attraction in spring.

Penstemons abound in the Northwest and can be raised from collected seed or taken as cuttings, which root rapidly in pots with plastic bags over them. Some herbaceous ones we've had good luck with are *Penstemon richardsonii*, a Cascade Mountain form with violet-blue flowers rather than the usual rose-pink, and *P. albertinus* from the Bitterroots, with numerous eight- to ten-inch spikes of small bright blue flowers. The large-flowered shrubby penstemons are favorites with many Northwest gardeners. We have found the lavender-flowered *P. cardwellii* and its white-flowered cultivar 'John Bacher' among the most permanent and satisfactory. *P. fruticosus* 'Charming', a light true pink instead of the usual lavender, is another choice selection. Hybrid penstemons such as 'Pat' with rich rose-pink flowers and 'Edithae' with rich purple flowers have done much better for us than *P. rupicola*, one of their parents.

Plants of shrubby penstemons that had been reduced to a vegetative existence by increasing shade have recently been given a new lease on life in a new sunny rock garden built over an irremovable madroña

stump with chunks of concrete from the former front walk. Concrete chunks posing as rocks for the rock garden are not as bad as they sound—particularly when one has no access to limestone. They have been installed as ledges with the flat surfaces facing inward at an angle and only the broken edges visible. Penstemons planted under and between the concrete "rocks" have all done well except for one which was down slope from a small bearded iris plagued with botrytis. Shrubby penstemons often dwindle from a mysterious die-back vaguely attributed to soil fungi, but this is the first time we have seen an obvious source of trouble. One would perhaps do well to avoid planting them with irises or tulips. Full sun, perfect drainage, and a mulch of rock chips aid in discouraging fungi; Benlate treatment also helps.

For ground cover we've tried a couple of native strawberries, and prefer the alpine and prairie *Fragaria virginiana* with its evergreen blue-green leaves and clusters of small white flowers, over the more vigorously runnered pale green *F. vesca*, which seldom blooms (at least in shade) and tends to gallop over choicer plants.

This is by no means an exhaustive list of the Northwest natives that can be grown easily in the Seattle area. Gardeners with more favorable conditions than ours, or with more time to devote to soil preparation and maintenance, should be able to find many other small natives worthy of inclusion in their rock gardens.

BROOMS AND ROCK ROSES

LESTER HAWKINS

Too often, brooms and rock roses are thought of as quick-growing shrubs that are, to be sure, showy in their flowers, but otherwise rank and somewhat weedy in their habits. This unjust reputation has been perpetuated by the following vicious circle: we do not grow the best species and the reason we do not grow them is because of the faults of those we do grow. Thus, for example, many gardeners, when they think of brooms, have an image of a rather stiff bush hung with brown pods ready to broadcast thousands of seeds in all directions. Such a gardener is not likely to discover the large numbers of beautiful brooms that have great elegance of form and set only small amounts of seed. Before we get to these better plants, however, let us take a brief overall look at these two great groups of shrubs and see what they have to offer us.

Brooms and rock roses share a preeminent place in the shrub flora of the Mediterranean, where together they number more than a hundred species, only a small fraction of which have appeared in our gardens. There is no argument that they tend to be showy plants; indeed some of them are among the most beautiful shrubs we can grow. They are, on the whole, su-premely well adapted to our climate and are among the easiest to cultivate and most reliably drought-tolerant of all garden subjects. Also—no small item to those who live outside cities—they are almost immune to the ravages of deer. There is no doubt that they have a lot to offer, and for my part at least, I would not want a country garden in which they did not play a prominent role.

It follows from all this that, if we are to capitalize on these qualities, we should know which to use and where to plant them to the best effect. Perhaps more than any other landscape subjects, they suffer from the current fashion for planting shrubs in masses of a single kind. Few rock roses can claim to be superior foliage plants. Yet they can be charming when used singly or in small groups in appropriate places. To plant them in masses is to display all their defects. Similarly, the best brooms are airy, graceful shrubs and can be planted here and there to lighten the quality of a land-scape, whereas bedded out, they look like weeds.

Those who know how the modern nurs-ery trade operates should not be surprised that the brooms and rock roses sold are often the wrong ones and often under the wrong names. Technical advances, mass production, everything that makes for ability to propagate plants by the hundreds of thousands, all conspire to narrow the lists and to discourage new introductions and experimentation; plants produced must be known, even when they are known infamously. We can only hope that the worst of this standardizing trend is over and that new ways of informing the public about a wider variety of plants will be found. The present notes on the range and uses of brooms and rock roses are made with this hope in mind.

BROOMS

Brooms, members of *Cytisus*, *Genista*, and allied genera,* comprise a very large number of woody plants ranging from shrubs twenty feet high to totally prostrate, sometimes minuscule, alpines. Of the more than a hundred species, well over half are worth growing; many of these are highly picturesque shrubs of beautiful habit, and almost all are extremely showy when in bloom.

Brooms are often thought to be short-lived. This is certainly not true of the dwarfs in our garden, many of which are sixteen years old and show no signs of declining. The record is less clear for the larger brooms, some of which have as-

*For the most part this guide is limited to the plants usually placed in *Cytisus* and *Genista*. It would be tempting to define broom so as to include such outlying genera as gorse (*Ulex*), the blue gorse (*Erinacea*), the fabled and rarely grown red gorse of Patagonia (*Anarthrophyllum*), our native broom (*Pickeringia*), and such Mediterraneans as *Calycotome*, *Petteria*, and *Adenocarpus*, but this would hopelessly complicate the task. There has been an increasing tendency to fragment the genera *Cytisus* and *Genista* into *Argyrocytisus*, *Chamaecytisus*, *Lygos*, *Monospartium*, *Echinospartium*, and others. We treat them all under *Cytisus* and *Genista*, the procedure followed by Hillier's *Manual of Trees and Shrubs*, Bean's *Trees and Shrubs Hardy in the British Isles*, and most other books of horticultural reference.

sumed a bedraggled appearance after eight or ten years. Others have done better, however; a fourteen-year-old tree of *Genista aetnensis* is twenty feet high and has in no way deteriorated. Without doubt, brooms do not belong in the class of permanent shrubs, but for the kind of plants they are—growing quickly and producing masses of flowers at an early age—they have a reasonable and worthwhile span of productive life.

The reputation brooms have for seeding in the wrong places is due to the habits of three of them, *Spartium junceum*, the Spanish broom, *Cytisus scoparius*, the Scotch broom, and *Cytisus monspessulanus*, the Montpelier broom, the worst offender. This last has gone wild over large areas of northern California and Oregon and is a serious threat to our native vegetation. It is ironic that it is one of the least desirable of brooms and need not have been introduced in the first place. We should emphasize that most species set almost no seed at all. *Cytisus multiflorus* and its numerous hybrids, for example, are never unsightly with seed pods. Unfortunately, nurseries are more apt to feature the hybrids of *Cytisus scoparius*, which are heavy seed bearers. Because of this problem, the brooms that set heavy seed crops and have naturalized extensively are omitted from the following discussion.

Brooms, I find, associate well with a very large number of shrubs. This is, of course, a matter of taste, but the better ones are never ungainly and can be used, as I have said, to add flowers and a graceful quality to an otherwise heavy planting of broad-leaved evergreens. I like to plant them here and there throughout a garden. Proper planning will insure a long flowering season. A few plants of *Cytisus* × *praecox* scattered strategically along a path will light up large areas with their creamy white flowers

Cytisus 'Carla', with ceanothus and other native shrubs in a planting designed by the author for a housing development at Novato, California

in late February and March. When these fade, *Cytisus multiflorus* and its hybrids take over until *Genista cinerea* and *G. aetnensis* come into bloom in early summer.

Following are some of the brooms that can unreservedly be recommended for Pacific Coast gardens.

MEDIUM AND TALL BROOMS

Cytisus multiflorus, the white Spanish broom or white Portugal broom, should come first by all means. It is an upright shrub to about ten feet with numerous slender gray-green branches that give the shrub a delicate look

even when not in bloom. It flowers in April or May with an abundance of small, pure white blossoms, and is, at that time, perhaps the most spectacular as well as the most charming of all brooms. Bean aptly says of it, "This beautiful broom is one of the most useful of hardy shrubs. Easily raised from seed and reaching its full beauty in three or four years [sooner in California], it is admirably adapted for planting in small groups in shrubberies, in association with the sturdier evergreens." We have a plant of *Cytisus multiflorus* from Portuguese seed that has a red spot at the base of the keel of the flower, giving the entire plant a pink cast. It promises to be a very beautiful plant.

Cytisus multiflorus is the most important parent of a large number of hybrids of great beauty. These plants set little or no seed and have a grace of habit and delicacy of flower lacking in the hybrids derived from *Cytisus scoparius* crossed with its bicolored cultivar 'Andreanus'.

Cytisus × praecox is the name given to a group of hybrids derived from the dwarf yellow *C. purgans* crossed with *C. multiflorus*. The original of this cross, *C. × praecox* 'Warminster', is the cultivar usually planted. It has the slender upright branchlets of *C. multiflorus* and the same gray-green color, but is dwarfer and denser, forming a dome usually less than four feet high. Its flowers are pale sulfur yellow and appear very early in the season.

The Warminster broom sets some fertile seeds and these may be grown and lined out for the selection of other plants. Several such selections have appeared in Europe: 'All-gold', of Dutch origin, has bright yellow flowers and is somewhat taller; 'Gold Spear' is a smaller plant with yellow flowers from Germany; 'Albus', from England, has white flowers, and 'Luteus', also from England, has clear yellow flowers.

Cytisus × praecox has also been used as a parent for other hybrids, particularly by the Dutch. A number of beautiful plants in lavender and rose shades have been produced and, since the program is gathering momentum, a still larger number can be expected in the future.

Cytisus × dallimorei is the name given to the first broom hybrid ever created by controlled cross-fertilization; it was the result of crossing *C. multiflorus* with *C. scoparius* 'Andreanus'. The original plant, *C. × dallimorei* 'William Dallimore' has the numerous small flowers of *C. multiflorus* except that they have rosy pink petals shad-

Cytisus 'Carla', a fine large shrub with brilliant flowers

ing to crimson. I have never seen this plant, but another of the *C. × dallimorei* hybrids, 'Geoffrey Skipwith', was imported into this country and grown for some years in the Strybing Arboretum in San Francisco. 'Geoffrey Skipwith' is a tall, graceful broom with tiny lilac flowers. Some years ago Victor Reiter pollinated this plant with itself; one of the resulting seedlings was a plant with the brightest red flowers of any broom I have ever seen. Victor gave us this plant and we have marketed it under the name 'Carla' in honor of Mrs Reiter. Subsequently we gave it to Leonard Coates Nurseries, which is producing it. It is, without doubt, the finest large hybrid broom now available in general commerce in this area. We have been back-crossing 'Carla' with *Cytisus multiflorus* in the hope of obtaining a red broom with the masses of very small flowers of that plant. One resulting seedling did have the small flowers, but with a color of such dark red that it must be planted so that the sun can shine through the flowers for full effect. We have called it

Genista aetnensis, *twenty feet tall, flowering during the drought year 1977. White flowers in foreground are romneyas*

'Garnet'. Meanwhile, of course, more crosses of the *C. × dallimorei* hybrid series are reported from Europe.

Some of the most interesting brooms we can grow come from the Canary Islands. Two of these are *Cytisus filipes* and *C. supranubius*. Both have the stout stems and almost leafless appearance of the Spanish broom, *Spartium junceum*. Both are around eight feet high and have white flowers, borne in clusters on *C. filipes* and abundantly along the stems on *C. supranubius*. The last species is particularly handsome and distinct with a tinge of rose to the petals; it is abundant on the peak of Tenerife and undoubtedly extremely drought resistant.

Another pair from the Canaries is *Cytisus palmensis* and *Cytisus proliferus*, both sometimes placed in the genus *Chamaecytisus*.

These two are tall shrubs to fifteen feet, very graceful, their long slender shoots bearing an abundance of white blossoms in late winter.

The best known of the brooms from the Canaries in California is *Cytisus × spachianus*, known in the nursery trade as *Cytisus fragrans*, *Genista fragrans*, *Cytisus racemosus*, or *Cytisus canariensis*. This is a large broom that will eventually become tree-like in its proportions. It bears its yellow flowers in racemes terminating leafy shoots, commencing in early winter and continuing often until summer. It has been popular for many years and many large specimens can be seen in San Francisco and Peninsula gardens, but it is somewhat tender and has largely died out in colder areas.

Cytisus multiflorus

Cytisus battandieri (*Argyrocytisus battandieri*) grows at an altitude of 5,000 to 6,000 feet in the Atlas Mountains of Morocco. It is an astonishing and unusual broom with large, silvery leaflets and heavy racemes of golden flowers five inches long with a strong pineapple fragrance. In good soil it makes a massive shrub eighteen feet high and almost as wide. When in full bloom in late spring it is a handsome addition to any garden large enough to accommodate shrubs of such monumental proportions. Unfortunately, *Cytisus battandieri* is deciduous and, in mild California gardens, tends to retain its slowly decaying foliage throughout winter and into spring. Also, the shrub sends up several very long stalks from its base and care should be taken to cut them out when they get old and unsightly. Despite these drawbacks, I have al-

ways found it worthwhile, but I am one of those gardeners who will sacrifice a certain amount of year-round neatness if the reward is sensational beauty for a time.

Another beautiful white broom that comes from the Iberian Peninsula and North Africa as well as the Canaries is *Genista monosperma* (*Lygos monosperma*, *Retama monosperma*). The plant is thin, graceful, and silvery, usually around six feet tall, although sometimes much more. A beautiful, aged plant at the old California Nursery in San Jose grew to be a tree. Its flowers are white, silky, and somewhat spidery in appearance with a dark contrasting calyx; they are delightfully fragrant. *Genista monosperma* is a well-behaved bush, narrow and upright in habit. It can be beautiful placed among or in front of darker evergreens. It, too, is only moderately hardy in cold areas.

Two more large shrubs of the genus *Genista* deserve attention. The first is the large *Genista aetnensis*, which can be made into a small tree by training it to a single trunk. This great broom develops a wide-spreading mop-head of weeping, nearly leafless branches, giving the plant an airy quality unusual even among brooms. It is effective as a specimen and also when several are planted together and allowed to fill a space in the garden with a large, twiggy mass of weeping stems. Its great virtue is its summer flowering; in the hottest and driest locations it will make a display of intensely fragrant yellow blossoms in July. This magnificent broom is seldom grown in nurseries, perhaps because of its initial slow growth as a container plant.

Also blooming in summer, but a much smaller shrub (to about eight feet) is *Genista cinerea*, which, as E. A. Bowles wrote, "puts on a show of the most dazzling clear yellow of any plant in my garden." Out of bloom it is a pleasing shrub with grayish white stems that are at first upright, then arch from about midway, somewhat like a very large version of *Genista lydia*. *Genista tenera*, from Madeira, is a closely allied shrub of similar habit.

SMALLER BROOMS

There is, perhaps, no need to stress the great value of small shrubs, and especially small flowering shrubs, for the garden. They can be used for edging paths, in front of larger shrubs to blend them into the landscape, to fill the spaces between large shrubs, or to create open spaces in the garden—spaces you can see across as you can a lawn, but that can be filled with a considerable variety of interesting and beautiful plants. Areas so used can be strikingly beautiful, yet they are among the easiest of all types of plantings to maintain. As H. G.

Hillier has said, "There is, perhaps, no other form of gardening which gives so great a return for so little effort." It is here that brooms really come into their own, for they are among the most reliable, numerous, easy, and showy of all classes of small flowering shrubs.

It should be noted, however, that the small brooms are not rampant spreaders and should be planted well away from plants that are, such as *Cistus salviifolius* or *Arctostaphylos uva-ursi*. Ideal companions are dwarf conifers, dwarf lavenders, *Arctostaphylos nummularia*, heathers, and small herbaceous plants.

Most of the smaller brooms come from the mountains or from rocky, desert-like wastes, where they are slow-growing but also long-lived. They vary remarkably in habit: some (from the most inhospitable sites) are spiny tufts; some have a semi-prostrate mounding habit; some are totally prostrate; and some spread slowly by horizontal shoots to form clumps and mats; yet others are upright with the characteristics of large shrubs scaled down to smaller size.

The small gorse-like brooms are from poor-soil areas and bristle with spines and thorns, but they are not as forbidding as this may sound (they may be to rabbits, but not to animals of our size who do not propose to eat them). They are numerous, each with its own picturesque habit; in some, the branches themselves divide into a spine-tipped mass, while in others the branches have side shoots equipped with spines. *Genista horrida* and *G. hispanica* are examples of the former; *G. sylvestris*, *G. falcata*, and *G. anglica* of the latter. Given a poor soil, good drainage, and an open exposure, all produce brilliant displays in late spring or early summer. *G. hispanica* is a shrub of about one and a half feet; Bean says that it produces in May and June a

Genista tournefortii, *a dense, dwarf shrub to about one and a half feet. The branching habit is similar to that of* G. sylvestris, G. anglica, *and* G. falcata

"more gorgeous display of golden blossom than any other dwarf shrub." He goes on to recommend planting several together to produce "a most brilliant color effect." *Genista horrida* is somewhat smaller and silvery rather than bright green. The dry parts of the Spanish Pyrenees are said to be alight with its golden flowers in July. *G. falcata* is a larger shrub with masses of tiny flowers in dense panicles.

In many ways the most beautiful of the smaller brooms and undoubtedly the most useful for general landscaping purposes is *Genista lydia*. It is, for us, a shrub less than a foot high, but slowly growing to several feet across, the main branches horizontal and close to the ground. The many slender branchlets are upright at first, then bend toward the ground in regular arcs, giving the entire plant a graceful weeping effect. In spring the shrub becomes a bright gold patch on the ground. It is one of the most solidly floriferous of all small shrubs, extremely showy even among brooms, and, luckily, fairly easily found. *G. lydia* is the medium-sized member of a series of related brooms; *G. cinerea* has the same floriferousness and habit of growth on a larger scale, and *G. januensis*, the Genoa broom, on a smaller.

Of the numerous small upright brooms, not spiny, perhaps the most picturesque is *Genista radiata*. It is an apparently leafless shrub that sends out numerous branches

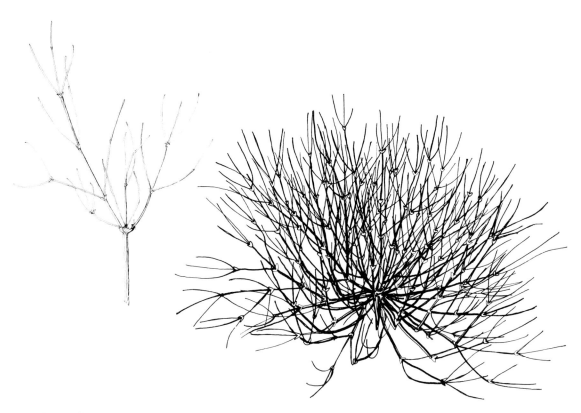

Genista radiata, *which has the branching habit of the slower* G. horrida *and the larger* G. ephedroides

that finally divide into upright branchlets; the result is a perfectly rounded mass of green stems radiating outward. Since each stem produces about six deep yellow flowers, the plant is showy. *G. radiata*, as we said, appears to be leafless; it does produce leaves early in the spring, but these soon fall and short shoots take over the photosynthetic activity of the leaves. This is one of the slowest growing of all brooms; it eventually forms a dome three feet high, but for some years is a much smaller plant. It should be noted that *Genista radiata*, though showing its close relationship to *G. horrida* in its opposite rather than alternate branching, is from the mountains and would not survive in the hot stony places that are the habitat of the gorse-like genistas. *G. radiata* has a variety, *nana*, an alpine for the rock garden, and a larger cousin, *G.*

ephedroides, from the coasts of Sardinia, Corsica, and Sicily.

Cytisus hirsutus is a low, spreading shrub of excellent habit, lovely in late spring with its radiating clusters of large yellow flowers stained brown in the center. Ours is a perfectly rounded dense shrub four feet across and two feet high. It is, unfortunately, one of the leafy brooms and deciduous; throughout most of the winter it is a mass of slowly yellowing leaflets, which, of course, is perfectly acceptable when other deciduous shrubs are about. *C. hirsutus* is closely related to a number of other *Cytisus* species of similar habit, *C. ciliatus*, *C. supinus*, *C. ratisbonensis*, *C. glaber* (*C. elongatus*), and *C. eriocarpus* (*C. absinthoides*). Most of these are not Mediterranean natives, but occur in colder areas with more summer rainfall in central and eastern Europe.

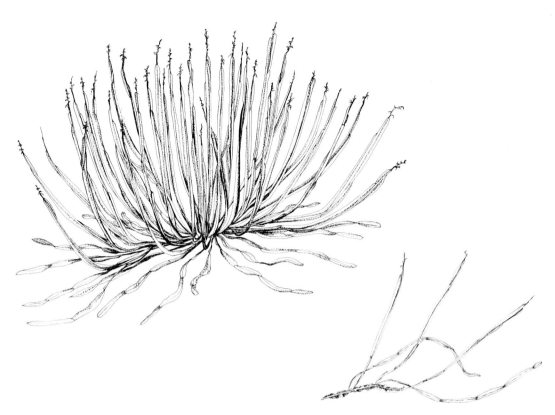

Genista sagittalis, *showing the winged foliaceous stems also typical of* G. delphinensis

Cytisus emeriflorus, from the mountains around Lake Como, is another small, leafy broom to three feet, showy in flower. *Cytisus purpureus* is a low shrub from the Southern Alps and the mountains of southeastern Europe with purple flowers. It is not showy, but the cultivar 'Atropurpurea' has flowers of a striking deep purple and is a handsome anomaly among dwarf brooms. It is a low, semi-decumbent, rather thinly habited shrub used sometimes in English gardens as a ground cover beneath taller shrubs. In our experience, *Cytisus purpureus* and its slightly more vigorous bi-colored hybrid, *C. × versicolor*, require special care; they are not drought-resistant, and they must be pruned to prevent legginess. Extra care should be taken to ensure that they are not overrun by more vigorous neighboring plants.

Some medium-dwarf brooms are the products of hybridizing low alpine plants with taller ones. The most famous example is *Cytisus × kewensis*, a hybrid of the tiny *C. ardoinii* and *C. multiflorus*. This shrub is one of the glories of English gardens, where it is sometimes seen as a graceful weeping plant six feet across and only a foot or so high, a mass of large, pure white flowers in spring. Unfortunately, as Sydney Mitchell noted long ago, it does not do well in California gardens, but is more suitable for the Pacific Northwest. I have found, however, that when planted on a north bank it makes a worthwhile dwarf shrub, provided it is not compared with its English counterparts. Another famous old hybrid is *C. × beanii*, a semi-prostrate shrub to eighteen inches, with *C. ardoinii* and *C. purgans* for parents. A few new dwarf hybrids are now appearing; *Cytisus* 'Peter Pan', with rose flowers, and *Cytisus* 'Lilac Time' can occasionally be found in Pacific Coast nurseries.

Some of the larger prostrate brooms are excellent for ground cover and dwarf shrub plantings. One of the best of these, *Genista sagittalis*, has perfectly prostrate, winged foliaceous branches, from which rise numerous flattened winged stems, each carrying a cluster of yellow flowers about an inch and a half across. This broom was considered too coarse for the rock garden by Reginald Farrer, and indeed it is; but covering the ground in front of larger shrubs it has a curious and delicate character.

Cytisus procumbens forms low patches several feet across with slender arching shoots six to eighteen inches high. It blooms in numerous cylindrical racemes three to six inches long and is closely allied to *Cytisus decumbens*, the most prostrate of all *Cytisus* species. Since the latter lies absolutely flat on the ground, it is also good for large areas in the rock garden, but it spreads so wide that I have found it excellent for bank cover.

A broom that can be used either as ground cover or in the rock garden is *Genista sylvestris* (*G. dalmatica*), which forms dense spiny tufts only a few inches high but two or three feet across. The plant sends out horizontal rootstocks from which the flowering stems rise a few inches out of the ground. Similarly spreading is *Cytisus diffusus*, which in spring forms a beautiful sheet of gold on the ground.

DWARF BROOMS FOR THE ROCK GARDEN

A number of brooms are such dainty plants that they can be cultivated adequately and seen at their best only in rock garden conditions. Most of these are diminutive versions of some of the shrubs already discussed. Thus, *Genista delphinensis* is almost identical in all details to *Genista sagittalis* except that it is about one-fourth the size in all its parts. Similarly, *Genista januensis*, the tiny broom that grows with *Campanula isophylla* on the cliffs around Genoa, is a miniature version of *Genista lydia*.

The gorse-like brooms also have their small counterparts: *G. aspalathoides*, from Algiers and Tunis, is a spiny bun about six inches high. Farrer calls it a "worthy golden flowered peer to *Erinacea pungens*." *Genista boissieri* is like *Genista horrida* with the added attraction that the gold of its flowers is backed with shining silver calyces.

Genista libanotica and *Genista villarsii* make dense mats like *G. sylvestris* (*G. dalmatica*), while *Genista pilosa* will creep gracefully along the surface of a rock like *Cytisus decumbens* except that it is an altogether smaller and more delicate plant.

There are many other elegant diminutive brooms: *Cytisus ardoinii*, *Cytisus pygmaeus*, and *Genista tinctoria* 'Plena' are all rock garden subjects of the first rank, but perhaps their greatest value is that they will flourish in areas with hot summers and a long growing season, conditions that severely limit the number of alpines that can be cultivated successfully.

MORE BROOMS AND ROCK ROSES

LESTER HAWKINS

For the fastidious, rock roses must be maddening. The taller kinds, with few exceptions, tend quickly to become rangy bushes with foliage that is coarse and glandular, or hairy or sticky with resin. The spreading ones are more densely clothed, but most of them billow out in all directions and refuse to confine themselves to an allotted space in the garden. Moreover, it is difficult and perhaps inadvisable to resort to heavy pruning in an effort to cure these defects. I think we should recognize that no rock roses are really suitable for the small, tightly controlled garden. These are plants for roomier and airier places, rocky hillsides, for example, or along driveways leading to country houses. Given these appropriate and spacious settings, all the so-called drawbacks disappear and they become wildly picturesque and singularly beautiful shrubs with an abundance of charm—which is, after all, rarely a stilted and highly confined quality.

Since rock roses tend to spread and to gangle they cannot be planted with impunity here and there among other shrubs like brooms. They are best clothing hot, dry banks, or tumbling over rocks as if in the chaparral, or billowing out from an island planting of drought-resistant shrubs, always, of course, given plenty of room. A number of memorable plantings come to mind: *Cistus creticus* spilling out from a south-facing wall by the back door of a farmhouse, dozens of pink, saucer-shaped flowers rising above its fine, soft, green leaves; a hillside planting of California natives with the deep rose flowers of *Cistus albidus* in the background; an island of *Cistus × purpureus* and a clump of brooms with *Cistus × corbariensis* and *Cistus salviifolius* 'Prostratus' billowing out on all sides; a bank of *Phlomis fruticosa* rising above a few plants of *Cistus hirsutus*. Given the kind of home they require, rock roses are a pleasure to plant and their possibilities are endless.

They are year-round performers in country gardens. For the kind of plant they are (drought-resistant, Mediterranean natives that bloom in late spring) they have a long flowering season. In Occidental, California, scattered flowers begin to appear around the first of April; by the middle of May the entire garden is flooded with thousands of these delightful, large-petaled, single flowers; then they taper off until by the middle of June there remains only a sprinkling of flowers, still very pleasant in their overall effect. It should be noted,

Cistus × paladin *'Blanche'*

Halimium atriplicifolium

however, that rock rose flowers last only until about two o'clock in the afternoon, after which the bushes are strewn below with fallen petals, itself a pleasant sight. The next day a new crop of flowers appears. This has one great advantage, however, that is seldom pointed out, which is that the flowers are always new and fresh when you see them. In the heat of summer the plants give off a resinous fragrance and a number of brown seedpods will have appeared, more obvious in some species than in others, but objectionable only to those, more to be pitied than condemned, who haven't yet grasped the unique qualities a garden in a climate of dry summers can have. In the winter, the plants remain sturdily evergreen and quietly go about their job of preventing erosion on banks, suppressing weeds, and providing a pleasant background for winter-flowering bulbs.

Rock roses are of the easiest possible culture, given good drainage. The only rule is to water them very little in the summer months. Like many ceanothus, rock roses will often appear at first to respond to frequent irrigation, but the excess water vastly increases the chance of die-back, induces lanky growth, and shortens the life of the plants. In my experience, plants grown in more natural conditions remain healthy and good-looking for a long time—many now seventeen years old in our garden show no sign of decline.

As I have already indicated, rock roses resent severe pruning. They can be pruned lightly, but the problem is when to do so. They flower late in spring and do not, in the natural way, grow afterward. If the usual rule is followed and the shrubs are pruned after flowering, the resulting stubs will remain all summer. If winter pruning is resorted to, on the other hand, you have to know that you are cutting out potential flowering wood. In general, I find that the only pruning necessary is that which protects a path from encroachment and eliminates dead wood and lopsided growth. If heavy pruning is called for, the plant is wrongly placed.

The term rock rose has been applied at one time or another to virtually all members of the Cistaceae. Here I shall be speaking mostly of members of the genera *Cistus*, *Halimium*, and the bigeneric hybrid *Halimiocistus* and shall append a note on the helianthemums, which are important plants for West Coast gardens. The principal genus, *Cistus*, consists of about twenty species, but includes a much larger number of hybrids, since these plants intermingle freely both in the wild and in cultivation. This promiscuity makes it difficult to name accurately many of the plants we have in cultivation. Almost everyone who has raised these plants knows that it is exceedingly difficult to get seed that is true to name even when it comes from seemingly impeccable sources. By now we have learned to be suspicious even of cultivar names. Many years ago we received a plant from an arboretum labeled *Cistus* 'Paladin'. It was a lovely plant, but since its large flowers were pure white and 'Paladin' has blotched flowers, we examined it more closely and determined it must be the cultivar 'Blanche', a hybrid of *Cistus ladanifer* and *C. palhinhae*. It is therefore with considerable trepidation that I assign names to the plants we have grown. My only real qualification for speaking of them is that as a working gardener I have planted many kinds in many locations and have observed their behavior. Unfortunately, as a group, rock roses are not apt to have highly knowledgeable devotees as do rhododendrons, although there have been a few among

Cistus × skanbergii

French and English gardeners. It is, however, to be hoped that one day someone will undertake the delightful task of remedying the defects in our knowledge.

WIDELY SPREADING ROCK ROSES

Cistus salviifolius 'Prostratus' is the correct name of the plant sold in California nurseries as *Cistus villosus* 'Prostratus'. It is among the best of all woody ground covers and is, in my opinion, at once the most useful and most beautiful of all low, spreading shrubs available for California hillside gardens. Like our native *Baccharis pilularis* 'Twin Peaks', it is dense and high enough to shade out weeds. Its small leaves are soft gray-green and in spring it is covered with a multitude of white flowers an inch and a half across. When an island planting scheme is used and the intervening spaces treated with preemergent herbicides, *Cistus salviifolius* 'Prostratus' will billow out on all sides in a most attractive way. A single plant will spread up to fifteen feet and planted at the top of a high wall will drape down a considerable distance.

A bank of helianthemums used as ground cover among taller shrubs at Western Hills Nursery

The intergeneric hybrid × *Halimiocistus sahucii* is almost as useful and equally attractive. It is a cross between *Cistus salviifolius* and *Halimium umbellatum*. It has somewhat smaller flowers than *C. salviifolius* 'Prostratus', more linear leaves, and more upright stems, but it is still a low plant. It does not spread so vigorously as its *Cistus* parent and is not so useful for suppressing weeds. Nonetheless, it is a valuable and extremely floriferous ground cover.

Another *Halimiocistus*, × *H. wintonensis*, has yet to be introduced into California. It is presumed to be a hybrid between *Cistus salviifolius* and *Halimium lasianthum*; it has the maroon-blotched yellow flowers of the latter. It is somewhat taller than its *Cistus*

parent but spreads widely and has beautifully colored flowers two inches across.

Cistus × *corbariensis* is a natural hybrid between *C. salviifolius* and *C. populifolius*, which has been reproduced many times in the south of France. It is one of the most beautiful and most serviceable of rock roses. Unfortunately, it is usually planted as a compact shrub and kept that way by persistent pruning; one often sees these bushes squared or rounded off with electric hedge shears. Left to its own devices the shrub will cascade a considerable distance down a hillside; a plant in our garden is now about twelve feet across and a little over two feet high. When not in bloom it is a good, densely clothed shrub, midgreen in color. It has no off season, no display of brown seedpods in summer, and no obvious leaf drop in winter. The shrub is extremely hardy, being one of the few rock roses to live undamaged through the most severe English winters. The flowers are white, over two inches across, and exceedingly numerous.

There undoubtedly exist other widely spreading rock roses in Europe, mostly hybrids with *Cistus salviifolius* as one parent. These plants should be searched out and imported for their landscape value for California country gardens. It should be noted that, if you want to speed up the process of covering a lot of ground, three or four plants placed quite close together will save a couple of years and still attain that cascading form that is so satisfying in a garden.

MODERATELY SPREADING ROCK ROSES

Cistus hirsutus is a somewhat spreading, almost mounding shrub whose leaves are covered with whitish hairs, giving the entire plant a pleasant light green look. It is usually less than three feet high and somewhat wider. Three or four plants grown in a clump will result in an attractive mound about six feet across. The flowers are white, one and a half inches across, and plentiful.

Cistus × lusitanicus is a hybrid of *C. hirsutus* with the upright-growing, large-flowered *C. ladanifer*. Its cultivar 'Decumbens' is a moderately spreading bush to three or four feet by four or five feet with larger, longer, and more gummy leaves than *C. × corbariensis*. This plant is notable among spreading rock roses for its large flowers, two and a half inches or more across with a crimson blotch near the base of the petals.

Cistus parviflorus is one of the prize rock roses with small, grayish leaves and with flowers, a little over an inch across, of clear pink without the admixture of violet usual in colored rock roses. Our seedlings grew to about two feet by five feet in five years and their flowers varied from light pink to deep rose.

Cistus × skanbergii is a natural hybrid of *C. parviflorus* and *C. monspeliensis*. It is a low, spreading shrub with the grayish leaves of *C. parviflorus* and flowers of a most unusual shade of pale pink. This exquisite plant is one of the most charming rock roses, refined far beyond most of its kin and worthy of a prime place in a small garden.

Cistus crispus is another low, moderately spreading shrub with bright purplish red flowers one and a half inches across and small leaves with undulating margins. It will grow to two feet and spread about five feet. It often occurs in nature with *C. albidus*, and where this happens the two hybridize to produce *C. × pulverulentus*. Selected forms of this hybrid have long been grown in England under the names 'Sunset' and 'Warley Rose'. It is interesting that a plant in the arboretum of the University of California at Davis labeled *Cistus crispus* is, in fact, almost identical with plants of *C. × pulverulentus* 'Warley Rose' imported by California gardeners from Hillier and Sons Nursery in England—another instance of the difficulty of getting true-to-name seed of *Cistus* species. 'Warley Rose', incidentally, is a very good rock rose with deep rose-red flowers somewhat larger than *C. crispus* and with larger undulate leaves. Among other *C. crispus* hybrids the most promising are *C. × crispatus*, a hybrid with *C. creticus* with pink flowers and *C.* 'Anne Palmer', which received an award from the Royal Horticultural Society as the best man-made hybrid for the year 1960.

Two species of the genus *Halimium* are also low, moderately spreading shrubs, excellent for ground or bank cover. *H. alyssoides* grows to about the size of *Cistus crispus* and has small, narrow, grayish leaves and pure yellow flowers. *H. umbellatum* is more rounded in habit with small leaves, dark green above, and masses of small white flowers. There is also a prostrate form of *H. ocymoides*, which has bright yellow flowers with a black or purple blotch at the base of the petals, but I have not seen it.

Many low, moderately spreading rock roses await introduction into California. We have obtained a plant of *Cistus × florentinus*, a hybrid between *C. salviifolius* and *C. monspeliensis*, but it is still too young to judge. *C. × obtusifolius* also sounds promising, being the offspring of spreading parents, *C. salviifolius* and *C. hirsutus*.

Low to Medium Height, Upright Rock Roses

Perhaps my favorite of all rock roses is *Cistus albidus*, at least in the form we know it. We have grown seedlings of *C. albidus*, and they vary in both flower and foliage color. The best forms have large (nearly three-inch-wide) deep rose flowers, perfectly set off by leaves that are covered with a dense, whitish, starry down giving the whole plant a pale green cast unlike any other color I have seen in nature. Our plants are about three feet high and almost as much across. If some seedlings are allowed to grow around a parent plant, the result will be a rounded clump, broader than high, giving the appearance of a wide, spreading shrub.

Cistus creticus (*C. villosus*) is an extremely variable species, which botanists have divided into a number of subspecies and varieties. The form we grow has flowers much like *C. albidus* but with much finer, light green, less downy foliage. It makes a pleasantly rounded, rather ferny-looking bush to two and a half or three feet. Excepting only *C. albidus*, I find it the most beautiful of rock roses and an extremely graceful object in the landscape.

Three of the most popular cistus hybrids are all descendants of *Cistus creticus*. These are *C. × purpureus* and the cultivars 'Doris Hibberson' and 'Silver Pink'. The other parent of the first was *C. ladanifer*, and of the last two, *C. laurifolius*. In all cases the color of the flowers was derived from *C. creticus*. *C. × purpureus* makes a stiff, rounded bush to three or four feet with deep reddish purple flowers with a still darker blotch at the base of the petals. *Cistus* 'Doris Hibberson' makes an upright bush of about the same height with flowers a delightful shade of clear pink. It appears pleasingly compact in containers, but tends to grow into a stiff, sparse shrub and the fastidious should beware of it. The plant sets no seed, holds its flowers high above the foliage, and completes its annual growth before blooming; the combination of these factors means that, after blooming, the plant bristles with bare flower stalks and pedicels. *Cistus* 'Silver Pink' is a more compact shrub, growing only to about two and a half feet, with similar clear pink flowers, but less obvious bare flower stalks after blooming. Because of their stiff habit, however, I find all three of these popular hybrids inferior to *Cistus creticus*, which suggests that a search for superior natural forms of this variable plant may be more rewarding than hybridization as a means of increasing our stock of good garden plants, at least for California, where *C. creticus* is perfectly hardy.

A most beautiful rock rose is *Halimium atriplicifolium*, which we consider one of the most valuable plants in our garden. It is an all-over silvery white bush around four feet high, upright in habit with upward-pointing, broadly ovate leaves two and a half to three inches long and with two-inch golden yellow flowers that appear over a long period on sunny days in spring. It blooms in cymes at the end of long stalks, and these may be cut off after flowering, although they need not be if the garden has a sufficiently wild look. In some forms the yellow flowers are spotted brown at the base of the petals. *H. halimifolium* is a similar plant, but not so outstandingly silvery.

Halimium lasianthum subsp. *formosum* and *Halimium ocymoides* are other handsome, yellow-flowered rock roses. Both grow two to three feet, have flowers with a dark basal blotch, and are upright but with stems that sometimes sprawl or take off at odd angles. They are almost archetypical of the kinds of shrubs, so numerous in Mediterranean climates, that have astonishing beauty in spring, then sink unnoticed into the drought-enduring landscape for the long summer. For horticultural purposes, the chief difference between these two plants is that *H. ocymoides* has smaller leaves and is more inclined to sprawl.

Of all members of the Cistaceae we have grown from seed, perhaps the most delightful surprise has been *Halimium commutatum* (*H. libanotis*), which sounds most ordinary in botanical descriptions, but proves to be an outstandingly beautiful small shrub. It is upright, dwarf (under two feet), with small, green, recurved leaves; the entire plant is surprisingly compact and well-behaved. The surprise is the clear lemon yellow of its abundant flowers, remarked on by almost all visitors to the garden.

There are many more small to medium-height rock roses. *Cistus monspeliensis*, for example, has distinctive long, bright green, linear leaves and small white flowers; *Cistus symphytifolius*, from the Canary Islands, is more tender and has gray-felted leaves and pink flowers in long-stalked panicles standing above the foliage; *Cistus palhinhae* has large clammy leaves and white flowers three to four inches across, enormous for a plant less than two feet high. These are all useful plants for the wild garden or for the rock rose enthusiast, but all are, for various reasons, less commendable to the average gardener than the plants I have described at greater length.

TALL ROCK ROSES

All the tall rock roses I have seen are sparse, rangy plants not to be recommended for specimen planting; they have no great beauty of trunk, as manzanitas have, and I have not been able to prune them into small trees as I have the larger species of *Ceanothus*. However, many of them are spectacular in flower and useful when a chaparral effect is wanted and when placed in the center of islands, growing out of lower plants such as *Cistus corbariensis*.

The best tall rock rose we have grown is *Cistus* 'Blanche', with pure white unblotched flowers, a hybrid between *C. ladanifer* and *C. palhinhae*. It will easily attain eight feet and its great white flowers, four and a half inches across, are produced in abundance in the middle of May. The plant is infertile and produces none of the large brown seed pods so noticeable in both its parents. It is also bushier than either parent, although it can scarcely be called compact. It has the peculiarity of opening more of its flower buds at one time than any rock rose I know, which means that, while its display is spectacular, it flowers for only about eight days. Other members of this same cross, made by Captain Collingwood Ingram in England, are 'Paladin' and 'Pat', both of which have blotched flowers; all three plants have received awards of merit from the Royal Horticultural Society.

Of all tall *Cistus* species, *C. ladanifer* produces the largest flowers. These are four inches across and have a crepe like texture and conspicuous yellow stamens. As a shrub, however, *C. ladanifer* is apt to be sparse and rangy. Moreover, it produces its flowers on lateral branches along the upright woody stems and these are later loaded with seedpods. *C. laurifolius* is similar in habit to *C. ladanifer* but has smaller flowers.

Cistus × cyprius is generally thought to be a cross between *C. ladanifer* and *C. laurifolius* with blotched flowers three inches across. It has a bushier habit than either of its parents and ages somewhat more gracefully. The English think highly of it and it is undoubtedly worthy of more extensive trials in the West.

Cistus populifolius is another tall, rangy plant with large, light green, poplar-shaped leaves and white flowers two inches across. I find this shrub has a pleasantly wild quality and am looking forward to receiving a plant of its variety *lasiocalyx*, which has larger flowers. A hybrid between *C. populifolius* and *C. ladanifer* is *C. × aguilari*. It has bright green, lanceolate leaves four inches long and three-and-a-half-inch flowers, blotched on some plants and pure white on others.

HELIANTHEMUMS: SUN ROSES

The following brief glance at helianthemums is included here because they, too, have been called rock roses (by Farrer, for example) and because they will round off our brief survey of the garden possibilities of the cistus family.

The genus *Helianthemum* includes more than a hundred species, most of which are low evergreen shrubs, although some are herbaceous perennials and a few are annuals. Three are native to California and, where they occur, are abundant after fires. *H. scoparium*, one of these, I have found to be a pleasant subject for the lowland rock garden. It is a wiry, diminutive subshrub that blooms vigorously for a time with tiny yellow flowers.

With the exception of a few alpines, most of the cultivated helianthemums are hybrids, derived mostly from *Helianthemum nummularium*, a delightful plant, crossed with *H. apenninum*, *H. croceum*, and others. They come in an astonishing array of colors from deep red through orange and various shades of yellow to white and have foliage varying from deep green to silver. All are very low—less than six inches high—with a spread of from two to five feet.

These are not plants for rough, neglected places; to remain in good health, helianthemums require something like rock garden conditions—good drainage and some summer water. Given this extra care, these are excellent plants to grow among the taller, more rampant rock roses and will vastly extend the color range. The helianthemum collection in the gardens of the Royal Horticultural Society at Wisley contains thirty-two kinds, mostly differing color forms, and we have sixteen of them. The great charm of these plants lies in the way they hold their colorful cistus-like flowers above the foliage on thin, delicate, stems; they not only put on a fantastic floral display, but also invite close inspection and compare favorably with the best alpines.

SOUTH AFRICAN BULBS AT HOME

ROBERT ORNDUFF

DURING his visit to the Atlantic coastal areas just north of Capetown, South Africa, in September 1773, British horticulturist Francis Masson wrote: "The whole country affords a fine field for botany, being enamelled with the greatest number of flowers I ever saw, of exquisite beauty and fragrance." Much of the floral display that so impressed Masson, whose mission was to collect plants and seeds for Kew, was contributed by members of the iris, lily, amaryllis, hypoxis, and oxalis families, all of which produce bulbs in the horticultural sense (but not always in the botanical sense). Many bulbs from the Cape are already familiar in horticulture; species or hybrids of *Lachenalia, Ornithogalum, Babiana, Ixia, Sparaxis, Watsonia, Tulbaghia, Gladiolus, Nerine, Freesia,* and *Oxalis* are widely grown for their showy flowers produced in the spring or early summer. Rarely seen, however, are members of the genera *Ornithoglossum, Albuca, Massonia, Wachendorfia, Cyanella, Geissorhiza, Spiloxene, Gethyllis, Hessea, Lapeirousia, Romulea, Galaxia, Homeria, Ferraria, Moraea,* and others that are equally ornamental and that deserve to be more widely grown. Furthermore, only a few members of the familiar genera named earlier are known in culti-

vation; many other members of these groups are equal, if not superior, to their better-known representatives.

In the southern hemisphere spring of 1970, and again in 1974, I visited South Africa for research purposes, and from these visits amassed a sizable collection of South African bulbous plants. These are housed at the University of California Botanical Garden, Berkeley. I cannot provide any surefire recommendations for successful cultivation of these plants in captivity, but my surprise at the unexpected field conditions under which they grow prompts me to offer a few observations that may stimulate adventuresome bulb growers to experiment more widely.

Most South African bulbs are centered in the winter-rainfall area, particularly concentrated in the southwestern part of Cape Province. Over most of this area the summers are warm, if not hot, and without rain. Winters are mild, though not always frost-free, and the little rain that falls does so during the winter months. Thus, in rainfall patterns, this region resembles much of California and a few other parts of the globe that have a Mediterranean climate. The growing cycle of Cape bulbs is geared to this highly seasonal climate, but

Ferraria crispa (F. undulata)

In the lower and middle elevations where bulbs are most common, the soil is composed of somewhat heavy clays or sometimes of fine or coarse sands. I would judge that, on the average, these soils are acidic to neutral, and are rarely if ever alkaline—something of a surprise in view of the general aridity of the region. They are also generally poor in nutrients.

Most rain in the region falls between April and September. Despite the overall arid nature of most of the southwestern Cape, during good years, vast areas are inundated for most of the winter months. Many species of *Galaxia*, *Spiloxene*, *Romulea*, *Oxalis*, and *Gladiolus*, even though bulbous, are essentially aquatic during the growing season. It is virtually impossible to view them close at hand without getting wet feet. Cold feet come later in the season, when many of these areas are occupied by armies of tiny, black, biting flies that can drive away all but the most avid (or anesthetized) individuals.

Most of my own collection of several hundred South African bulbs are treated alike. Nearly all have been planted in small (four- or six-inch) pots filled with fine beach sand. A few genera, notably *Cyanella*, have been planted in heavy clay. Pots are housed in a fiberglass greenhouse in which night temperatures are maintained at 50° F. (due to the heating system in this house, but I think 40° F. would be better) and in which daytime temperatures may reach 100° F. or more in the spring. Watering is started in mid-September and selectively terminated as foliage in pots begins to yellow. Generally, all watering has ceased by mid-April, which approximately coincides with the cessation of the rainy season in the San Francisco Bay Area. Weak liquid fertilizer is applied periodically during the growing season. The chief problems encountered are local infesta-

the flowering cycle is not, and something can be found in flower during almost any month of the year. Some species of *Oxalis*, *Spiloxene*, *Romulea*, and *Lachenalia* produce flowers shortly after the first heavy rains; others, such as members of *Ixia*, *Sparaxis*, *Watsonia*, and *Ornithogalum*, flower in mid-season; and still others, such as other species of *Lachenalia* and *Ornithogalum*, various ground orchids, and *Cyanella*, flower near the end of the rainy season. A few bulbs, such as *Amaryllis belladonna*, *Boophone*, *Brunsvigia*, and *Gethyllis*, produce flowers in summer or autumn long after rains have ceased. Fires are common in much of the scrubby Cape veld, and serve to stimulate flowering of species of a number of genera, such as those of *Amaryllis*, *Moraea*, *Watsonia*, *Cyrtanthus*, and *Boophone*. How this last observation can be applied horticulturally is unclear.

Hesperantha vaginata

Geissorhiza rochensis

Boophone bulb in rock crevice, North Cape Province

tions of mites, floppy growth from low light intensities or high temperatures, or both, early in the growing season, and a tendency for the bulbs of many to subdivide into numerous tiny bulblets and to cease flowering as a consequence. Those that subdivide must be repotted every third year or so to encourage flowering.

A friend who has planted some of these bulbs directly in the ground in Palo Alto has had none of these difficulties and finds their flowering period overall to be considerably longer than when grown in a greenhouse.

Propagation is by bulblet production or by seed. Both methods can produce flowering plants as soon as a year after division or planting. Seeds should be planted in the fall and the seedlings watered as long as green foliage is maintained. Dormant bulbs of seedling or adult plants should be kept dry and cool during the summer; I believe that most of my losses are a result of a combination of extremely dry soil and very high air temperatures. In the wild, most South African bulbs are generally deep-seated (up to twelve feet in the case of one *Oxalis*) and thus are probably not subjected to high summertime soil temperatures even though air temperatures may be excessive. My collection is sprinkled lightly with water every few weeks in the summer in an attempt to reduce loss of plants.

Seeds or bulbs of a wide range of South African species are obtainable commercially. If you receive bulbs directly from South Africa, they will have to be acclimatized to the reversed season of the northern hemisphere. My own collections were shipped to Berkeley in February (summer in South Africa), planted, and watering began in March. This represented unusually early autumn rainfall for my bulbs fresh from South Africa, and most responded by producing leaves if not flowers. In mid-April, the increased day length and daytime temperatures signalled to these plants that the abbreviated winter was over and they went into dormancy as watering ceased. In the following northern hemisphere autumn, watering commenced and most bulbs began growing again, now seemingly completely attuned to the reversal of seasons. A few species never adjusted, however, and were lost.

For those who visit South Africa and intend to collect in the wild, I should mention that provincial permits are necessary and that ordinary citizens (to say nothing of law enforcement officers) are considerably more knowledgeable about, and protective of, their native plants and the laws governing their collection than in the United States. I recommend using commercial sources of seeds and bulbs, and, on the basis of what I've seen in the wild, giving a few of the uncommonly grown but stunning bulbs a try in the hope that you'll succeed. The riches of South Africa's bulbs have been scarcely tapped—the peacock hues of *Spiloxene*, the fluorescence of *Lachenalia* flowers, the intense fragrance of *Gladiolus tenellus* or *Gethyllis* species, and the exquisitely complex flowers of *Ferraria*—or of *Antholyza ringens*, which provide a perch for the pollinating sunbird—deserve to be more widely known in cultivation. Many genera, such as *Lachenalia*, have ornamentally corrugated or boldly striped leaves. *Gethyllis* and a few other genera have erect leaves that resemble corkscrews and are as interesting in leaf as in flower. Seeing the conditions under which most of these novelties grow in nature helped me provide satisfactory growing conditions in cultivation and, I think, is an incentive toward cultivation of a greater variety of species than are now grown.

CEANOTHUS OF CALIFORNIA

MICHAEL NEVIN SMITH

THE genus *Ceanothus*, or wild lilac, typ-
ifies the rich diversity of plants in California. Elsewhere in North America the
wild lilacs are a scattered handful of mostly
unexciting shrubs and trees. Yet, on reaching our borders, they explode into a vast
array of forms: windswept emerald carpets on coastal bluffs; unyielding, rough-
textured brush for which chaparral is
cursed by would-be mountaineers; mats
that hug the forest floor; picturesque small
trees; and dense shrubs with clustered tiny
blossoms so dazzling they seem to radiate
their own light. Leaves may be broad or
pencil-narrow, smooth-surfaced or warty,
lacquered or dull, and plain-edged or
toothed like holly. Flowers vary from the
more familiar blues and purples, through
pink, to white, often eluding capture on
photographic film.

As a group, the ceanothus are by no
means new to cultivation. They have long
been popular in Europe; many fine selections were listed in the early nineteenth
century and at least some of these European selections enjoyed favor here in the
early 1900s. However, little of this material
has been of Californian origin, in spite of
extensive British collection from 1830 to
the 1880s.

Only in the past thirty years or so has
there been a serious horticultural review of
the genus as it occurs in California, led by
such institutions as the Rancho Santa Ana
Botanic Garden and the Saratoga Horticultural Foundation, and a few dedicated
individuals. Even so, most Californian species and hybrid selections have come to us
by rather haphazard routes. Some, including popular selections of *Ceanothus griseus
horizontalis*, Carmel creeper, and *C. gloriosus*, Point Reyes ceanothus, were snatched
almost randomly from the wild and may
represent little more than the average, aesthetically speaking, of their type. Others
have originated as chance hybrid seedlings
from mixed plantings. Controlled crosses
have been rare or nonexistent, partly because of the difficulty of working with small
flowers. Clearly, much remains to be done
with the Californian ceanothus to realize
their full potential as landscape and garden plants.

LANDSCAPE APPLICATIONS

Clearly a group so diverse must have a variety of uses in the landscape. The smallest
of the matting kinds of ceanothus are
charming in the rock garden. More vigor-

Ceanothus *'Concha'*

ous low-growing types are popular as ground covers. Plants of mounding habit may be employed for looser, more billowy cover, particularly on banks and hillsides. Those of more erect habit are often featured as free-standing shrubs. Those that grow like trees are graceful alternatives to the flowering plums, olives, and other too-familiar small trees of California landscapes. Whatever their habit, most kinds are valued for both foliage and flower.

Whether short or tall, most ceanothus grow broad and are clearly most at home in large country and commercial landscapes. It takes frequent pruning—to which some respond well, others poorly—to confine them in small tract yards. The development of a new generation of ceanothus, more moderate in growth, is a challenge for future selection and breeding.

CULTURAL NOTES

Ceanothus are encountered from the edge of our coastline to the high Sierra, yet their surroundings are remarkably similar in important respects. Little, if any, rain falls in the late spring and summer months, when water loss by transpiration is greatest

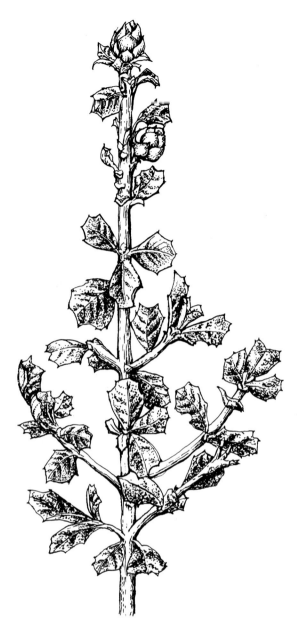

Ceanothus maritimus

rely on whatever they can bring up with deep roots. It is not surprising that many ceanothus are valued for low water and nutrient demands in roadbank plantings and similar situations.

Despite the Spartan conditions under which they have evolved in the wild, ceanothus respond as do few other plants to constant moisture and good nutrition under commercial nursery cultivation, often growing almost too profusely. However, an army of fungus root pathogens, to which ceanothus have not been required to develop resistance in the wild, also flourishes under such conditions. The chemical controls applied routinely in the nursery are unavailable or impractical in the open landscape. The sudden decline for which ceanothus are noted nearly always results from attack by one of these pathogens.

The remedy is not necessarily to prepare special soil mixes for ceanothus and isolate them for less frequent watering. Some of the larger-leaved coastal species, when transferred to hot-summer areas of the interior, require supplemental watering to offset increased loss by transpiration, often insuring their own demise. The more satisfactory course for gardeners in these areas lies in selecting appropriate plants—those that can stand heat and drought or those more disease-resistant (usually called garden-tolerant) individuals of normally tender species. Both kinds exist, and several will be described in the section that follows.

Ceanothus are subject in still other—avoidable—ways to attacks for which they have evolved no defenses. Close spacing of plants—particularly ground covers—for an instant, finished look is a common sin. Branches pile up, foliage is shaded to death, and water is trapped between stems and leaves, creating an ideal medium for predatory water molds, which devas-

(although the drought is eased for some coastal species by fog drip). In addition, the soil is sandy or rocky and generally infertile, allowing ceanothus to escape competition from many more demanding plants. They often grow on a steep slope; surface water is quickly shed, and the plants must

tate twigs and occasionally even large branches.

Invasion by a still more virulent organism, known as apricot pathogen, is promoted by making cuts into mature (barked-over) wood, particularly in winter, and not sealing the cuts immediately. This organism girdles and kills ceanothus limb by limb. Even with proper sealing, heavy cuts should be considered a last resort among pruning techniques, since mature tissue in many plants becomes inactive, heals slowly, and seldom develops new shoots.

Several species of ceanothus are members of chaparral communities, renewed periodically (until the advent of fire tankers) by fire. Even unaffected by disease, plants of these species may gradually decline after ten to twenty years, filling with dead twigs—accumulations of many years—which may weigh down large branches and break them. This is the sense in which certain ceanothus are genuinely short-lived, a criticism applied indiscriminately to the entire genus. Yet many, particularly the arborescent ones, will thrive thirty years or more, longer than many gardeners will be around to enjoy them.

Given the moderating influence of the sea upon winter temperatures, it is surprising that any coastal species should be cold-hardy. Yet some, like *Ceanothus gloriosus*, have survived winter bouts of 0–10° F. The less surprising fact is that there are also tender species, sometimes, but not always, identifiable—like *C. griseus* var. *horizontalis*—by succulent growth. Estimated minimum temperatures given in the descriptions that follow should therefore be heeded. Even these refer to short, occasional bouts, not extended nightly low temperatures.

Additional basic information on the cultivation of ceanothus is found in the *Sunset New Western Garden Book*. Greater detail will be found in *Ceanothus* Part 1. *Ceanothus for Gardens, Parks, and Roadsides*, by M. Van Rensselaer, and *A Systematic Study of the Genus Ceanothus*, by Howard E. McMinn, published in 1942 by Santa Barbara Botanic Garden.

Some Ceanothus Described

The list that follows contains some of the best known ceanothus; others that are just now entering the trade; and some that are, frankly speaking, obscure. All, however, are plants that I feel have significant ornamental potential; many, in addition, serve such utilitarian purposes as erosion control and revegetation of barren sites.

As an aid to sorting out a very complex group, I have used a tool provided by taxonomists: division of the genus into two subgenera, *Ceanothus* and *Cerastes*, which have obvious vegetative distinctions. In general, plants of the section *Ceanothus* have alternate, slender, flexible twigs and alternate, rather thin-textured leaves, often deeply veined or even warty—but never margined with spines. Plants of the section *Cerastes* are marked by generally stouter, often quite rigid, opposite branches. Their leaves are also opposite, normally thick and smooth-surfaced, and often with holly-like marginal teeth or spines.

Section Ceanothus

Ceanothus arboreus, Catalina ceanothus. A large shrub or smooth-barked tree of up to twenty-four feet, often quite picturesque in form. It is clad with broad leaves, white-felty below and dull green above. The branched flower clusters measure up to five inches long, but are normally pale blue to off-white in color, adding only slightly to the year-round beauty of the plant.

Above and left: Ceanothus *'Frosty Blue' in Rancho Santa Ana Botanic Garden. Right:* Ceanothus *'Concha'*

Catalina ceanothus has been largely replaced in cultivation by its darker-flowered hybrids with *Ceanothus griseus* and *C. cyaneus*, most of which lack its grace of form and distinctive soft textures. Certainly it deserves greater favor as a tree of character for the larger landscape. It is long-lived, often to thirty years or more, and succeeds in heavier soils with occasional summer watering. It is hardy to 10–15° F.

Ceanothus 'Blue Buttons'. This is a hybrid of uncertain parentage, selected and recently introduced by the Rancho Santa Ana Botanic Garden. It is rigidly branched, becoming a beautifully crooked-trunked small tree of up to thirteen feet, with equal or greater spread. The leaves are small and dark, forming a thin veil over purplish twigs. In mid-spring the plant is well covered with small, button-shaped clusters of light blue flowers.

While its garden tolerance and hardiness are unproven in general cultivation, 'Blue Buttons' has thrived for many years at Rancho Santa Ana with sprinkler irrigation every few weeks in summer. Like *Ceanothus arboreus*, it is most attractively displayed as an individual specimen tree, its striking form viewed and appreciated at close range.

Ceanothus 'Concha'. A hybrid probably involving *C. impressus* and *C. papillosus* var. *roweanus*, this plant deserves far more attention than it gets. It is a shrub of up to six by nine feet, with gracefully arching branches. The foliage is dense and symmetrically arranged, with a distinctive sheen, each narrow, dark green leaf measuring about an inch. It is a dependable and heavy bloomer, producing a dazzling display for several weeks each spring. The blending of dark blue flowers with reddish buds renders an overall, glowing purple.

'Concha' is a most adaptable shrub for the home or commercial landscape, restrained as necessary by light pruning or even shearing. It is considerably more tolerant of heavier soils and summer watering than *Ceanothus* 'Julia Phelps', with which it is often confused, and longer-lived in the landscape. It has survived winter freezes of 10° F. and high summer heat, though it is at its best near the coast.

Ceanothus cordulatus, mountain whitethorn. A most interesting plant of higher mountain ranges nearly throughout California, it is mounding or sprawling in habit, reaching a maximum of six feet by perhaps twelve to fifteen feet in age. The rigid and intricate branches are nearly white, with a sprinkling of blue-green oval leaves. The white flowers in summer add little to the beauty of the plant.

This is an attractive and undemanding shrub for mountain homes and an excellent rough cover for roadbanks and open slopes. Almost nothing is known of its landscape tolerance at low elevations.

Ceanothus 'Dark Star'. This, one of the most impressive hybrid selections of recent years, was introduced by Kenneth Taylor of Aromas. It is believed to be a chance cross of *C. impressus* and *C. papillosus* var. *roweanus*. Out of bloom it is a spreading mass of tiny, dark green, stippled leaves reaching four to six feet by seven to nine feet, or perhaps even more. For over a month in spring, it becomes an equally dense mass of cobalt-blue flowers, borne in small round clusters.

The home gardener will like 'Dark Star' for its dazzling floral displays and foliage texture, restraining its growth through frequent tip pruning. However, it will be most at home in the large country or commercial landscape where it can roam at

Ceanothus *'Gentian Plume'*

will. It is still early to assess its climatic range and garden tolerance; thus far, it has thrived in a wide range of soils, with and without summer water.

Ceanothus dentatus, cropleaf ceanothus. Beautiful in the wild, this species has been cultivated very little in California. It is one of the smallest of the shrubby ceanothus, one and a half to four feet tall and slightly broader. Its twigs are densely set with small, very narrow, dark green leaves, among which round, dark blue flower clusters appear in spring.

Cropleaf ceanothus seems to me most promising as a parent, with the goal of developing smaller-scale hybrid plants for the home garden. The few selections tried thus far have exhibited poor tolerance of garden conditions, but this need not be an invariable trait.

Ceanothus diversifolius, pine mat. A charming forest dweller of the Sierra Nevada and north Coast Ranges, pine mat is perfectly prostrate, slowly spreading to perhaps six feet and rooting as it travels. The small, fuzzy, gray-green leaves give the plant a soft, pleasing texture. Sky-blue flowers in round clusters decorate the plant in middle to late spring.

This would seem a most worthy candidate for trial in the rock garden or as a small-scale ground cover, assuming that speed is not essential. Given a little shade and occasional summer watering, it seems to thrive at sea level.

Ceanothus foliosus, wavyleaf ceanothus. This is a highly variable species, occurring on dry slopes of the coast ranges nearly throughout the state. It is usually spreading or mounding to about three by six feet. The twigs are quite slender and clad with small glossy, wavy-edged leaves. Plants of

Ceanothus horizontalis

C. foliosus var. *vineatus*, Vine Hill ceanothus, are both lower and broader, with less wavy leaves. The blossom clusters of both, while small, offer some of the most brilliant blues and purples of the genus.

These are rugged plants, tolerating considerable drought, heat, and even cold (to 10°F. or less). They are admirably suited for decorating summer-dry banks and slopes and should certainly be considered for highway plantings in hot-summer areas. Their response to irrigated garden conditions has been as variable as the plants themselves.

Ceanothus 'Frosty Blue'. This is my personal favorite among recent introductions by the Rancho Santa Ana Botanic Garden. As seen at the garden, it is an almost spherical shrub or shrub-like tree of up to thirteen feet. The deep green leaves are dense, glossy, and crinkled in texture. Its most distinctive feature—for which the plant is named—is the glittering contrast between white bracts of the bud clusters and deep blue flowers, borne profusely in mid-spring.

'Frosty Blue' offers considerable promise as a large, free-standing specimen shrub, tall screen, or even giant hedge; it responds well to shearing. Alternatively, a bit of early thinning to expose the graceful, smooth-barked trunks can give it the bearing of a small oak. Thus far it appears exceptionally resistant to the diseases that plague many ceanothus, thriving in a variety of soils with varying irrigation levels. We should reserve final judgment on its tolerance for a later date.

Ceanothus 'Gentian Plume'. One can hardly avoid a mixture of admiration and disdain for this plant. It is sparsely branched and foliaged and given to rampant, weedy growth when young; yet well-grown larger specimens have gracefully arching trunks twenty feet tall, and the large, broad leaves are wonderfully shiny. It is similarly sparse in bloom, yet its branched clusters may reach ten inches in length, loosely set with brilliant gentian-blue flowers. A large plant can make a stunning display.

Planted as a garden specimen, 'Gentian Plume' has shown tolerance of heavier soils and summer watering. However, we have yet to learn its ultimate limits of garden and climatic conditions.

Ceanothus griseus, Carmel ceanothus. Most gardeners are familiar with this species only by way of var. *horizontalis*, the Carmel creeper of the ground-cover trade. Yet the original species has much to recommend it. It is usually seen along the northern and central California coast as a round to spreading shrub three to nine feet by six to twenty feet, its green branches clad with large, rounded, deeply veined leaves, shiny green on their upper surface and grayish beneath. The branched inflorescences range in hue from white to deep blue.

With its massive size, Carmel ceanothus is admirably suited for large commercial landscapes and highway plantings. However, pruned early, often, and lightly, it can serve as a large specimen shrub for the home garden. It is happiest near the coast, requiring supplemental summer irrigation and often falling prey to root diseases in warmer climates. Existing selections will survive winter lows of 10–15° F.; further selections from northern forms may result in still hardier material.

Plants of *Ceanothus griseus*, including var. *horizontalis*, may be troubled by scale and other sucking insects. Both are also extremely attractive to deer.

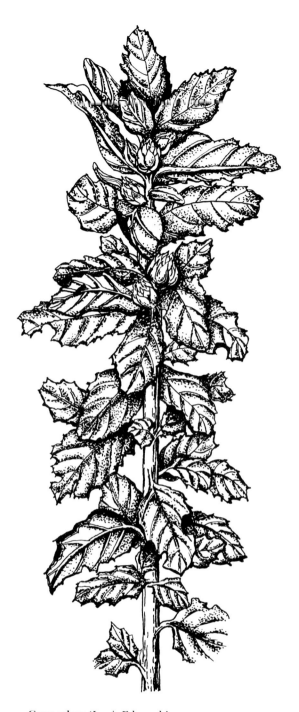

Ceanothus *'Louis Edmonds'*

Ceanothus griseus 'Louis Edmunds'. This plant deserves far greater recognition. It combines the features of dark, glossy foliage, long blooming season, bright blue flowers, and excellent performance in heavier soils and with summer watering. The main branches are wide-spreading and nearly prostrate, the side branches nearly erect, to form a dense mass of up to six by twenty feet. It seems reasonably tolerant of summer heat.

Ceanothus griseus 'Santa Ana'. This is a more open shrub with relatively thin, arching stems and smaller dark green leaves. With occasional light pruning or shearing it can be a pleasing, airy dome of four to ten feet by ten to twenty feet. 'Santa Ana' is truly outstanding for large, dense flower clusters of as deep and glowing a blue as any ceanothus in cultivation.

With reputedly excellent tolerance of heavier soils and summer watering, as well as good response to shearing, this selection should perform admirably in the home garden. It has thrived in occasionally high summer heat at Rancho Santa Ana Botanic Garden.

Ceanothus griseus var. *horizontalis*. Carmel creeper. Used in vast numbers as a large-scale ground and bank cover, this has become the most familiar ceanothus of the landscape trade. It is a prostrate, widely spreading variant of the species, native to a tiny stretch of coast south of Carmel. It resembles other plants of the species in foliage, though the leaves are usually larger and rounder. The pale blue flower clusters add little to its charm.

Most of the plants sold are unnamed and represent an indeterminate number of selections. Many of them appear to be 'Hurricane Point', an exceptionally vigorous cultivar growing rather loosely to four feet by twenty-five to thirty feet. While it tolerates heavy soils and thrives with either summer watering or drought along the immediate coast, it usually perishes within two to five years elsewhere.

Ceanothus griseus var. *horizontalis* 'Yankee Point'. Plants from two separate clones may be offered under this name. The cultivar has proven decidedly more rugged than other selections, though it too should be summer-irrigated away from the immediate coast and avoided wherever summers are chronically hot. It is relatively compact, eventually reaching three feet by nine to sixteen feet. Both foliage and flower color are darker than those of other selections. I hope that commercial growers will propagate this in greater quantity to replace inferior alternatives.

Ceanothus hearstiorum. A most unusual plant, found on the Hearst Ranch in San Luis Obispo County, it is almost completely flat, with branches radiating from the base to form a loose, dark green mat up to six inches by eight feet. The narrow leaves are warty in texture, like those of *C. dentatus* and *C. papillosus*. The small, round flower clusters are light to medium blue.

The most obvious use for this species is as ground and bank cover—certainly of more refined texture than *Ceanothus griseus* var. *horizontalis*. While it might be spaced close enough to permit intermeshing, and thus make a more or less solid cover, it would seem a shame not to expose its attractive starlike pattern of growth. One might also try cascading it over rocks and walls. It is said to tolerate ordinary garden conditions, though its climatic limitations must be better defined by future trials.

Ceanothus impressus, Santa Barbara ceanothus. Viewed from a distance in the coastal chaparral of Santa Barbara County, plants

Ceanothus thyrsiflorus *Snow Flurry*

of this species appear a billowing, nearly formless mass three to eight feet tall and six to fourteen feet broad, its branches hidden by dark green foliage. A closer look reveals pleasing textures in the tiny leaves, crinkled and rolled on their margins. In spring one sees only showers of deep blue, the small blossom clusters almost overlapping.

This fine shrub is not for everyone. Its considerable spread and variable, sometimes poor, response to frequent pruning put it beyond the bounds of most home gardens. The stress of high summer heat, winter cold below 15–20° F., and summer-wet, heavy soils quickly renders it an unsightly pile of brush. It has few peers, however, for the decoration of large banks, open slopes, and other spaces in sandy soils near the coast, where it may spread without restraint.

Although virtually all of the plants available are vegetatively propagated and include some highly ornamental selections, only the following are distinguished by name:

Ceanothus impressus 'Puget Blue'. Once offered by several growers but now almost vanished from the California trade, this selection is moderate in size, reaching four by eight feet, more in very rich soils. It is reputed to thrive in heavy soils and with summer moisture. Otherwise it is similar to other plants of the species.

Ceanothus *'Julia Phelps' with* Osteospermum fruticosus, *an African plant that associates well with ceanothus in low-maintenance plantings*

Ceanothus thyrsiflorus *on San Bruno Mountain, San Mateo County, California*

Ceanothus integerrimus

Ceanothus impressus var. *nipomensis*. Occurring on the Nipomo Peninsula north of Santa Barbara, this variety is distinguished for the non-botanist by larger overall size (to nine feet or more tall) and broader, flatter leaves. I have seen plants at Rancho Santa Ana Botanic Garden with rather open, gracefully arching branches and beautiful lavender flowers.

Ceanothus 'Joyce Coulter'. This popular plant originated as a garden hybrid, thought to involve *C. papillosus* var. *roweanus* and *C. griseus* var. *horizontalis* 'Yankee Point'. Mounding to about three feet high, it spreads to ten to twelve feet. The branches are thickly clad by nearly rectangular dark green leaves possessing a crystalline texture and sheen. Large, medium blue flower clusters, while never really covering the plant, are produced over many weeks in spring.

'Joyce Coulter' is admirably suited for covering large spaces, whether on sloping or on level ground. Responding exceptionally well to pruning, it may also be employed as an ornamental shrub or a low hedge for the home garden. Its tolerance of heavy soils and summer watering is outstanding (in fact, water is required for good performance in hot-summer areas). One can fault this plant only for tenderness to cold; some foliage is shed at about 20° F., and serious damage may occur at 15° F.

Ceanothus 'Julia Phelps'. Despite a temperamental disposition, this garden hybrid has probably been more planted and admired than any other bush-form ceanothus. It is fountain-like to dome-shaped, roughly four to six feet tall and up to ten feet broad. Its branches are densely packed with tiny, stippled, dark green leaves. In mid-spring small roundish blossom clusters merge into a solid blanket of glowing blue-violet over the entire plant.

'Julia Phelps' is at its best near the coast, planted on sandy slopes and left to its own devices in summer. It is the spring traffic stopper of highway plantings in the San Francisco Bay Area. It is perhaps unfortunate that it is also highly prized as a garden specimen, for it seldom persists for long except with excellent soil drainage and summer drought. Evidently many gardeners feel that even a brief reign justifies an effort with this spectacular plant.

Ceanothus papillosus, wartleaf ceanothus. It is equally at home in redwood forest, oak woods, and chaparral but defies neat description. It ranges from five feet to sixteen feet in height and may be erect or mounding, loose or compact. Its most constant feature is its long, narrow, warty-textured leaves, often sparkling dark green on their upper surface. The flowers, borne profusely or sparingly in spring, are generally deep true blue.

A particularly attractive version of this species is its variety *roweanus*, which is marked by dense growth, quite narrow, closely set, square-tipped leaves, and flowers of usually intense blue. Plants from seed collected on Mt. Tranquillon, Santa Barbara County, were once sold as *C. roweanus* and produced such outstanding hybrids as *C.* 'Joyce Coulter' and 'Julia Phelps'.

Garden use and tolerance for this species will vary with the plants selected. More compact forms—especially those of the variety *roweanus*—should be attractive individually, as small to medium specimen shrubs, in groups on banks, or in other large plantings. Since these forms inhabit primarily dry chaparral, they will probably take heat and drought but not heavy soils and summer watering. More erect, open forms, largely of the forest, might be trained as small trees for shady and probably moist conditions. Winter hardiness should range from 10° F. to about 20° F., depending on origin.

Ceanothus 'Ray Hartman'. Gardeners even passingly familiar with the genus will recognize this plant as the common tree-form ceanothus of private and commercial landscapes. A hybrid of *C. arboreus* and *C. griseus*, it begins life as an almost spherical shrub, thrusting out rapidly in all directions to become as much as twenty feet tall, and approximately as broad. Its foliage is most attractive, suggesting its parent *C. arboreus* in shape and size but with leaves more polished above, covering the branches well. In spring the plant is heavily

Ceanothus *'Joyce Coulter'*

laden with large, branched flower clusters of a distinctive shade, the pink bud-scales blending with medium blue blossoms to give an overall impression of bright lavender.

Though it may require careful and frequent pruning to remain in scale, even as a tree, for the smaller home landscape, 'Ray Hartman' is in all other respects one of the most satisfactory ceanothus hybrids yet discovered. It has proven itself in heavy

Top: Ceanothus *'Ray Hartman'. Above left: A fine pink-flowered form of* Ceanothus integerrimus, *and right: squaw mat (Ceanothus prostratus) in fruit, both photographed in the Siskiyou Mountains, California*

soils with summer watering, high heat as well as winter cold to 10–15° F., and some drought. One may see it effectively combined with fremontodendron in bank plantings along various San Francisco Bay Area highways. With early pruning to develop the necessary trunk height, it might even be employed as a shade and street tree.

Ceanothus 'Sierra Blue'. A hybrid involving *C. cyaneus* and exhibiting some of its best features, this has been for many years one of the most popular large ceanothus. It is nearly erect in habit, quickly reaching a height of ten to twelve feet, with somewhat smaller spread. The bark remains smooth and green for several years, enhancing a generally youthful appearance. Still more striking are the highly polished, oval leaves and profuse spring blossom spikes, each up to eight inches long, of bright true blue.

Like others as showy and large, 'Sierra Blue' is cast most frequently in the role of specimen shrub in both commercial and home landscapes (the latter with frequent pruning). It may also be effectively grouped in bank and hillside plantings, where drought will curb its rapid growth. Like 'Ray Hartman', it seems to tolerate a broad range of garden and climatic conditions, proving itself one of the best of hybrids for southern California. Its reputation for weak-rootedness and short life span is difficult to weigh; like many ceanothus, it has behaved differently in various settings.

Ceanothus thyrsiflorus, blue blossom. This roams our coastal hills and valleys from Santa Barbara County to southern Oregon, changing its character and hybridizing with several other species to produce a confusing and fascinating array of forms.

It is commonly encountered as a round to nearly vase-shaped shrub or smooth-

Ceanothus *'Julia Phelps'*

barked tree four feet to over twenty feet tall and as broad or broader. The stems of recent years' growth are green, forming an attractive backdrop for darker green leaves of variable size, shape, and spacing, usually shiny above. Compound blossom clusters of two and sometimes four inches or more transform the plant into a cloud of pale to deep blue or snow white for several weeks each spring.

Whatever its guise, blue blossom is one of our most ornamental species of *Ceanothus*. Its taller forms may be adapted, through various degrees of pruning, to both smaller and larger landscapes. Its attractive trunks are easily shaped and exposed as desired. Lower forms may be individually displayed or grouped as a hilly cover for large open spaces. It is generally

Ceanothus gloriosus *'Emily Brown'*

long-lived and tolerant of a broad range of soils and watering regimes (in hot-summer areas it will probably require supplemental irrigation for good health). Although the species is considered most at home near the coast, various selections have thrived with 100° F. heat and 10° F. cold.

Ceanothus thyrsiflorus 'Millerton Point' was recently introduced by the Saratoga Horticultural Foundation. It is treelike, with a round, full crown of shiny foliage, growing to at least nine feet tall and twelve feet broad. It is wreathed in spring with large clusters of white flowers.

Attractive even as a foliage tree, 'Millerton Point' in bloom provides a welcome change from the usual ceanothus blues. It may be used effectively for contrast with blue- and lavender-flowered selections. We should reserve judgment of its cultural tolerance for a later date, though it has thrived thus far under a wide range of landscape conditions.

Ceanothus thyrsiflorus 'Skylark'. This is my own name for a plant of obscure origins— justified, I hope, by a desire to distinguish it from others in the trade. It is exceptionally compact, growing domelike to about four feet by six to seven feet. The leaves are dark, thick textured, and slightly curled. The flowers are borne in medium-sized clusters of dark blue, beginning after nearly all other ceanothus have finished their show, and continuing for several weeks.

It may be used as a more upright form of *Ceanothus griseus*, although it is adaptable to smaller quarters. Thus far it has shown exceptional resistance to disease and has passed unscathed through 10° F. cold and 115° F. heat. 'Skylark' should prove to be one of the most rugged of the blue blossoms.

Ceanothus thyrsiflorus 'Snow Flurry'. Never a commercial success, this selection by Joseph Solomone is my personal favorite among white-flowered ceanothus. It can be a dense, round tree twenty feet tall in the most favorable locations, or a shrub four to six feet tall, with slightly greater spread, when subjected to severe heat and drought. The dark, lacquered leaves suggest *C. griseus* in shape and veining (and that species may indeed be a parent). Medium-sized, snow-white blossom clusters nearly blanket the plant in spring.

This fine plant is perhaps best as a tree,

since it is too pretty to cast upon a parched, distant bank where its natural vigor could be stifled. Like 'Skylark', it has shown excellent tolerance of both climatic and cultural extremes in its few plantings. Let us hope that it will soon be tried in many more.

SECTION CERASTES

Ceanothus cuneatus, buckbrush. Common to the chaparral nearly throughout California except along the immediate coast, this is a stout, stiffly arching shrub three to nine feet in height and usually broader than tall. Its branches, lined with short spurs carrying a thin haze of quarter- to three-quarter-inch wedge-shaped leaves, weather silvery gray. In early and mid-spring the plant is massed with short clusters of white to pale lavender or pinkish flowers, whose rich perfume can be almost overpowering.

Buckbrush has been employed largely as a utilitarian cover for roadbanks and bare slopes; its relish for heat, drought, and impoverished soils is almost unequaled except by desert plants. It is also ornamental in this role, offering pleasing colors and textures. One might even try it, with careful pruning to accentuate its trunk and branch structure, as a small specimen tree. From experience in the nursery I would expect it to be tolerant of most soils and some summer watering.

Ceanothus divergens var. *confusus*, Rincon ceanothus. Perhaps revealing a bias in favor of little things, I would class this as one of the gems of the genus. It is encountered on dry, rocky slopes from Sonoma County to Lake County as an incredibly dense, rigid mat or ankle-deep mound, spreading to three feet or less. Its thick green to gray-green, holly-like leaves are interlaced as if to fend off marauding animals. In bloom,

Ceanothus *'Millerton Point'*

it may be covered or lightly dotted with small clusters of blue to lavender flowers.

This is a plant to delight the rock gardener, pressing itself to the earth and following its contours. It would also be charming as a small colony in a hillside planting. It seems to be reasonably easy to grow, given well-drained soil, in sun or light shade. Summer watering should be restricted. As in nature, it should tolerate harsh extremes of heat, cold (probably to 5° F.), and drought.

Ceanothus gloriosus, Point Reyes ceanothus. Of all the low-growing ceanothus in this section, this is by far the most rapid and luxuriant in growth. It is planted extensively as a ground cover near the coast, where it occurs in scattered locations from Marin to Mendocino County.

Point Reyes ceanothus grows as a loose mat or low mound, ranging up to one and a half by eighteen feet in the cultivated selections. Its branches are closely lined with deep green, toothed, three-quarter to two-inch-long leaves which have an attractive sheen. In spring the plants are sprinkled or well-clothed with clusters of pale to deep blue or violet flowers.

Used properly, this is a massive and beautiful cover for large landscapes. One might even restrain it sufficiently for the average garden, as it responds well to light pruning and shearing. It relishes the cool, moist climate of the immediate coast and thrives there even in heavy soils, with or without summer watering, and has even shown promise in the Sierra, surviving short bouts of 0° F. weather. However, plantings rarely succeed where summers are hot; supplemental watering is required under these conditions and plants are quickly attacked by fungus root and stem rots.

Most of the plants grown today appear to belong to one of two clonal selections, unfortunately not distinguished by name. One is flat, its lateral branches usually under one foot high, with very deep green leaves under one-half inch long. The other is exceptionally vigorous and taller, with larger, lighter green foliage. Both have disappointingly pale flowers.

Ceanothus gloriosus 'Anchor Bay'. Selected and propagated by the Saratoga Horticultural Foundation, plants of this cultivar are less rampant and more compact than either of the two preceding unnamed selections. The leaves are an inch long and the flowers are a few shades darker than those of other current selections, though still no cause for excitement.

Ceanothus gloriosus var. *exaltatus* 'Emily Brown'. The only selection to achieve widespread use, this one seems to capture all of the best features of the subspecies. It grows at a moderate, controllable pace, ultimately reaching one and a half to three feet by six to ten feet. Though its branches are well covered with thick, crisped, deep green foliage, they form a sufficiently open network to give a filtered view of attractive, grayish older trunks. I would have this plant for its flowers alone; in mid-spring they create a stunning display of glowing blue-violet.

'Emily Brown' has long proven its ease of culture under average garden conditions, even far from its coastal haunts. It has survived short bursts of 10° F. weather unscathed, and further testing may reveal still greater tolerance.

Ceanothus gloriosus var. *porrectus*. Restricted in the wild to a small area of Marin County and only recently introduced to cultivation, this is the least known form of *C. gloriosus*. It is spreading to mounding in habit, growing to one to two and a half feet by perhaps seven feet. Slender stems and smaller, densely packed foliage give it finer texture than is usually seen in *C. gloriosus*.

Virtually all we know of this ceanothus in cultivation is from plants propagated from a single unnamed selection by the Saratoga Horticultural Foundation. It has already reached the largest dimensions given here, with masses of rich, deep green foliage. The bright blue flower clusters have been only spottily borne in cultivation. Attractively employed as a tall ground and bank cover, this selection has shown good tolerance of heavier soils and summer watering in its first few years of landscape use. However, its limits for heat, cold, and drought are not known.

It should be worthwhile to make further selections of *Ceanothus gloriosus* var. *porrectus* for both foliage and flowers, testing and comparing their performance under a variety of landscape conditions.

Ceanothus prostratus, squaw carpet. This makes a perfect deep green mat, three to seven feet broad, spilling over rocks and stumps and rooting as it spreads. Its leaves are small and toothed, resembling those of a miniature holly. In early summer the plant is bedecked with numerous small, flattish clusters of light to deep blue flowers. The reddish seed capsules that follow are also quite attractive.

Thriving in poor sandy soil and rooting wherever the branches touch the ground, squaw carpet is as useful for erosion control as it is delightful in its role as an ornamental ground cover or even rock garden plant. It stands considerable summer heat and drought in its native ranges. Plants grown at sea level, though pampered with gritty soil and careful watering, nearly always succumb to fungus root rots. This is not an uncommon experience with high-altitude natives.

There is some hope of success with *Ceanothus prostratus* var. *occidentalis*, which descends to 2000 ft. or lower, from Sonoma to Mendocino County. However, it has been tried very little and my own first efforts have failed dismally.

Ceanothus rigidus 'Snowball'. A delightfully whimsical shrub, domelike and nearly six feet tall in some sites, flattening itself into low drifts up to fifteen feet broad in others. The foliage is dense, dark, and shiny, contrasting nicely with the gray of mature branches. In bloom it is a solid mass of snow white.

'Snowball' is said to tolerate a wide range of landscape conditions, though the combination of heavy soils and frequent summer watering should probably be avoided. Its climatic range is not well established; however, it has taken plenty of summer heat at Rancho Santa Ana Botanic Garden and elsewhere. It is a striking subject for individual display and for planting in groups on open hillsides and banks, always looking fresh and bright. With light clipping to restrain its spread, it might even accept the confines of the home garden.

PERENNIAL PLANTS: PLANNING, PREPARATION, AND CHOICE

ED CARMAN

GARDENING experience begins for many with annual plants because of the quick and showy results they give. After several years of replacing them each season, annuals pall and something more saving of time and work is looked for. It is then that ideas of perennial plants seem to cast a spell, or at least to suggest plants that will live and flower forever—and with no care.

Dreams of perennial plants have, perhaps, been reinforced by the perfection of magnificent borders seen in England or of those in the East or the Northwest of this country; many are led to believe that they have found the answer to their gardening problems. This, we soon sadly find, is not the case. Before we put perennial plants in place of annuals, consideration must be given to their special needs.

Space is the first, and I believe the most important, consideration in planting perennials. Generally speaking, annuals are more compact and tidy while giving a great show of seasonal color. With less and less space available around modern houses and the demand for as much color as possible, annual bedding plants are in many cases the best choice. To develop a colorful planting of perennials one must devote at least two or three times the amount of space that would be necessary for annuals. This additional space is required because perennial plants occupy a certain amount of space whether in bloom or not. Each has a definite flowering time so some plants will be in full bloom while others are past or just starting. Also there is a period in the winter when the space occupied by most perennials is desolate.

Equally important is the effect desired of any particular area. If as much color as possible is needed in a restricted space then annuals should certainly be used. If the area calls for a single green ground cover there are many perennials that are suitable. Consider the area and results wanted when making a choice between annuals and perennials.

The greatest single factor for a really successful perennial planting is, of course, climate. If we give a little thought to where the most notable plantings of them can be seen we realize that they are blessed with frequent summer rains. Summer rains help to keep up the humidity, which in turn maintains the foliage and flowers in prime condition. Many of us who live on the Pacific Coast south of the Oregon border must realize that we are gardening for the

Bigeneric hybrids between Venidium *and* Arctotis. *Cultivars shown are 'Terra Cotta', 'Rosita', 'China Rose', 'Torch', and 'Flame'*

Anigozanthos manglesii

most part in almost desert conditions. We have no summer rain, the air is dry, sunlight intense, daytime temperatures generally high, and nights cool in many areas. If we are to grow perennials successfully under these conditions we must modify our climate to try to duplicate that which favors these plants.

Hedges make an excellent background and help to protect plants from hot dry winds. Trees, if at some distance, also help to break the wind and give broken shade, especially important in the afternoon. We must be careful not to plant where there is risk of invasion from large roots. Most perennials have strong root systems but will not do their best when in competition with the roots of trees or large shrubs.

Perennials, like most other plants, do best in soils that drain well yet contain humus or clay sufficient to retain water for good growth. Very heavy clay soils can be improved and their humus content increased by working in organic matter of all sorts. A further advantage is gained by building a mound or raised bed of amended soil. By raising the planting level above the general level we allow the winter water to drain away from the crowns of plants where excess can cause loss from rot and water mold during dormancy.

With these considerations in mind the planning of the perennial planting, if it is to be of any size, should be set down on paper. It is quite simple to change or move plants on paper but much more troublesome after they are planted. Nursery and seed catalogs with descriptions and pictures of unfamiliar plants can be a great help in planning. Some have cultural directions and planting diagrams showing combinations of plants that can be duplicated or rearranged to suit your own situation. When you are ready to put plants in the ground there are still some decisions to

be made. If starting plants from seed, extra time must be allowed, as most perennials will require one winter in the ground before flowering. Divisions will sometimes take about the same amount of time to become established. Even when setting out container-grown plants it will take two seasons for a perennial planting to achieve a look of maturity.

After four or five years in the ground many perennials should be lifted and divided and then reset. Plants most in need of dividing are those that have strong sucker growth and make large clumps in a short time. Other perennials, after a couple of years in the ground, make large clumps which become so crowded that the centers tend to die out. Generally there are many small rooted plants around the outside of the clump, and these may be transplanted and will quickly make new flowering plants. Some plants benefit from a severe pruning as soon as they have finished flowering, and new growth will quickly cover the bare old stems. This also helps to maintain the shape of the plant.

Where winters are more severe than on the Pacific Coast and with a somewhat shorter growing season, there may not be quite so much trimming, cutting back, and dividing to be done, although no matter where a perennial planting is established there will certainly be work involved. As the plants die down for a winter rest the old stems and foliage must be cleaned up and can be included in the compost pile. This is the time in Pacific gardens when most of us will want to incorporate some annuals to continue color through the winter. After clean-up and cutting back there will be space between your plants to set out established winter-blooming annuals that have been grown on in pots ahead of time. By potting the annuals at the time they might have been set out in the ground you will be

Inula hookeri

able to get all of the bloom from the fading perennials while the winter annuals are making a good root system and top growth in pots.

Where there is a very limited growing area we should consider grouping perennials among shrubs or in foundation plantings. Whether a traditional border or group planting is intended there are many lists of perennials from which to choose for your garden. To supplement the lists we suggest a few plants that may be a little out of the ordinary.

SOME UNUSUAL PLANTS

Anigozanthos, from Australia, is particularly good in the coastal areas. It will stand some frost but must have excellent soil drainage. *Anigozanthos flavidus*, with green and red forms, should do well for several years without dividing, while *A. manglesii* probably should be divided at least every second year. These will give a vertical accent with the flowering stems standing four to six feet above the heavy grass-like foliage. The flowers will also dry and hold their colors well. Another upright grower with strong vertical lines is *Macleaya cordata*. This is also rather invasive, so give it plenty of space and be prepared to remove underground suckers frequently. It has large blue-gray lobed leaves that make a good background. Its small white flowers in branched panicles are short-lived, but the reddish orange seeds maintain their form till the foliage dies down. It is particularly effective if planted so the sun can highlight it from the back.

Carex buchananii also is most effective in backlight. The narrow copper-bronze leaves with curled tips seem almost translucent. The plant forms an upright, slow-spreading clump about two feet tall. The

plant does seed readily, so it may be desirable to keep the heads picked off to avoid too much of a good thing.

From Arizona and Mexico we have a fairly new introduction in *Tagetes lemmonii*, an almost woody marigold that, given the right conditions, will bloom all year long. It grows to about six by six feet in two seasons and has single golden yellow flowers that cover the plant. A minty fragrance is released when the foliage is brushed. If frozen, *T. lemmonii* will be killed, so a few cuttings, which root easily, should be kept inside for the next summer. Also from Mexico is *Cosmos seemannii*, with leaves so finely divided that it looks like a conifer. It forms a bright green mound about three by three feet with magenta flowers in late summer extending above the foliage on six-inch stems.

An old-timer that has not been used much is *Verbena* 'Flame'. It grows about a foot tall and spreads easily to six feet, producing flowers of a good red color all summer. *Verbena* 'Flame' should do well on a bank or spilling over a retaining wall as it is fairly drought tolerant. A sunny, well-drained spot is the best location for the so-called curry plant, *Helichrysum angustifolium*. It has fine gray leaves that really do smell like curry, and small yellow flowers in terminal clusters. A rather open, mounding plant, it needs a severe trim at least once a year. A similar situation will suit *Ballota pseudodictamnus*—a tight, two-foot, upright grower with heart-shaped leaves that are almost white. The not-too-showy whorled flowers are white with rose markings.

For partial shade *Thalictrum aquilegifolium* 'Purple Mist' makes a good show in the spring. The rose-purple flowers are in fluffy panicles about three feet above the clean blue-gray foliage. This could be combined with another old-timer, not seen frequently, *Rehmannia elata* (*R. angulata*). With various shades of reddish pink foxglove-like flowers, this plant has a long summer season and carries the same colors as the thalictrum. If the old flower spikes are not cut the seed will self-sow and make a spreading patch. There is also a white form of rehmannia that must be propagated by divisions so is not widely available. Another old-timer with the same reddish pink flower tones is *Teucrium chamaedrys*. This has been widely used as an edging, which can be informal or clipped like boxwood. This will do well in a hot, sunny area and has a long summer flowering season.

Of quite a different color is *Origanum vulgare* 'Aureum', which has leaves between yellow and chartreuse. It also can be used as an edging or, with contrasting background, to provide a low spot of color at the front of a planting. This must have sun and be in good growth for the best foliage color. A more upright clump of much the same yellow green is provided by *Milium effusum* 'Aureum', Bowles' golden grass. This should grow about two feet high in a good tight clump and will want regular watering. Its golden grass foliage is most effective in front of deep green plants or in a pond-side planting. A rather bold composite is *Inula hookeri*. The three-inch flowers have fine, dark yellow rays surrounding a flat-crowned center. It will grow three feet high and as wide, but the many flower heads on each stem may need some staking. It provides a good show of color in the late summer and fall.

For those with plenty of space there are the recent imports from England called venidio-arctotis. They are hybrids between *Venidium* and *Arctotis* grown from cuttings and named 'China Rose', 'Flame', 'Rosita', 'Terra Cotta', and 'Torch'. The three- to four-inch flowers are displayed above gray foliage. Constantly blooming, they grow rapidly to about a foot high and at least three feet across in one summer. A few cuttings should be rooted and held in a protected area for planting out the next summer in case of winter loss.

Those just beginning gardening should start with plants that are easy to obtain from seed or cuttings and that make a good show. As experience and knowledge accumulate, something new can be tried each year. Just because we are growing perennials we should not feel bound to keep everything or to grow the same things year after year. Some areas and combinations of plants will give just the right effect when first planted. These should be kept, but don't be afraid to remove those that don't suit the situation, and try something else.

We should keep in mind that in working with plants time is most important. All plants have their inner timing set in relation to the seasons. We must allow for this, and, with patience, we will enjoy the many years of beauty that perennial plants provide in our gardens.

HEATHERS IN THE NORTHWEST

DOROTHY METHENY

As I write, near the end of October, there are still good crops of flowers on some summer-flowering ericas. Late-flowering callunas are glowing with long racemes of blossom, and others, later still, are just coming to purple bloom. Specks of color show here and there on the earlier winter bloomers and I know the abundance they promise. Hardy heathers are satisfying and easy garden plants where soil and climate suit, and their merit in the garden is being recognized.

They are not natives of the western hemisphere, though several are reported to be naturalized in coastal areas such as Nantucket Island, near Cape Cod. Where our Pacific Coast provides the maritime climate and acid or neutral soil in which they often naturally thrive, they are easily adaptable for a wide variety of garden situations. They are all small-leaved shrubs of the heath family, the Ericaceae. Their heights range from two inches to ten or more feet, but their flowers—white, pink, red, or purple—are always bell-shaped with united petals.

Because of their great variety of form, one or another of the heathers is suitable for ground cover, hedging, or specimen planting in a moist part of the rock garden.

They can also be used as an evergreen frame for intensely brilliant-flowered plants, such as some of the evergreen azaleas, or for grouping with deciduous trees and shrubs, with brooms, or with small conifers. Many gardeners who, in a more leisurely age, grew annuals or other care-demanding plants are now turning to heathers for their long season of garden color.

HEATH AND HEATHER

As common names, the words "heath" and "heather" are often loosely applied to plants that are perhaps fine-textured small shrubs but are no more heath or heather than the Christmas rose (*Helleborus niger*) is a rose.

Some purists would admit only callunas and ericas, but our heather garden also includes daboecia and *Bruckenthalia spiculifolia*. It could, with equal justification, include manzanita, huckleberry, salal, kalmia, rhododendron, and pieris, for all are members of the heath family.

"Where the place?" the first witch asked. "Upon the heath," replied the second, "There to meet with Macbeth." A geographical heath was the grim setting

Left: The author's garden in April. Below: Erica × veitchii. Bottom: A group of spreading heathers, including callunas and ericas with bronze, pink, and yellow foliage

Shakespeare provided for the sinister doings of his three witches. And such a heath is defined as a tract of wasteland; an open level area clothed with a characteristic vegetation consisting principally of calluna and erica. Our heath and heather plants are also natural inhabitants of moors, downs, bogs, scrub, and subalpine meadows. A feature these have in common is that they are infertile land. If their soil is supplied with nutrients, other hungrier plants march in and elbow the heathers out.

In Scotland, where there is more than enough of it, heather provides food for a few sheep and cattle. There it has been found that land can be reclaimed by spreading oyster shell sand, to reduce the acidity, and fertilizer. The sheep trample these in and grass seed is sown in the spring. This eliminates the heather and encourages a good crop of grass, providing fodder for much larger herds. The lesson from this is that heathers do better without fertilizer.

Plant them as nature does, with their lower branches at ground level. Even so, their very fine feeder roots will multiply close to the surface, where they are easily damaged by cultivating tools. A good mulch of peat or similar material will eliminate the necessity for cultivation and hand weeding. Eventually the plants will grow close enough together to discourage weeds. Like many other plants, heathers need to be kept moist until their roots are thoroughly at home.

Plants of flowering size are frequently sold in four-inch, half-gallon, or gallon pots, and there is no reason why they can't be put in at any season when the soil is workable. Because their roots quickly become one-foot diameter balls in many cases and will not move easily when mature, they are best planted as youngsters, paying due heed in siting to the eventual size of the plant.

The character of the plant dictates its use. The so-called tree heaths are fine-textured, upright shrubs. The small cushion and other compact callunas also have special uses, but the great majority of more or less upright-growing heathers, from about six inches to two and one-half feet in height, are most effectively used in massed plantings. In this way magnificent billowing effects with variations in foliage and flower color, height and line can be achieved with no other plants. Unity and variety are obtained with the utmost ease in heather gardens.

LOW-GROWING HEATHERS: WINTER-SPRING FLOWERING

Perhaps the most commonly grown heathers in North America are forms of needle-leaved *Erica herbacea* (*E. carnea*) from the European Alps. They are especially valuable for their tolerance of virtually any soil, including even limy clay. They perform well in partial shade, are reliably hardy, and are esteemed also because their flowering season extends through the dullest months of winter and early spring, regardless of weather. The only thing I have found to discourage them is the direct blast of automobile exhaust. Various forms have earlier or later, shorter or longer periods of flower. Most are in the six- to nine-inch height range, but others are more compact. The most widely grown are the cultivars 'Springwood White' and 'Springwood Pink', both reasonably fast-spreading ground covers. Another old reliable is 'King George', bearing its deep pink flowers from December to April, a season when it can harmonize nicely with *Cyclamen coum*. Other enticing forms are available. The flowers of many of these open pale and the color intensifies as the season progresses. They can be trimmed back afterwards or not, as the gardener prefers, but not later than early June when next winter's flower buds start forming.

Another widely used winter-flowering shrub is *Erica × darleyensis*, often mislabeled *E. mediterranea*. A hybrid of *E. herbacea* (*E. carnea*) and *E. erigena* (*E. mediterranea*), one of the tree heaths, it carries the sturdy tolerance of adversity and long flowering season of the former parent along with the strong-growing trait, though not upright habit, of the latter. The original plant of this cross, now given the cultivar name 'Darley Dale', was welcomed for its virtues and enthusiastically disseminated. It is a strong grower to one and one-half feet high and three or four feet across. If examined closely its small bells appear to be a presentable shade of pink, but for some reason, at normal viewing distance it seems to me to be a muddy mauve. Its newer cultivars have much better color and should be planted instead. This vigorous plant needs to be trimmed well back in April or May.

If you are so fortunate as to be able to acquire and keep a plant of *Daboecia azorica*, you will see it all but completely hidden by brilliant cherry-red bells for three weeks or so in May and June. It is a choice alpine from high volcanic peaks in the Azores, but apparently its home is not high enough to confer reliable hardiness. If the temperature in our garden drops to 20° F. or less it may be damaged. It is a low shrub with branches stretching out parallel with the ground, thickly furnished with fresh green, quarter-inch-long, ovate leaves. The quarter-inch bells in erect, four-inch or longer racemes, rise to about eight inches above ground. My original plant had achieved thirty inches in diameter after five years before being cut back to the ground by a freeze. Now it is back to thirty inches again. If we have that always expected bad winter again, at least we can hope for survival among its volunteer seedlings, as they seem to suffer less.

LOW-GROWING HEATHERS: SUMMER-AUTUMN FLOWERING

Sometimes before the flowers of *Daboecia azorica* are spent *D. cantabrica* will begin to show its colors. This so-called Irish heather is a native of a small area in western Ireland and around part of the Bay of Biscay, growing only in peaty bogs. I assumed at first that it wouldn't do on my sandy hillside, but with plenty of peat incorporated in the soil it has been a great success, the adverse situation seeming to produce a much handsomer plant than the straggler of the bogs. It grows one or two feet tall, depending on variety, and somewhat broader. The flowers, produced all summer, are lantern-shaped, three-eighths inch in diameter, and can be light lavender-pink, dark purple, or white. Those of cultivar 'Praegerae' are cherry pink. Unlike those of callunas, ericas, and bruckenthalias, flowers of daboecias drop from their racemes when spent. *D. cantabrica* is said to be slightly less hardy than the callunas, but I have not seen evidence of this.

A recently introduced hybrid of the above two species is *Daboecia × scotica*, its two available cultivars being 'William Buchanan' and 'Jack Drake'. To this cross *D. azorica* contributes smaller stature and purplish red bells; *D. cantabrica* provides the more upright habit and hoped-for greater hardiness.

A good, easily grown, and uncommon little shrub from mountains of the Balkan Peninsula and Asia Minor is *Bruckenthalia spiculifolia*. Some don't consider it a heather, but it looks very much like one. It also retains its spent blossoms and is happy in heather conditions. A slowly spreading, very hardy plant growing eight inches high, its erect stems are clothed with small needle like leaves and topped in June and July with compact racemes of small, clear pink bells. It sometimes grows naturally in part shade and will do so in the garden, where it can fit into a peaty alpine spot.

In mid-summer, Scottish heather, *Calluna vulgaris*, joins the scene; one species only and literally hundreds of cultivated varieties. The vast majority of these originated in the wild where they have been found by assiduous heather-hunters. One Pacific Northwest nursery lists eighty-five or more of them and there are more and reputedly better ones still to be imported. As it is, we can choose from them, small cushions three or four inches high, spreading ground covers four to twelve inches high, and stay-put shrubs two or three feet high. Foliage can be deep blue-green, golden, or tawny orange. Most callunas flower in July, August, and September, but a few flower later and are welcome in autumn.

Callunas are distinguishable by their minute one-tenth inch or less long, more or less overlapping, oblong-ovate leaves; and by their one- to twelve-inch spikes of small roundish flowers. The flowers may be single or double in form and their color ranges through white, lavender, pink, purple, and red. Their natural area stretches from Scandinavia to the mountains of Italy and the Balkans, and all of the cultivated varieties except a few of southern European origin (e.g. Ingwersen's 'Elegantissima') are hardy. Rehder assigns them to Zone IV, which suggests they tolerate any weather the Pacific Northwest coast has to offer. They are not tolerant of lime, prolonged drought (if they appear wilted it may already be too late to rescue them), or

undrained heavy clay. In order to keep them in good fettle, those with erect flower spikes need to be cut back below flowering level before vigorous growth commences in the spring.

This same rule of annual trimming, preferably in March, applies to the low-growing, summer-flowering ericas. Over 600 species of *Erica* have been described. Most of them are natives of southern Africa, generally in the mountains, and so far as I know none has been found hardy in areas colder than coastal northern California. Many of them have flowers that are much larger than those of their hardy cousins, and their colors are those of the rainbow. Sadly, my attempt at growing them in the garden ended in winter defeat.

Blessedly there remain those hardier ones, about a dozen species, a number of hybrids, and many cultivars to enliven our plantings. I have already mentioned the winter-flowering *Erica herbacea* (*E. carnea*) and *E.* × *darleyensis*, but there are several that flower in summer.

SUMMER-FLOWERING ERICAS

Erica ciliaris, the Dorset heath, is a native of damp places near the southwest coast of England, around the Bay of Biscay, Portugal, and adjacent Spain. It is more tender than most of the low-growing hardy ericas. Its cultivated varieties range from about nine inches to one and one-half feet tall, and it has quarter-inch long, ovate, more or less hairy leaves in whorls of three, grayed in color according to hairiness. (The gardener's rule of thumb about gray-leaved plants for dry places is not valid for heathers.) The three-eighths-inch-long, bottle-shaped bells are in upright terminal racemes from July through October or longer, and several good color forms are available: the white 'Stoborough'; delicate pink 'Wych'; pink and white 'David Mc-Clintock', a vigorous eighteen-inch bush; intense purplish red 'Mrs C. H. Gill', the only one to succumb to protracted cold in 1972 in my garden; and wonderful bright salmon pink 'Corfe Castle'. I also have a planting of the original form, with vivid purple flowers still brilliant at the beginning of November. In spite of its wet natural habitats, *E. ciliaris* will do well in any soil if plenty of peat has been provided for its roots, and if it is not allowed to dry out.

Conversely, *Erica cinerea*, twisted heath, also called Scottish heath and bell heather, is a very hardy plant of drier situations from southern Norway, across Britain and western Europe, down to the Mediterranean. I have seen it growing naturally from a high cleft in a big rock in Scotland, but it is not subjected there to prolonged summer drought. I have also seen it, mixed with other heathers, in wet muck in Cornwall, but not without adequate drainage. It will take either full sun or part shade. Its plump round bells are small but neon-brilliant and wonderful for painting garden pictures. Its scarcely flowering but nevertheless popular cultivar 'Golden Drop' is a moderately spreading four- to six-inch-high creeper with foliage that alternates between gleaming gold in the summer and dark mahogany red in winter. Given acid soil, *E. cinerea* can be said to be a tolerant plant, but because of a rangy root system, nursery growers sometimes find it tricky to transplant. I have never seen an objectionable color form, and there is a selection from white through a delicious range of pinks to dark red and purple. The colors never seem to clash, so one needs only to place them for height, which can be from four inches to one and one-half feet.

Erica mackaiana, with bright pink flowers and small ovate-lanceolate leaves in whorls of four, is a plant from the edges of bogs in only two small areas in western Ireland and northern Spain. Also with pink flowers, *E. mackaiana* 'Plena' is a low, spreading, not very showy plant which has the distinction of being the only double-flowered hardy erica.

Erica tetralix, the cross-leaved heath, got its name from having its eighth-inch-long leaves in criss-cross whorls of four. Depending on the amount of hair on the leaves, the foliage appears from dark gray-green to light silvery gray. The flowers are small ovate bells in terminal clusters held above the foliage with good clear colors and no sign of mauve among them. But these terminal clusters come and go through a long season from June to September or October, and some gardeners dislike the presence of browned bells on stem tips along with fresh ones. In such a dark-red-flowered kind as 'Con Underwood' the browned bells are less apparent; in others the spent flowers turn a lighter tan color and thus distract less from the fresh flowers. In any case, if you are one of those invariably drawn to lovely gray foliage, and have come to think of brown as one of nature's warm colors, the browned bells won't prevent you from enjoying *E. tetralix* through its long season. Besides those already mentioned, some favorites are 'Alba Mollis' (white), 'Daphne Underwood' (shocking pink), 'Darleyensis' (salmon), and 'Ken Underwood' (cerise). The soft blue-green foliage of 'L. E. Underwood' makes a lovely foil for its clear pink little bells.

Erica tetralix is another of the hardy heathers. Its home territory extends north even to Iceland and far up the coast of Norway, and includes Britain and northwestern Europe. It grows in acid bogs or, now and then, in pine woods.

Erica umbellata, from Portugal and Spain, has small, pinkish red flowers in umbels of three. It is not very hardy, and I hope that it will survive the winter in my garden, near the house, close to the chimney. Plants of it elsewhere in the garden have died, and it hasn't been happy potted in the cold frame. It stands drier places and some shade.

Erica vagans, the Cornish heath, takes its name from the Latin word for wandering. In other words, it is a spreading shrub, with some of its branches lying on the ground, rooting as they go. Where heathers are grown it is an old garden favorite, frequently known only by such cultivar names as 'Mrs D. F. Maxwell' (bright cherry red), and 'St Keverne' (clear pink). The cleanest white-flowered one is 'Lyonesse'. There are others, none startlingly different except 'Nana', six to eight inches high with white flowers, which is much more compact than the rest. Some plants of *E. vagans* have unexciting mauve flowers, and the only excuse for using them in the garden is that they keep such color as they have till Thanksgiving. Its natural habitat is around the Bay of Biscay, but it is hardy nevertheless. It will do well in any acid soil and will stand some shade.

Erica 'Stuartii' is not widely known or grown in this country, but is one of my favorites because of its neat, compact habit and its generous star-like cluster of small but bright, light pink and deep rose flowers from June to September. My seven-year-old plant is nine inches high and has slowly spread to a diameter of one and one-half feet. Presumed to be a hybrid, its origin is uncertain.

Erica × *watsonii* 'Dawn' (*E. ciliaris* × *E. tetralix*) is a deservedly popular heather. It is a compact plant growing about nine inches high with new foliage tips a charming bright dawn color in spring. Its plentiful bells are three-eighths inch long and a good rose color, and its flowering season is five summer months long.

Erica × *williamsii* (*E. tetralix* × *E. vagans*), is valued for its good yellow-green foliage. After eighteen years in my garden it is a foot high and about three feet in diameter. The pink flowers are sparse.

TREE HEATHS

Tree heaths are not trees but shrubs with linear leaves and more or less upright trunks from one foot to twenty feet high. Only one of these, *Erica terminalis*, Corsican heath, flowers in summer. It is a native of several central and western Mediterranean locales, but is hardy, having suffered no damage from temperatures as low as 8° F. It is erect in habit, from three to eight feet tall, with terminal umbels of clear pink flowers from June to September. It will grow in virtually any soil and flowers well in part shade. It is sometimes used as a hedge and trimmed.

There are five tree heaths that flower in winter and spring. All have feathery foliage. *Erica arborea* is the most chancy of these for cold endurance. It is likely to succumb in temperatures below 20° F., especially with no protection from snow. It is naturally wide-ranging around the Mediterranean and there are even isolated stands in the mountains of central Africa. In warmer climates it can reach a height of twenty feet, and it bears masses of fragrant, small white flowers in spring. Fortunately it has a reliably hardy form, *E. arborea* 'Alpina', an erect, four- to eight-foot shrub discovered at 4,000 feet in mountains in eastern Spain. It has foliage of a cheerful light green and its flowers are even more fragrant than those of other plants of the species. *E. arborea* is reported to have been found in woodland, but in Seattle a plant shaded by deciduous trees to the south leans away from them. It will probably stand lime in the soil.

Erica australis, the Spanish tree heath, differs from the others in its larger cylindrical bells, pink, flared at their tips and about one-third inch long. These appear in profusion in February, March, or April, depending on the weather. It can be cut to the ground by a severe cold snap, but rises again from the roots even after 8° F. Its cultivated variety, 'Mr Robert', is considerably hardier, suffering only a few scorched branch tips from such cold. It has pure white flowers and a sturdier, upright center with ascending side branches. Either can achieve a height of nine feet in our climate.

Plants of *Erica erigena* (*E. mediterranea*) are bushy and vary in height from two to six feet. It is yet another native of the Bay of Biscay area and is found also near the west coast of Ireland. It is reasonably cold resistant, tolerant of many soils, including some with lime, and will produce copious pink or white flowers even in shady locations.

Erica lusitanica, Portuguese heath, has feathery, upright branches and pyramidal masses of flowers one foot or more long. The flowers appear in late autumn as light red buds and gradually expand, from below upward, to small white bells, providing a delicately exciting vision from November-December to March-April, depending on the weather. Unfortunately it seems that ability to endure temperatures below 20° F. varies from one individual to another. In this climate it is wise to plant it where sudden loss won't leave too painful a gap. It is said to reach heights of ten or twelve feet in the wild, but is four or five feet less in our gardens. It is tolerant of many kinds of soil and does well in some shade.

Erica × *veitchii* (*E. arborea* × *E. lusitanica*), of which 'Exeter' is the only cultivar, made a chance appearance in Veitch's nursery in 1905. Fortunately, it was not rooted out and discarded, because it is now a garden stalwart. It has the feathery, fresh green foliage of *E. arborea* var. *alpina* and great masses of small white bells in spring. It grows eight to ten feet tall, increasing in breadth also as the years pass. It appears undismayed by any bitter weather.

Pruning tree heaths is best avoided, but if it becomes necessary, cut whole stems from the base, following which fresh new shoots will rise. Cut out old trunks when they die off.

Do not attempt to move a tree heath after it has attained flowering size; it will almost certainly die.

The question of sun versus shade is probably a relative one; the warmer and drier the climate the more the shade is necessary for the health of the plant. Some may not flower well in reduced sunlight.

Desert peach, Prunus andersonii

CALIFORNIA PLANTS FOR CENTRAL VALLEY DRY GARDENS

WARREN G. ROBERTS

R AINLESS summer skies and increasingly scarce supplies of irrigation water are facts of life in California's Central Valley and other interior valleys. The prudent landscaper in these regions will, therefore, want to use plants that don't need watering. Fortunately our own native flora includes a number of attractive, easily maintained plants that are well adapted for dry landscaping in California's heartland.

There are many good reasons for installing dry landscapes, that is to say, gardens and other attractively planted outdoor areas that receive water only from the winter rains.

We live in a water-scarce environment, and demand for water increases as more land is urbanized or cultivated. Getting and transporting more water is increasingly difficult because our state is surrounded by ocean, desert, and mountains, and competition for water in western North America becomes ever stronger. Agriculture, which will continue to need huge quantities of water, is of course very important to our economy. Our mountain valleys, with their endangered species and magnificent natural landscapes, are threatened with more dams.

Severe droughts such as that in 1976–77 will happen again. We need to conserve water however we can.

There are horticultural reasons also for using less water. Irrigation water in large areas of interior California contains salts that tend to accumulate in the soil and cause damage to plants. Common symptoms of damage include chlorosis, or yellowing of foliage as soil becomes more alkaline, and dead areas on the tips and margins of leaves as soil salinity increases. Local soil conditions may aggravate drainage problems; hardpan, compaction, and dense clay prevent leaching of offensive salts. Many plants well-adapted to surviving dry, hot weather do not tolerate wet soil in summer, especially near the root crown. These plants may be susceptible to fungi that thrive in warm, wet soil, or they may be dormant and unable to resist the attack of these diseases.

Why should we consider using California's native plants for dry landscaping? Many of them are beautiful, useful landscape subjects, perfectly adapted to our cool, wet winters and hot, dry summers. They appeal to our sense of local history and of what is appropriate. Some of these native plants are easily available in most

Beavertail, Opuntia basilaris

PLANTS ADAPT TO DROUGHT

nurseries, and others can be found without too much searching. Particularly, they need no care or irrigation after they are transplanted properly and cared for during the first year.

Many California plants survive and thrive, in spite of the rainless summers, because of adaptations to drought easily seen in the leaves. Gray-green or silvery leaf color reflects light so that the plant stays cooler and loses less water. This whiteness may be caused by a white waxy surface or a felty mass of hairs or scales. A waxy or resinous surface also helps seal the leaf against water evaporation. Plant hairs slow the movement of air and trap moister air next to the leaf. Some leaves are placed so that they expose only the edge to the full sun, or they may be thick with more mass in proportion to surface. Leaves may temporarily curl or fold with water stress. Many plants lose all or most of their leaves with the start of the dry season. Sometimes the dried leaves stay on the plant to shade the stems, but these look untidy and such plants won't be recommended for landscaping. Some desert plants have no functional leaves or very few, and food production takes place in green stems instead. Leaves of some plants are succulent and able to store water. Other leaf modifications that allow plants to withstand drought are less obvious. Microscopic pores called stomates, through which leaves lose water, may be few in number and located only on the cooler underside of the leaf or in pits. Stomates may open only when it is cool and dark, and they may be capable of closing tightly.

Chemical or structural adaptations in leaves also aid in drought survival. Some plants have cell sap that is slimy or saturated with sugars or salts and strong leaf cells. These devices help in meeting the water needs of the plant.

Stems may also be modified to help the plant succeed in the face of drought stress: reflective, flaky, or waxy bark; spines or plant hairs that shade the stem and slow down air movement; capacity for storing water; low growth, less subject to the drying effect of wind; stems or branchlets that are deciduous with drought (these plants resprout from the root crown or from dormant buds on larger stems); or underground stems like tubers and corms.

Partial dormancy during drought is another mechanism by which some plants survive. Others wait out the drought underground as bulbs or fleshy roots, or as seeds in the case of annual plants. But for most plants to be attractive during the summer they should look alive and that means green.

The most successful landscape plants that don't need to be watered in the summer have extensive, deep, widespread root systems that can take water from a large amount of soil. These roots are fast growing and have high potential for water absorption. Plants may also have surface roots for absorbing dew and the occasional summer rain, and fleshy roots for storage of water.

In order to claim sufficient area for their root systems some plants produce growth-

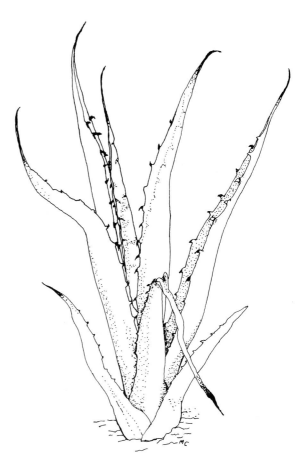

Agave deserti

inhibitor (allelopathic) chemicals to control competition, or they may produce their own leaf mulch to reduce evaporation of water from the soil. This leaf mulch often contains the chemicals that discourage the germination of seed of potential rivals for soil water.

LANDSCAPING IN THE VALLEY

The quantity of really useful California plants adapted to unirrigated landscapes in the Central Valley is somewhat limited. Summers here are hot and dry, winters are cold, spring is short, and hot, dry winds are common. Soils vary tremendously from

Encelia californica

San Francisco Bay Area may need weekly or monthly watering in our Central Valley. Some plants that are fast growers, or trees, or short-lived when watered, will be slow or dwarfed or long-lived when grown without watering. Use of California native plants for dry landscapes is increasing, but more observations and more research are needed to produce information on their production and landscape use for our water-scarce environment.

Although pests are not an aesthetic problem with the plants that we are considering, other problems could develop. Because some plants are flammable it is best to use low-growing ones or to avoid planting near buildings in high fire-danger areas. However, the reduction of irrigation will also result in reduced growth and less accumulation of potential fire fuel.

Diseases such as root and crown rots are often aggravated by excessive summer irrigation or poor planting techniques. Pruning can increase the danger of cankers on some natives such as ceanothus, manzanita, or fremontodendron and should be avoided as much as possible. Tip prune only, and do it just after the rainy season.

Many drought-adapted plants lack the bright green color we have come to expect in our irrigated landscapes. For the lush green effect just those plants that are very green may be used. The green plants sometimes gain importance from contrast with gray ones. A lush oasis in a small part of an otherwise dry landscape is a device often employed with success.

Some plants become less attractive as the dry season progresses. Occasional irrigation may be helpful; one to five deep waterings during the summer will generally improve the plants' appearance considerably. Water is saved if plants with similar water and shade requirements are combined.

coarse sands to heavy clays, and alkaline and saline soils and hardpan are common. Most successful unirrigated landscapes that use California native plants are in coastal or foothill and mountain areas where moister climates prevail, or in habitats with a high water table. This reflects the fact that most of our native landscape plants come from these areas. We are lucky that some are adaptable to the Valley and that the Valley itself also has some attractive, drought-tolerant natives.

Plants that may be recommended as good performers in dry situations for one area may be unsuccessful in others. For example, plants that need no irrigation in the

Helping Plants Along

There are horticultural techniques that increase the usefulness of these drought-tolerant California native plants. Without summer irrigation for plants the water already available to them in the ground must be conserved. A good way to do this is by avoiding or decreasing competition for it. This may mean not planting too closely, especially with plants that need to draw water from a large volume of soil. Weed control is also very important. Herbicides that destroy weed seedlings before they emerge from the soil and those that move throughout the weed before killing it completely are the most useful chemicals. Dense shade also eliminates most weeds. But the most effective soil water saver is a good mulch, sometimes called top dressing. This will not only eliminate weeds and buffer the soil from temperature extremes but will also decrease evaporation of water from the soil. Mulching materials include wood chips, fir bark, pine needles, fine gravel, or coarse sand. Even a mulch of dust is effective—recreated each year by cultivating the soil at the beginning of summer. For best results mulch should be three to four inches deep. Asphalt paving, sometimes known as Detroit mulch, has been used successfully and can be made to divert rain runoff to plants that need lots of water.

Improvements of the soil will often help ensure success for the dry landscape. Alkaline soils are a common problem and organic matter, sulphur, and aluminum sulphate can be used to lower the pH. Check the soil pH occasionally and add material to counteract alkalinity as needed. If necessary, improve the soil structure: for poorly drained, clayey soils, add organic matter—use organic mulch such as wood chips—and gypsum; for saline soils, leach; for hardpan (caliche) or compacted soil, break through to allow deeper root growth and more storage capacity for rain water. If the soil is very sandy, add clay or loam to improve water retention.

The amount of water that plants will need can be reduced. We have found shade to be important in reducing the amount of water used by plants. Many native plants succeed on dry sites if they are protected from full sun, especially in the afternoon, or if the plants' root zone is shaded—especially important for shallow-rooted plants. But plants providing shade may also compete for water. Afternoon is the hottest and most drying time of day. Many plants tolerate dry Valley conditions if they are planted on the east or north side of some shade source or on a north- or east-facing slope. This reduces the amount of water needed by plants as well as reducing the amount of salts accumulating in the soil or in the plant, an important consideration if the irrigation water is at all saline. Anything that will decrease the force of hot, dry winds, which periodically move through the Valley from mid-spring to fall, will aid in water conservation. Even pruning can be used, as an emergency measure, to decrease transpiration.

Planting is best done just before or during the rainy season. This reduces transplant shock and allows the plants' roots to establish at greater depths so that summer drought is not as damaging. It will be necessary to prune off all circling or kinked roots if a plant has been grown in a can, and at the same time remove a corresponding amount of foliage to reduce transpiration until the roots recover. When planting, soil should be prepared so that water penetrates and is retained at greater depths. Alter the planting soil as little as possible in order to avoid interface problems. Irrigation basins and mulching will help the plants become established, and take care

Blue oak, Quercus douglasii, *and field of wildflowers*

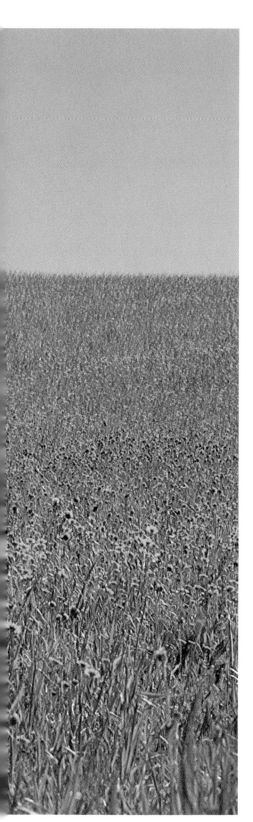

Phacelia viscida

Fremontia, Fremontodendron californicum

that soil will never accumulate above the root crown.

When irrigating new plantings, use pure water if there is a choice, or use water with more calcium salts and less sodium. The saltier the water, the less should be used. However, when watering, do it seldom but deeply for better leaching. Adding plenty of water at each, infrequent, irrigation will

also encourage deep root growth. This is especially important for recent transplants that have been accustomed to frequent, shallow irrigation. If emergency watering is needed once the new plants are established and a serious drought is occurring, do it in the spring.

At the University of California Arboretum in Davis on the Yolo and Solano County line, where the climate is representative of California's interior valleys (about twelve inches of rain each year, temperatures approximately 18° F. minimum, 115° F. maximum, and high evapotranspiration rate) we have had success with growing native California plants. By success we mean that the plants need no supplemental irrigation and yet remain attractive and vigorous all year, with no problems and no maintenance. Any plants that need tedious yearly pruning, have serious disease and pest problems, or are unsightly during dormancy are not included in the accompanying list.

The drought-tolerant native plants recommended here for the Central Valley and other interior valleys are listed under the headings Tolerate Full Sun and Protect from Afternoon Sun. Both lists are compiled with the assumption that the plants will be watered as needed for the first year after planting and that thereafter they will receive only the amount of water that falls each year as rain; nor will these plants require additional sources of water such as might be provided by a high soil water table.

Recommended Plants

California plants for landscaping in the Central Valley
that require no irrigation when established.
D = deciduous in winter, PD = partly deciduous in winter,
S = deciduous in summer, PS = partly deciduous in summer.

TOLERATE FULL SUN

Trees

Aesculus californica (California buckeye)	D, S
Cercidium floridum (palo verde)	S
Chilopsis linearis (desert willow)	D
Fraxinus dipetala (California flowering ash)	PS, D
Pinus sabiniana (digger pine, gray pine)	
P. torreyana (Torrey pine)	
Prosopis glandulosa var. *torreyana* (mesquite)	PS, D
P. pubescens (screw-pod mesquite)	PS, D
Pseudotsuga macrocarpa (big cone Douglas fir)	
Quercus douglasii (blue oak)	D
Q. engelmannii (mesa oak)	PD
Q. wislizenii (interior live oak)	PD
Washingtonia filifera (California fan palm)	

Shrubs

Adenostoma fasciculatum (chamise)	
A. sparsifolium (red shanks)	
Agave deserti (California maguey)	
Arctostaphylos manzanita (common manzanita)	
Atriplex canescens (wingscale)	
A. polycarpa (allscale)	
Justicia californica (chuparosa)	D
Brickellia incana (white brickellbush)	D
Ceanothus cuneatus (buckbrush)	
C. megacarpus (bigpod ceanothus)	
C. spinosus (greenback ceanothus)	
C. verrucosus (warty-stem ceanothus)	
Chrysothamnus nauseosus (rabbit bush)	
Dendromecon rigida subsp. *harfordii* (Santa Cruz Is. bush poppy)	
Echinocereus engelmannii (hedgehog cactus)	

Encelia californica (coastal brittle-brush)	
E. farinosa (incienso)	
Ephedra species (Mexican tea)	
Eriodictyon species (yerba santa)	
Forestiera neo-mexicana (desert olive)	
Garrya veatchii (silk-tassel bush)	
Isomeris arborea (bladderpod)	
Larrea tridentata (creosote bush)	
Lepidospartum squamatum (scalebroom)	
Lycium brevipes (desert box-thorn)	
Mahonia nevinii (San Fernando barberry)	
Nolina species (nolina)	
Opuntia species (prickly pear)	
Pickeringia montana (chaparral pea)	
Prunus andersonii (desert peach)	D
P. fremontii (desert apricot)	D
Quercus dumosa (scrub oak)	
Q. dunnii (spiny-leaf scrub oak)	
Q. durata (leather oak)	
Q. turbinella (scrub oak)	
Q. wislizenii var. *frutescens* (dwarf interior live oak)	
Rhus ovata (sugarbush)	
Simmondsia chinensis (jojoba)	
Yucca schidigera (Mojave yucca)	

Herbaceous annuals and perennials could include species of the following genera: *Allium, Bloomeria, Brodiaea, Calandrinia, Chlorogalum, Clarkia, Collinsia, Dichelostemma, Eschscholzia, Gilia, Lasthenia, Layia, Lupinus, Mirabilis, Muilla, Nemophila, Phacelia, Stipa, Triteleia, Viola, Zauschneria.* Beds of annuals and perennials look better if mown at the beginning of summer.

PROTECTION FROM AFTERNOON SUN

TREES

Cupressus forbesii (Tecate cypress)

C. sargentii (Sargent cypress)

Juglans californica (southern   D
California black walnut)

Juniperus occidentalis (western juniper)

Lyonothamnus floribundus (Santa
Catalina ironwood)

L. floribundus var. *asplenifolius* (Santa
Cruz Island ironwood)

Pinus attenuata (knobcone pine)

P. × attenuradiata (Monterey
knobcone hybrid pine)

P. coulteri (Coulter pine)

P. jeffreyi (Jeffrey pine)

P. ponderosa (ponderosa pine)

P. monophylla (single-leaf pinyon)

P. quadrifolia (four-leaf pinyon)

P. edulis (pinyon)

Prunus lyonii (Santa Catalina cherry)

P. lyonii × P. ilicifolia (hybrid holly-leaf
cherry)

Quercus agrifolia (coast live oak)

Q. tomentella (island oak)

SHRUBS

Arctostaphylos (manzanita) species:
    A. bakeri,
    A. densiflora,
    A. pajaroensis,
    A. rudis

Baccharis pilularis subsp. *consanguinea*
(coyote bush)

Carpenteria californica (carpenteria)

Ceanothus (ceanothus) species:
    C. arboreus,
    C. incanus,
    C. jepsonii,
    C. oliganthus,
    C. purpureus,
    C. rigidus,
    C. sorediatus,
    C. thyrsiflorus,
    C. 'Concha',
    C. 'Joyce Coulter',
    C. 'Ray Hartman'

Cercis occidentalis (western redbud)   D

Cercocarpus betuloides subsp. *blancheae*
(mountain mahogany)

Chamaebatiaria millefolium (fern bush))   PS

Comarostaphylis diversifolia (summer
holly)

Eriogonum arborescens (Santa Cruz Is.
wild buckwheat)

E. giganteum (Santa Catalina wild
buckwheat)

Fallugia paradoxa (Apache plume)   D

Fremontodendron species (fremontia)

Garrya (silk-tassel) species:
    G. elliptica,
    G. flavescens var. *pallida,*
    G. fremontii

Haplopappus canus (felt-leaf hazardia)

Heteromeles arbutifolia (toyon)

Juniperus californica (California
juniper)

Mahonia (mahonia) species:
    M. amplectens,
    M. dictyota,
    M. fremontii,
    M. haematocarpa,
    M. higginsiae,
    M. pinnata

Ornithostaphylis oppositifolia (palo
blanco)

Pinus contorta (beach pine)

Prunus ilicifolia (holly-leaf cherry)

Ptelea crenulata (western hop tree)   D

Quercus garryana var. *semota* (shin oak)   D

Rhamnus californica (coffeeberry)

R. crocea (redberry)

Rhus integrifolia (lemonade berry)

R. laurina (laurel-leaf sumac)

R. trilobata (squaw bush)   D

Ribes aureum var. *gracillimum* (golden   D
currant)

R. indecorum (white-flowered   PS
chaparral currant)

R. malvaceum (chaparral currant)   PS

R. roezlii (Sierra gooseberry)   D

R. speciosum (fuchsia-flowered   PS
gooseberry)

Rosa californica (California wild rose)   PS, PD

R. *californica* 'Plena' (double California rose)	PS, PD	**PERENNIALS AND HERBACEOUS ANNUALS** (These don't need mowing)	
Salvia clevelandii (San Diego wild sage)		*Calochortus* species (mariposa lily)	S, D
		Datura meteloides (toloaché)	D
S. *leucophylla* (coastal white sage)	PS	*Dodecatheon* species (shooting star)	S
		Dryopteris arguta (wood fern)	
Styrax officinalis var. *californica* (California styrax)	D	*Dudleya* species (dudleya)	
		Eriogonum umbellatum (sulphur wild buckwheat)	
S. *officinalis* var. *fulgens* (southern California styrax)	D	*Heuchera maxima* (giant alum root)	
Symphoricarpos rivularis (snowberry)	D	*Leptodactylon californicum* (prickly phlox)	
Torreya californica (California nutmeg)			
Trichostema lanatum (woolly blue curls)		*Montia perfoliata* (miner's lettuce)	annual
		Monardella species (deer mint)	
VINE		*Muhlenbergia rigens* (deer grass)	
		Oenothera deltoides var. *howellii* (Antioch dunes evening primrose)	
Aristolochia californica (Dutchman's pipe vine)	D	*Penstemon heterophyllus* (chaparral penstemon)	
GROUND COVERS		*Pholistoma auritum* (fiesta flower)	annual
		Sisyrinchium bellum (blue-eyed grass)	S
Baccharis pilularis subsp. *pilularis* (dwarf coyote bush)		*Solanum parishii* (broom nightshade)	S
Ceanothus griseus var. *horizontalis* (Carmel creeper)			
C. *maritimus* (Hoover ceanothus)			
Ribes viburnifolium (Catalina currant)			

SUPERPOPPY

ART TYREE

HUGE flowers of glistening white petals with yellow centers waving head-high over blue-green foliage erupting from rock piles: not a backdrop for some ballet fantastique, but one of California's native botanical treasures, the Matilija poppy, *Romneya coulteri*. Named for a canyon in Ventura County from which it has now largely been removed, Matilija poppy is as rare in the wild as it is spectacular. It grows now along its narrow range in southern California and northern Baja California in such scattered localities that few have seen it in the wild.

These giants of the poppy family are perennial, each winter sending up new growth from underground rootstocks. The attractive lobed, blue-green leaves grow along robust stems that may reach over six feet high. The flowers, which open in late spring, are often five inches or more in diameter. They have four white petals that are pleated or wrinkled like crepe paper, crowned with a bunch of rich yellow stamens. This floral color scheme prompted from earlier Californians the name "fried egg plant." The flowers have a delicate spicy fragrance.

After flowering, the plants set seed and go dormant until next season's rains. They increase in size, forming large colonies by means of runner roots. Whether the Matilija poppy ever propagates by seed in nature is somewhat of a riddle; seed is produced abundantly, but seedlings in the wild are unknown, though brush fires probably trigger embryos into germinating and burn the seed-killing fungus from the soil. The poppy's preference is for gravelly, loose, but deep soils in canyons, draws, and escarpments where there is likely to be moisture below long after the surface has taken on its seasonally dry appearance. In nature it is found away from direct coastal influence, but grows well under cultivation in coastal areas, flowering longer there—sometimes well into September.

Romneya coulteri gathers in one of its largest concentrations in the Trabuco Wash area of Orange County, extending from the slopes of Santiago Peak to O'Neil Park. Colonies also grow in neighboring Silverado Canyon, Ortega Pass, and parts of Riverside County. A slightly different form occurs in parts of Santa Barbara and Ventura Counties, San Diego County, and Baja California. Designated *Romneya trichocalyx*,

Matilija poppy, Romneya coulteri

(but by some *R. coulteri* var. *trichocalyx*), it differs from *R. coulteri* in having generally narrower leaf lobes and rounded flower buds with bristles, rather than beaked, smooth buds. Further, the petals have a somewhat regularly pleated pattern, rather than the crumpled appearance of *R. coulteri* flowers.

Romneya trichocalyx can be seen in scattered canyons along State Highway 94 near Dulzura in southern San Diego County. It is conspicuous, too, in the canyons behind Ensenada. There is some variation among plants in growth as well as in arrangement and size of flowers. In Trabuco Wash there are two especially interesting individuals. One has dense growth and heavy flowering, the other opens its flowers in attractive clusters. The cultivar 'White Cloud' propagated by Paul Scott of Duarte is probably of hybrid origin; it combines robust growth with abundant large flowers.

A favorite in England for a century, Matilija poppy has a horticultural history in its homeland beginning at least as early as the days of Madame Modjeska, the wealthy Polish lady of the theater who retired to the wilds of Orange County in the first quarter of this century. She insisted on having the plant on her estate in the canyon in the Santa Ana Mountains. To her gardener, an adventurous English Quaker named Theodore Payne, she gave the task of propagating and cultivating the spectacular poppy. No easy plant this; Payne discovered that the seed could be induced to germinate only if straw had been placed on the seed bed and burned.

Having mastered this and other specialized propagation techniques required for California plants, Payne not only provided Madame Modjeska with her prized poppies, but went on to found a nursery spe-cializing in native plants, which he ran until he was nearly ninety years old.*

Matilija poppy is a superb ornamental plant, if given space so that its colonizing habit is an asset instead of a nuisance. It is especially useful on slopes, cuts, and fills, where its wandering roots stabilize the soil.

Good companion plants are monkey-flower (*Diplacus* species), penstemons, and the California fuchsia (*Zauschneria* species), all of which are smaller than *Romneya* and flower with it.

With Theodore Payne's seed propagation method, germination, often rather spotty, occurs in about thirty days. Use only a moderate amount of fuel; about an inch of loosely spread pine needles over the seed bed will furnish the heat to trigger germination. In infancy plants are distressingly vulnerable to damp-off fungus, water mold, and root disturbance. It seems impossible to avoid losing at least half of the seedlings despite vigilance. Seedlings should be kept moist at the roots and dry around the leaves. Peat pots are good for seedlings, as they allow air circulation around the roots and minimize transplanting disturbance.

A more certain method of propagation is by root cuttings taken in November or December. It may need a major excavation to reach the lateral roots, which sometimes run as deep as two feet. The roots to use are horizontal runners with a diameter of about that of a pencil. Cut them into two- to three-inch lengths and plant them horizontally in pots of coarse growing mix, keeping them moist and lightly shaded while roots and shoots develop. They should not be planted out in perma-

*Now the Theodore Payne Foundation, Inc., a non-profit organization distributing native plants at 10459 Tuxford Street, Sun Valley, Ca. 91352.

nent sites until plenty of roots have formed in the containers.

Should you be fortunate enough to find a plant in a nursery, put it in soil that has been loosened with an addition of organic soil amendment or pumice. It is best to plant it container and all (with a few extra holes punched in the bottom of the container) in order to avoid breaking tender new roots. The roots will find a way through the holes.

Water plants several times a week during the first season's growth, after which they will take care of themselves with no watering other than rainfall. You can encourage them with a winter top dressing of compost or processed sewage sludge, but nothing stronger. Extra watering at flowering time extends the season. After flowering, the stems may be cut back to about a foot high, making the plant more tidy and encouraging compact growth the following season.

PART FOUR

THE GARDENER'S CRAFT

WATER USE BY PLANTS

S. L. GULMON & H. A. MOONEY

WATER is essential for plant life because it is the primary constituent of all living cells. In cells depleted of water, most of the complex molecular interactions involved in organism function cease. Water also maintains plant cells in a distended, or firm, state (cell turgor pressure), which provides mechanical support for leaves and green stems and pressure on cell walls, which is necessary for cell elongation and plant growth. In some cases, water evaporating from cell surfaces within the leaves and passing out through openings (stomata) in the leaf surfaces performs a cooling function that protects leaves from high temperatures.

All green plants use light energy to reduce atmospheric carbon dioxide gas to organic molecules, which are then used as sources of energy or as building blocks for plant structure. Consequently a leaf must be an open system to exchange gases with the atmosphere. As carbon dioxide enters the leaf through the stomata, water vapor in the intercellular spaces within the leaf is similarly free to pass out. This passage of water, called transpiration, is the process by which plants lose over ninety percent of the water taken up by the roots.

It is easy to conceive of means by which

plants might restrict the loss of water vapor from within the leaf—by reducing stomatal openings, for example. Such restrictions would, however, also impede the entry of carbon dioxide. This need to allow rapid carbon dioxide entry while restricting water loss is basic to plant growth and survival, and in this chapter we discuss some of the mechanisms plants use to achieve it.

WATER IN THE SOIL

Desert plants often have enlarged fleshy roots or stems, or thick, succulent leaves, in which water is stored for use during dry periods. Most trees normally contain two to six days' supply of water in the trunk sapwood. In general, though, plants depend on the water stored in the soil to supply their needs.

Stored soil water is the water that is held in soil against the force of gravity by matric forces—forces arising from the attraction of water molecules to the surfaces of soil particles. The smaller the particles, the larger the water-holding surface in a given volume of soil. For this reason, soil texture affects the amount of water from rain or

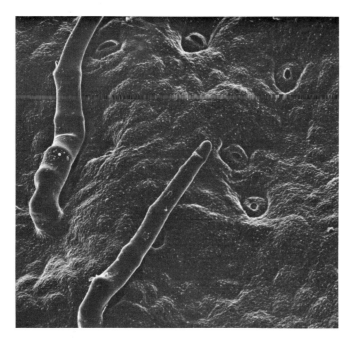

Scanning electron micrograph of the leaf surface of Simmondsia chinensis, *native to the southwestern U.S. The small holes are stomata and the finger-like projections are leaf hairs. Magnification 400×*

irrigation that will be stored for plant growth.

Sand holds the least water—only sixteen gallons per cubic yard. Clay, with the smallest particle sizes, holds up to 120 gallons per cubic yard, but many of the spaces between clay particles are too small for roots to enter, so over half this water is unavailable to plants. Loam soils, which contain from forty to seventy percent sand and from twenty to forty percent clay, offer the best compromise between total water storage capacity (sixty to ninety gallons per cubic yard) and interparticle spaces large enough for roots to explore.

THE ROOT ZONE

As roots take up water from the soil, the remaining water is held progressively more tightly to the soil particles; liquid flow through soil to dry zones is limited. Consequently, all the water available to a particular plant is contained in a volume defined by the outer limits of extension of its roots, the root zone.

The root zone of a plant is determined in part by genetic factors. Plants native to arid environments generally have deeper or more widely spreading root systems than those native to areas with moister climates. Evergreen shrubs from the California chaparral, such as California lilac, coffeeberry, toyon, and manzanita, and plants from other summer-dry climates, such as oleander, olive, and strawberry tree, all have deep and extensive root systems that help make them more resistant to drought.

Root zones are also affected by environmental conditions occurring during the period of growth. Roots grow toward moist soil, and will not grow into dry soil, so a plant's root zone will be concentrated where there is moisture. Frequent, shallow irrigation results in shallow root systems with less stored water available to plants. Also, plants tend to use up the water near the soil surface before beginning to tap deeper stores. Deep, infrequent irrigation forces plants to use water stored at depth. Finally, root growth may be restricted by physical factors that impede penetration

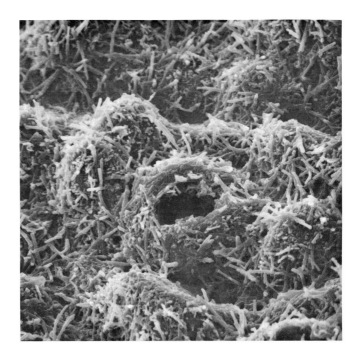

Scanning electron micrograph of the cuticle of Eucalyptus socialis *showing heavy deposition of wax particles. The opening is a single stomate.* E. socialis *is a shrub-type eucalyptus native to south-eastern Australia. Magnification 200×*

into the soil, or by lack of oxygen in heavy, compacted, or waterlogged soils. In such cases water, though abundant in the soil, is unavailable to plants, which may exhibit symptoms of drought stress.

WATER IN THE PLANT

The pathway for water from the soil through the roots and stems and out of the leaves to the atmosphere is a continuous one. In the course of this passage, water changes from the liquid state in the soil to gas (water vapor) in the atmosphere. The physical laws governing this process are the same laws that describe evaporation of water from an open pan. As anyone who has ever hung laundry to dry knows, evaporation is greatly speeded by high temperature, low humidity, and strong wind. These same conditions induce greater rates of transpiration from leaf surfaces. The effects of each are additive, so that when all three conditions prevail, plants can lose a great deal of water.

Water in a plant, however, is different from water in an open pan in two important respects. First, a pan of water holds a certain volume, which is progressively depleted. The plant, however, draws water in at the roots and loses it at the leaf surfaces, and thus represents a flux, or movement, of water. Secondly, water in a pan (or in wet laundry) evaporates freely from the surface, whereas water from the soil must move across a boundary of living cells at the root tips. This boundary constitutes a resistance to water movement; the water can flow into the plant only at a limited rate. Just as the balance of a checking account will shrink if spending exceeds deposits, leaves will develop a lack, or deficiency, of water, called a water deficit, if the loss of water by transpiration exceeds the uptake by roots.

The magnitude of the leaf water deficit depends on the rate of water loss relative to the rate of uptake. The latter rate depends in part on the root resistance, which varies greatly among different plants. Those with dense, finely divided root systems generally have lower root resistances than those

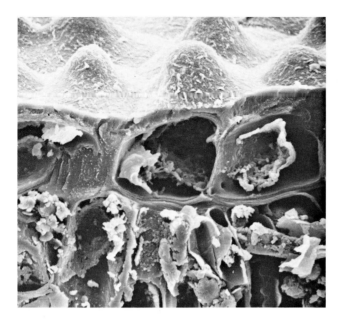

Scanning electron micrograph of a cross-section of a leaf of Eucalyptus socialis. *Note the large epidermal cells at the leaf surface. The exposed walls of these cells form the cuticle. For this picture the cuticular wax was removed. Magnification 1500 ✕*

with simple, elongated systems. During periods of high transpiration, plants with high root resistances may undergo leaf water deficits even in fully wetted soil.

Leaf water deficits concern us further for three reasons. First, when leaves of a particular plant reach some deficit value, there is insufficient water to maintain cell turgor, and the leaves wilt. The deficit value that induces wilting differs considerably among species of plants. Plants native to dry habitats frequently sustain much greater leaf water deficits without wilting than those from moist areas. Such drought-tolerant leaves and deep roots are characteristics often seen together in plants most recommended for low-water gardens.

Secondly, the magnitude of the leaf water deficit represents the pulling force that a plant can exert against the matric forces that hold the water in the soil. Leaves deficient in water exert a stronger pull than leaves that are fully turgid. As pointed out earlier, remaining soil water is held more strongly as it is depleted. Thus plants whose leaves tolerate high water deficits without wilting, in addition to being more resistant to drought damage, can use more of the water stored in the soil than can plants that wilt more readily. Such plants need less frequent irrigation because there is more water available to them.

Many drought-tolerant plants maintain high effective water deficits by concentrating sugars and salts in the cell sap. These solutes enable leaves to exert a stronger pull on the water in the soil. Such plants may also have thick, rigid leaves that do not collapse when cell turgor is lost. Tough, thick leaves are thus a good indicator of a drought-tolerant species.

Leaf water deficit also acts as a signal that plants use to control water loss through the stomata.

WATER LOSS FROM LEAVES

When fully saturated, one cubic yard of loam soil contains about fifty-five gallons of

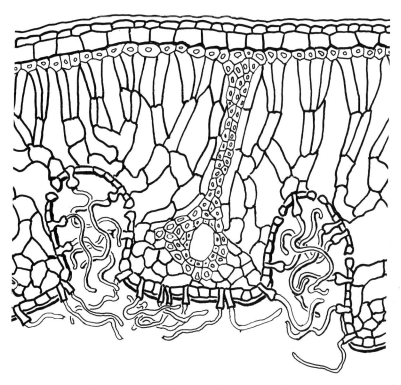

Cross-section through the leaf of Banksia marginata, *a shrub native to western Australia, which shows several features characteristic of drought-tolerant plants. The leaf is covered by a heavy cuticle on both surfaces, and the under surface is covered with hairs. Stomata are sunken in pits between rigid columns of mechanical tissue*

water available to plants. On a warm July day (85° F., forty percent relative humidity), a single corn plant growing in this yard of wet soil would use about 1.4 gallons of water per day. If the plot were covered by annual herbs with characteristically high transpiration rates, such as desert evening primroses, water use would jump to about 4.3 gallons per day. However, if we filled our plot with corn, daily water use would increase still further to seven gallons. By contrast, a six-foot toyon shrub would get by on a meager half gallon per day.

It is of interest to compare these figures with evaporation from bare soil. Fully saturated, our square yard of soil surface would lose about 2.3 gallons per day under similar weather conditions. But after about two days the dry surface soil would form a natural mulch and greatly reduce further evaporation. Thus soil watered deeply and infrequently loses little water from the surface. On the other hand, when frequent watering of shallow-rooted plants keeps the upper soil moist, mulch-

ing with bark fiber, plastic sheet, or other material will save water by reducing soil surface evaporation.

Variation in water use among the plants described above arises principally from differences in the number and size of their stomatal openings. A large number of wide apertures allows rapid water loss and concomitant rapid carbon dioxide entry. Water loss is controlled by closing the stomata in response to increasing leaf water deficit. When stomata are completely closed, transpiration losses are reduced, and leaf water content begins to rise. Of course, carbon dioxide entry is restricted during this time.

Some plants close their stomata at the onset of water stress whereas others, drought-happy plants, maintain open stomata and continuous carbon dioxide entry with much greater leaf water deficits. Many cereals and other grasses of dry habitats rarely open their stomata at all. Still others, including the potato, cabbage, and onion, do not shut their stomata until the leaves wilt. These plants are not adapted to drought, but are from cool climates and seem to have evolved in areas where water shortage seldom occurs.

Many plants lose water through the leaf surface layer, or cuticle, even when the stomata are completely closed. Tomatoes and beans, for example, lose up to twenty percent of their total water flux directly through the cuticle. Such plants tend to have thin, soft leaves. Leaves of plants grown in the shade also lose more water through the cuticle than leaves of similar plants grown in the sun. Thus a plant that is moved to a sunnier location may suffer leaf damage even if roots are undamaged and receive ample water. Plants with high cuticular water loss are extremely susceptible to drought stress. Water loss continues even after leaves wilt, and irreversible damage may occur rapidly if water is not supplied. These plants do not do well in a low-maintenance garden except in moist climates, and should be restricted to small areas that receive frequent attention.

The phenomenon of midday wilt on warm, sunny days is often observed in plants such as fuchsias, impatiens, cinerarias, and artichokes. These plants have high rates of cuticular water loss and may have sluggish stomata and high root resistances as well. Midday wilt occurs even in thoroughly moist soil because it is due to plants' inability to restrict water loss, or take it up rapidly enough, during conditions of high potential evaporation.

ADAPTATIONS TO WATER STRESS

When water is insufficient for growth, some plants simply allow the leaves to dry and fall. New leaves are produced on the return of moist conditions. Many coastal California native plants, such as the sages (*Salvia* spp.) and the bush sunflower (*Encelia californica*), as well as the California buckeye, are deciduous during drought.

A somewhat less drastic response to water deficit is collapse, or folding of leaves. This reduces the interception of radiant energy from the sun and the consequent heat load on the leaves. (Compare the heat on your body when lying in the noonday sun with that felt when standing up.) Leaf folding also reduces the leaf surface area that is exposed to evaporation. This response is particularly effective where stomatal surfaces are folded together. Many species of the pea family with double rows of leaflets can be observed to fold the pairs together in response to water stress. Similarly, the redwood sorrel, a shade-loving plant, drops the three leaflets down and compresses them against each other whenever it is struck by a beam of direct sun passing through the forest canopy.

The best xerophytes, or drought lovers, have thickened, often waxy cuticles that restrict leaf water loss to nearly zero when the stomata are closed. Leaves may be covered with white hairs or other structures that reflect sunlight and reduce the heat load. Often these plants have rigid partitions in the leaves to prevent collapse when turgor is lost. Xerophytes generally have sparse canopies, since simply having fewer leaves reduces water loss. Though they do not thrive when the soil is very dry, xerophytes can withstand long dry periods without damage and resume growth when the rains return.

In sun, plants solve the water problem at the root or in the leaf. Those with deep and extensive root systems tap groundwater, or water stored at depth, to survive long dry periods. Most trees, when well established, survive droughts of considerable length by means of their large root systems.

At the leaf level, plants restrict water loss by closing their stomata. However, stomatal control serves primarily to regulate water use over short time periods. During a protracted drought, cuticular water loss would eventually cause leaves to wilt and then desiccate. Long-term survival thus requires that leaves be protected by thick, heavy cuticles. Finally, plants from the most arid regions not only survive drought but grow and flower under conditions that would cause most plants to wither and die. These plants have specialized leaves that tolerate high water deficits, while still allowing exchange of carbon dioxide and water vapor across the leaf boundary.

WATER CONSERVATION
IN THE GARDEN

ROBERT D. RAABE

I N a geography class nearly thirty years ago, one of the facts stressed by the professor was that water would be one of the first natural resources to be depleted if action were not taken to ensure a conservative use of it. Though difficult to believe at that time, much of California and parts of some of the other western states are in just such a predicament.* As a result of critical water shortages, reductions in water use of up to twenty-five percent are suggested for residences in many of the coastal areas. Although this sounds reasonable, the amount allowed in some areas is based on the number of members in a family and not on a percentage of water used in the past. Thus those who have large gardens or who garden intensively find they have reductions far more than twenty-five percent. At our house, we will have to reduce consumption about eighty percent. This means that we, along with many others, will have to conserve water in every way

possible in order to keep gardens at a minimum maintenance level. A number of approaches to water conservation are available. Many of them are applicable to saving water in the garden and some of them will be discussed here.

Methods of watering. Of the various methods used in applying water, some use far less water than others. In brief, ditch irrigation uses the most water and should be avoided. Overhead sprinklers use less but may water areas where no plants are growing. Hand watering is probably the best, for the water can be put where it is needed. Also there is less tendency to overwater using this system as contrasted with systems where water is turned on and the device left to be re-positioned at some later time. Soaker hoses also can be used, particularly where plants are relatively close together. When used, they should be placed upside down so the water is not sprayed into the air, allowing for evaporation. Drip irrigation systems are excellent for conserving water and can also be used to water individual plants. Time, effort, and expense need to be considered, but once in operation it is an easy way to irrigate. Although drip irrigation is most effective in sandy soils, it will

*This was written during the severe drought of 1976–77. It is included here because water use must diminish whether or not there is a drought; we have reached a point where more water is used, in total, than is provided by precipitation. In other words, we have a permanent water deficit that, from time to time, reaches drought proportions.

conserve water even in the heavier clay soils.

Kinds of plants grown. There are many lists of plants that can survive low levels of moisture, so most of these plants will not be included here. In general, the larger the plant, the larger the root system to explore for water and the less often it will have to be given water. Certain plants, such as some California natives, most prostrate junipers, and many plants native to South Africa and Australia, do not need summer water. In the absence of winter rainfall, these plants should be watered in the winter when there is less demand for garden water. Shrubs with deeper root systems will need less water than those with surface root systems, such as rhododendrons, azaleas, and camellias. Perennials that can tolerate low moisture levels include columbine, hollyhock, geranium and other *Pelargonium* spp., *Liatris* spp., *Rudbeckia* spp., candytuft, *Lychnis* spp., perennial poppies, some species of *Echium*, forget-me-not, coral bells, and plants from bulbs, corms, or rhizomes such as freesia, daffodil, narcissus, tigridia, gladiolus, agapanthus, watsonia, oxalis, amaryllis, cyclamen, iris, scilla, and sparaxis. Ground covers such as ivy, ajuga, periwinkle, St. John's wort, *Duchesnea indica*, *Ceratostigma plumbaginoides*, and ice plant can get by on small amounts of moisture. Some annuals that tolerate low moisture levels include sweet alyssum, marigolds, ageratum, petunias, annual poppies, nasturtium, annual candytuft, mignonette, fibrous begonias, calendula, valerian, portulaca, coreopsis, and gloriosa daisies. From your own experience, you probably can add many to this list.

Weeding and pruning. Plants are inefficient users of water and during daylight hours are constantly transpiring water through their leaves. Removal of weeds or any unwanted plants is extremely important. If time is too limited to pull the weeds, a hula or other type of scuffle hoe is suggested. These hoes have a long handle, on the end of which is a knife-like blade that can be pulled just beneath the surface of the soil to cut the roots and thus kill the plants.

Pruning small trees, shrubs, and ground covers also will help. This is a good chance to prune overgrown or poorly shaped plants. With some plants, it is important not to cut back too far or branches or whole plants may die. For example, when pruning bush daisies or fuchsias, do not prune beyond the last active bud. Once cuts have been made, new buds may be forced and additional pruning then can be done. Many plants can be cut back severely with little damage.

Removal of plants used as ground covers around other plants may be of help. For example, ivy, baby's tears, or other ground covers sometimes are grown under shrubs such as rhododendrons, camellias, and hydrangeas. Such ground covers should be removed as far as the drip line of the shrubs so that water added for them will not be used by the ground covers.

The use of organic material. Organic material in the soil performs many functions, one of which is to retain soil moisture. Organic materials such as leaf mold, decomposed manure, or compost can be worked into the soil. In addition, organic materials can be put on top of the soil as a mulch to prevent evaporation. Of the organic materials, compost may be the most readily available, for with the rapid composting method, a new batch of compost can be ready for use every three weeks. There should be no excuses for a lack of abundant compost to add to soils and to be used as a mulch around all plants.

Other cultural practices. There are a number of cultural practices that will help conserve water in addition to those already mentioned. These include such things as scooping the soil away from the bases of plants to make basins that will concentrate the water in the root zones. We have done this to all our rose plants and have filled the basins with compost to prevent evaporation. Plants that tend to be surface feeders cannot be treated this way, though a ditch can be made at the margin of the root system that will prevent runoff. On sloping land, soil, rock, brick, or wood dams or barriers can be put in to prevent runoff.

Another practice is to lower soil levels of beds so they are not above sidewalks or driveways. This may not always be feasible, but if not the soil should be removed along the edge so that any water running off the bed will collect in the ditch that is formed.

When planting vegetable gardens, make ditches for the rows and then plant into these ditches. This will not only concentrate the water in the root zone and prevent evaporation loss but plants will be less exposed and will lose less water through transpiration.

If winds are a problem, plant rows of vegetables at right angles to, rather than parallel with, the wind. The erection of small windbreaks, even of cardboard, will help prevent some water loss through transpiration.

The use of rocks or boards as stepping places in the garden will also prevent evaporation from the soil that is covered. Layers of polyethylene plastic will do the same, but eventually it breaks down in the sunlight and must be disposed of. Compost is better as a mulch.

Concrete retaining walls frequently will draw moisture from the soil. This can be prevented by removing the soil from the wall and painting it with tar or asphalt emulsion. This, however, raises the question of whether it is advisable to use one diminishing natural resource in order to conserve another.

Avoid growing plants in containers, for it takes more water to support plants with a confined root system than plants that can explore open ground. Some containers, in addition, are porous and there is evaporation from their surface. If plants must be grown in containers, change to plastic or glazed containers for they allow little evaporation. At the same time, remember that because such containers allow little air exchange, they need to be watched more carefully for they are more subject to excessive moisture and thus root rots may be more common.

Other cultural practices might include watering at night to prevent evaporation, mowing lawns more frequently to prevent transpiration, and avoiding soil spading prior to planting because this not only destroys soil structure but allows excessive evaporation of soil moisture. Deep spading each year is helpful in removing the roots of large trees near beds because roots tend to accumulate where water is available. Control slugs and snails, for extra water will be required to replace the growth damaged by such pests.

The use of gray water. Gray water, that is, water from the washing machine, dishwasher, shower, bath tub, lavatories, or kitchen sink, should be saved and used wherever possible. Some cities forbid this and local regulations should be observed. The main problem from using such water is that detergents are sodium salts of organic acids and soaps are sodium or sometimes potassium salts of fatty acids. Sodium is not used by plants, and when it accumulates in soils it may reach levels toxic to plants. Potassium also may reach toxic levels, though it is used by plants and also plants are slightly more tolerant of potassium than of sodium in the soil. The use of gray water will depend on how much it is mixed with water not containing these materials. It will also depend on which plants receive it. Acid-loving plants should not receive such water. Monocots and particularly many of the grasses seem quite tolerant of sodium. As an experiment, we used only the first effluent from the washing machine to water our lawn. Soils in this area tend to be rich in calcium, which is more active than sodium and so replaces it in the exchange reaction in the soil. This releases the sodium, allowing it to be leached. Had there been signs of damage to the lawn we would have spread gypsum, which is high in calcium, at about one pound per twenty-five square feet.

If planning to use gray water, do not use detergents or soaps that have boron, for this material is toxic to plants. If bleaches or materials containing bleaches are used, allow the water to stand in the open air one day before using it for irrigation. Bleaches are quite toxic but break down in the presence of light and air to form less toxic salts.

Problems that may arise. The main problems from lack of water are obvious. Other problems may also occur. The use of gray water or the lack of enough water to leach the soils may result in the accumulation of salts in the soil and this may result in excessive salts in the plants. Salt damage usually appears as a browning of the tissues around the margins of older leaves. Plants vary in their sensitivity to this. Salt damage is more likely to occur in container-grown plants than in those grown in open ground. Therefore, when using gray water, do not use it on plants in containers.

Another problem that will occur as a re-

sult of low moisture levels will be sunburn. Some plants, such as ivy, camellias, rhododendrons, hydrangeas, and fuchsias, are more susceptible to sunburn than others. Sunburn appears as a bleaching of the interveinal tissues followed by the death of these tissues. They may remain bleached or sometimes will darken depending upon the plant involved or on the colonization of tissues by fungi that invade only dead tissues.

Wilting may occur but is serious only if the leaves go beyond the permanent wilting point. Sometimes only parts of leaves go beyond this point before water is applied. When this occurs, the margins of the leaves on the older portions of the affected plants die. They do not turn brown as in salt injury but retain a dull green color and have a crisp, papery appearance.

Benefits. Although it is sometimes difficult to find good in a situation as serious as drought, some good will come of it. Some plants will have to go without water. Such plants as some California natives, most of the prostrate junipers, and some of the plants from Australia and South Africa will thrive far better than when they received too much tender, loving care. Already, one of the live oaks on the campus of the University of California, Berkeley, which was on its way out because of summer water, has started to show signs of recovery. One of the more important diseases in California is root rot of the prostrate junipers and particularly of the tams (*Juniperus sabina* 'Tamariscifolia'). It will be severely reduced as a result of the lack of water. This may even allow plant pathologists to work on some new disease problems, maybe even some that will result from the lack of water.

THE GENTLE ART OF DIGGING

GEORGE WATERS

WHEN animal manure was plentiful, digging was accompanied by the incorporation of great quantities of the rotted stuff into the soil. With changes in farming and reduction in horse traffic animal manure has become scarce; the practice of digging has also declined. Digging beyond the first spit is rare (a spit is the depth of soil equal to the length of a spade's blade—about eleven inches) and mechanical cultivators, most of which disturb soil to a lesser depth, are often used. One of the benefits of bulky manure, including compost, is that it opens soil to the passage of air, but digging alone can help in this, and soil denied the spade is poorer for it.

A well known gardener said, "We don't talk about digging anymore—only about cultivation." Used to mean turning the soil, the word cultivation covers the use of machines with rotating blades and other powered tools, as well as digging with a spade, but obscures important differences between the results from them. It would require a large rotary cultivator indeed, in some soils, to work the depth reached by a spade. While digging with a spade, the opportunity can be taken to work the second spit too; powered tools usually only compact this further. With any tool, cultivation is damaging to the crumb structure of the soil, but the pulverizing action of rotating blades is utterly destructive of it.

Is digging unpopular? I looked again at some recent books on gardening for what they say on digging. Several have little or nothing to say about it. Most have a drawing of a hole dug to receive the roots of a tree, but on digging—the systematic preparation of a large area of ground—they are generally silent. Perhaps the authors of these books feel that describing the work discourages new gardeners. How ironic if so valuable an exercise as digging, and one with additional practical benefits, is ignored, while writers in other spheres encourage us to improve our health by jogging. Authors of some gardening books give the impression that they are, themselves, unfamiliar with basic tasks such as digging. Others advocate gardening without digging, and there is much to be said for this, but reducing the frequency with which soil is dug requires the production of large amounts of compost—a task that is also physically demanding and that presents, as well, the need to find sufficient raw material for the compost.

Whatever methods a gardener adopts, it is difficult to avoid digging entirely. Even if

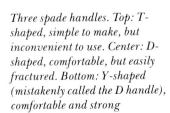

Three spade handles. Top: T-shaped, simple to make, but inconvenient to use. Center: D-shaped, comfortable, but easily fractured. Bottom: Y-shaped (mistakenly called the D handle), comfortable and strong

Short shafted spade with Y handle. The shaft is tapered, not stepped, to fit the socket. The forged blade is thicker where strength is needed

enough compost can be procured to keep the soil constantly covered inches deep with it—the first requirement for gardening without digging—the ground may be so compacted and infested with perennial weeds that digging is needed at the outset to correct these conditions. In addition to the benefits from digging already mentioned, there are others less tangible, but important to the gardener's well-being. It allows him opportunities to study the soil and become familiar with some of its occupants, and it gives time for peaceful contemplation of plans and reflection on successes and failures. Meditation requires yoga no more than a durable heart depends on jogging.

Would-be gardeners, lacking advice and example, tend to be overly eager. With ardor inflamed by onrushing spring, they attempt too much digging at once and quickly retire disillusioned and with aching muscles and sprains. Unaccustomed exercise must be limited to short periods, increasing in small increments as ability grows. Eventually only satisfaction and wholesome tiredness will result from several hours of digging. It is persistence, not hurry, that completes the job.

George Glenny, writing on gardening

Long-shafted tool with sheet-steel blade made rigid by turnovers at the shoulders and by the corrugation extended from the socket

early in the nineteenth century, said, "Never work with bad tools. The difference between the work done (with good and bad tools) in a month would buy a set of new ones." There are so many bad tools offered that finding good ones may call for diligence. My first spade was quite ordinary; it was not highly priced and little was claimed for it by the makers. Nevertheless

it served me well for thirty years and may be serving another still, for it was left behind in England, worn but undamaged. With it I had dug, and sometimes double-dug, many acres of ground. It survived misuse when tree stumps and large rocks were removed and endured occasional neglect when left overnight in the open. Once, when the shaft and handle seemed gray and rough, I brushed them with raw linseed oil to help make the wood smooth again; otherwise the spade had little care. I was fortunate to have come upon so good a tool in my early gardening days. Over the years I grew fond of its sturdy hickory shaft and familiar handle worn to my grip. The blade, polished by rich greensand, hungry gravel, and sticky marl, had the temper of a spring and rang like a bell when caught on a rock. It contributed to my pleasure in gardening; George Glenny understood that.

The best spades have blades of forged steel. Forging is a process of hammering metal to shape while it is hot. During the process the internal structure of the metal is aligned, making it stronger. Strength is also given to forged tools by allowing the metal to remain thicker where stress will be greatest in use. Spade blades are stressed most where the blade meets the socket into which the shaft fits, and the blade thickens toward that place over a roughly triangular area. Forged steel can therefore be recognized by the variation in thickness throughout the blade. Forged blades are also usually heavier than others, which are made from sheet steel. They also retain a better cutting edge, which allows them to enter the soil more easily. A file applied now and then to the back edge of the blade further improves cutting.

I prefer a spade with a short shaft, Y-shaped handle, and nearly flat rectangular blade with leading edge slightly curved.

The tool requires the user to stoop slightly, but picking perennial weeds and other debris from the soil during digging also bends the back, so the tool is well suited to the operation. Where grass or rank weeds are growing, they must be cleared from the surface or their matted stems severed during digging to prevent them anchoring the clods and pulling them from the spade before they are placed. Scraping the ground with the spade is sometimes the best way of removing weed stems, but thick growth, especially well-established grass that is to be turned under, is best severed as work proceeds. Stabbing the blade an inch or two into the soil cuts through the vegetation, measuring the width of the clod and releasing it for lifting. The stabbing stroke, with wrist turned through ninety degrees, is easily made with the short-shafted spade before it is inserted behind the clod.

Only by inserting the blade fully, and perpendicular to the ground, will soil be moved to a depth equal to the blade's length. Good spades therefore have plates on the shoulders of the blade so that it may be driven home more easily with pressure from the foot. They also have blade and shaft nearly parallel—although a little offset—so that, with the blade vertical, the handle remains conveniently near the user. The clod, loosened with a small backward tilt of the shaft, is lifted only slightly, moved to the trench made by the previously dug line, and tipped from the blade.

The long-shafted tool without handle and with pointed, scoop-like blade is less suitable for precision digging. It has advantages where soil is sandy and loose and is good for digging holes for tree planting. Leverage given by the long handle helps in lifting clumps of roots. Makers of these tools reduce the diameter of the shaft abruptly where the socket from the blade ends, so that the socket and shaft are flush.

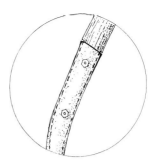

Shaft weakened by step cut to allow flush-fitting socket

The sudden change in diameter weakens the shaft, which is more likely to break near the socket. Shafts should have no steps but should be tapered to fit sockets, even if this gives a less smooth finish. Some garden tools now have tubular steel shafts. I have not used them and know nothing of their weaknesses.

Among books that I examined for references to digging is one with plenty to say on the subject. It is *The Self-Sufficient Gardener* (Doubleday, 1979) and the author, John Seymour, writes succinctly from great and varied experience. Bastard trenching, in which the soil below the first spit is also worked, but not removed, is described and clearly illustrated. Many gardeners, including some claiming to advise, confuse bastard trenching with double digging—a very different operation. Something said to be double digging is described in the *White Flower Farm Garden Book*. The description is accompanied by humorous comments about the effort required for the task and the reduced life expectancy of the digger. I am tempted to assume that the whole thing is a joke, for in it the gardener is advised to invert topsoil and subsoil (first and second spits). Subsoil becomes topsoil, it is said, because during inversion, compost and cow manure are mixed with it. If only it were so easy to produce topsoil from

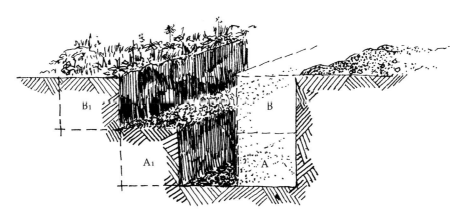

In double-digging, or trenching, work proceeds by moving soil at A₁ to A and that at B₁ to B. The soil at the bottom of the trench (the third spit) is worked as it is exposed

the dreadful stuff that usually lies below. Equally extraordinary is the advice to complete one trench and refill it before beginning the next beside it. This multiplies work when, with a little thought, each trench can be refilled with the soil taken from the next. How Amos Pettingill of White Flower Farm digs a second trench two feet deep, without the contents of the first falling into it, isn't explained.

Double digging, rarely attempted now, disturbs soil to a depth of about three feet. The diagram shows how this is achieved with least effort. Two trenches are first opened across the site, one two spits deep and three feet wide, the other one spit deep and eighteen inches wide. Top spit soil is kept separate from second spit; both are used in the final trenches. Work proceeds by moving the soil at A₁ to A and that at B₁ to B, working soil in the third spit, C, as it is exposed. First and second spit soil is not inverted by this procedure and there is much to be gained by keeping them at their original levels, whether or not manure is incorporated during digging.

It is not surprising that John Seymour ignores double digging in *The Self-Sufficient Gardener*; benefits from the aeration of subsoil can be great, but the work is tremendous. He does talk about the choice and care of tools and about many aspects of practical gardening ignored by others. The book is illustrated with useful and pleasing drawings and is directed toward those who wish to produce their own food.

Even the most intransigent soil is easier to work if the right moment is chosen. All are easier to dig when they are moist, but in clay soil the balance between too wet and too dry is critical. Clay soils adhere less readily to spades with stainless steel blades, but these are expensive. A good spade of the ordinary kind is easier to use in clay if the blade is frequently wetted from a bucket of water kept near. Some prefer a fork, rather than a spade, for clay soil. In England, where until recently every county had its own version of the spade, a blade with a large vee notch was favored for clay in some areas. The effect of the notch was to reduce the blade to a pair of triangular prongs that were easier to push into the clay and offered less surface to which it could stick.

Rapid Composting

Extra effort is needed to make compost in two or three weeks, but there are advantages in having it available quickly and in being able to process large quantities of material that might otherwise be wasted. Opportunities for vermin to nest in the heap are also reduced. Here is an outline of the process.

- Construct two bins each about 36 in. square, without bottoms or tops and with removable fronts. Spaces between slats to provide aeration are usually recommended for compost bins, but with this method aeration is provided during turning and it is more important to avoid loss of moisture and heat; therefore, leave no spaces between slats when making bins.

- Build a heap in one bin, mixing materials and avoiding all risk of leaves and grass clippings forming a matted layer that will inhibit the movement of air. Cover the heap with a heavy plastic sheet, tarpaulin or something similar to reduce heat loss.

- Woody material is ground or otherwise reduced to about half an inch. Soft stuff is included as it is, or cut up to facilitate handling.

- Including roughly equal amounts of dry woody stuff (twigs, cartons, paper, fallen leaves, etc.) and soft green stuff (grass clippings, kitchen scraps, etc.) gives the carbon-to-nitrogen ratio (approx. 30:1) needed for greatest activity in the heap.

- Moisten dry ingredients while building the heap.

- A soil thermometer may be used to measure the temperature in the heap. The information it gives is helpful and interesting, but not essential.

- The day after building the heap, or the one after that, turn it into the adjoining bin, with the outer parts of the old heap at the center of the new. Replace the cover.

- The heap should become hot (160° F.) at the center in 24 to 48 hours. If it fails to heat it may be too wet or too dry, or there may be insufficient green stuff to provide nitrogen. Turn the heap, correcting it as you go. Contents should be moist, but not wet; nitrogen can be provided in such things as fresh chicken manure, diluted urine, more green clippings, and sulfate of ammonia.

- Turn the heap into the empty bin every day or every other day. The oftener it is turned, the quicker the compost is made. When it fails to heat after turning, it is ready for use.

- The heat in properly made compost kills organisms that produce plant diseases, insects, and most weed seeds.

- The exercise of turning the heap is also beneficial to the gardener.

This information is extracted from *The Rapid Composting Method*, by Robert D. Raabe, 1981, leaflet 21251 of the Division of Agricultural Sciences, University of California.

A BEGINNER'S GUIDE
TO SLUGS AND SNAILS

GEORGE WATERS

No one new to gardening will remain for long unaware of the damage slugs and snails can do. These voracious little creatures are nocturnal feeders and the gardener may at first be unsure of the cause of damage to his plants, but the telltale silvery trail left by visiting snails and slugs will lead to the answer.

Damage done by slugs and snails can usually be recognized from the appearance of the wound. Their grazing mechanism is a sort of tongue, heavily equipped with teeth, called the radula. It resembles and is employed like a file, and damage on foliage, especially the heavy leaves of irises, often shows signs of the abrasive action by which plant tissue has been removed. It is not uncommon to find that the softer parts of leaves between the veins are eaten while the tougher tissue is left intact. Holes made in potatoes and in wheat seed invariably show an enlargement beyond the surface aperture, presumably because the softer tissue inside is preferred.

Young shoots of fleshy herbaceous plants seem to be their favorite food in the garden, but nothing is ignored. The bark may be stripped from a lemon tree by snails, and fungi, lichen, and even animal material have been found in the digestive tracts of collected slugs. Some slugs are cannibals.

Out of sight below ground, tiny slugs eat into bulbs and tubers. Thousands of tons of potatoes are lost every year because of slug damage and even the newly sown seed of spring wheat is sometimes destroyed, prior to germination, by slugs eating out the center. On farms slugs yield in economic importance to few other pests.

Slugs and snails are spread throughout the world. They belong to that enormous group of animals known as mollusks, and within this group they have relatives on land and in the seas and rivers, collectively known as gastropods. Most mollusks, in-

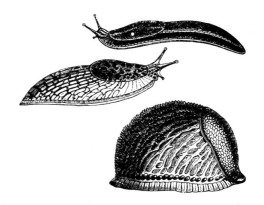

Arion ater *extended and in repose,
showing the mantle*

cluding gastropods, have a shell protecting part of their bodies, but slugs have evolved beyond that and are without shells. Some species of slugs show a patch on their backs that is differently textured from the rest of the back. The patch is called the mantle and is the vestigial location of the shell.

The lack of a shell has allowed slugs to succeed in a wider range of environments than can snails. The body shape is streamlined, allowing slugs to occupy cavities too small for snails; many slugs can therefore live below the soil surface. Having no shell, slugs need less calcium than snails, further extending their environment range.

The feature contributing most to the slugs' success (one shared with earthworms) is hermaphroditism. Within each animal are male and female organs producing ova and sperm simultaneously. Courtship and copulation nevertheless take place, usually at night, and sperm is exchanged, thereby effecting cross-fertilization. The sperm acquired during copulation can be stored and used gradually. In addition, some species can fertilize their eggs with their own sperm.

It is no wonder then that these creatures are so numerous and that they can multiply so quickly when their numbers have been reduced by disasters such as prolonged drought, or by onslaughts from determined gardeners.

Like the slugs themselves, their eggs are subject to desiccation in dry weather, but the main egg-laying season is autumn, when there is greatest chance of survival. Eggs are usually laid in small holes in the ground, enlarged and deepened by the parent if the soil is dry. Any number of eggs, up to a thousand, in groups of twenty to fifty, may be laid by a single slug in a season.

Their nocturnal habits protect slugs from predators to some extent, though they are eaten regularly by some birds, including starlings and gulls; but in no case do slugs represent a significant part of the birds' diet. Hedgehogs and some other small mammals eat slugs and so do certain insects such as carabid and staphylind beetle larvae, but by and large, the predators have little effect upon the slug population.

There are many things a gardener can do to control these creatures, although none is effective unless applied, diligently and frequently, each season. The first and most obvious method is to reduce the number of hiding places beneath which they can shelter during the day. Removing fallen leaves, large rocks, old flower pots, and other debris will reduce their numbers in your own territory. Soil frequently hoed between the crop rows offers fewer hollows for shelter and egg laying. The movement of the hoe will kill some slugs while the surface soil is kept drier and less attractive to the survivors. Applying irrigation water less often and less promiscuously will maintain in the garden a climate less hospitable to slugs and snails.

In some cases, simple sanitation of this sort may be enough to control slugs and snails, but if the plants you favor are also the ones preferred by them, direct attack is imperative.

A simple form of warfare may be practiced at night with the aid of a flashlight, when the larger and more easily seen of these nocturnal creatures may be picked off the plants by hand and destroyed. Simple traps such as inverted half-grapefruit skins can be used to lure them to cool, dark places where they can be easily destroyed. I heard of one old gardener who trapped them with fragile bridges of bait (bran) built over small containers of salt water. Bait stations, using bran, can be located at intervals among crops and visited regularly each night to remove and dispatch the

Helix aspersa *and eggs*

victims. A similar method, employing half a potato on a stick, can be used to catch the small subterranean slugs. Since the creatures breed so prolifically, however, these measures are only rearguard actions.

The use of sharp, scratchy material, like pine needles, cinders, and broken egg shells, spread around vulnerable plants to deter slugs and snails, is often advocated. Enthusiasm for this method seems greatest among young gardeners. With the skepticism bred of many battles, older gardeners believe the pests will reach their objective over any obstacle.

Slugs tend to be fewer in sandy soils than in heavier clay soils and this may have given rise to the idea that their soft bodies are in some way sensitive to abrasion. However, it is doubtful if this difference in population is because of the scratchiness of sand compared with clay. A more likely explanation is that heavy soils retain a higher level of moisture in the top few inches than does sand, and slugs and snails require a moist medium to remain active.

The effectiveness of scratchy material as deterrent gains no support from laboratory tests in which the rate of travel of slugs was found to be unimpaired, even when their foot surface was damaged.

Among delphinium growers in England, aluminum sulphate crystals, sprinkled on the ground between plants, were favored to combat slugs and snails. This is the chemical used to induce blue flowers on some kinds of hydrangeas; it can also help to lower the pH of the soil. It is doubtful if aluminum sulphate kills the creatures; it is probably an irritant tending to cause dehydration and inactivity.

Bran is attractive to slugs and snails and is used commercially, in combination with chemicals, to destroy them. Paris green, an arsenic compound, was once commonly used as the poison, but has now been replaced with other materials believed to be safer. Metaldehyde, the active ingredient in Corry's Original English Formula and some others, is still used. Unfortunately, metaldehyde is present usually only at about three percent concentration, and this allows many slugs taking the bait to recover in favorable weather. A metaldehyde concentration in bran of five percent is needed to ensure that slugs are killed by the preparation.

Carbamate compounds, originally developed as insecticides, have been found effective against slugs and snails and are generally more deadly for the purpose than metaldehyde. Carbamates, incorporated into pellets or granules of bran, are available as slug and snail killers produced by Forty-Niner, Ortho, and Best.

Neither carbamates nor metaldehyde, in granules or pellets of bran, is effective against the small black slugs living just below the soil surface. Severe infestations of these can be controlled with a liquid preparation of metaldehyde or a carbamate diluted with water and sprayed on the soil. However, all chemical preparations are expensive and inherently less desirable than the careful cultural practices mentioned earlier and should be employed only if all else fails. Carbamates are more toxic than metaldehyde to mammals and to other soil fauna, including earthworms; they must be used, if at all, with caution.

Terrestrial Slugs by Runham and Hunter, Hutchinson, 1970, contains a summary of the results of many studies of slugs, and much of the technical information for this chapter was drawn from it. The book also has a useful bibliography.

WILD SHRUBS FROM CUTTINGS

JOY SPURR

SOME of the most attractive and hardy garden shrubs are the natives that grow virtually in our own backyards. Wild shrubs have survived many centuries by adapting to the hardships of heat, cold, rain, salt spray, wind, and even volcanic lava and ice. Leveled by fire, drowned by flood, and uprooted by plow and bulldozer, still the wild shrubs endure.

Our gardens can benefit from the addition of wild shrubs. Their roots stabilize hillsides and their fallen leaves and twigs enrich the soil. Many kinds of animals use shrubs as a source of food, shelter, and nesting materials. Maintenance is minimum, pests and diseases few. The variety they offer in texture and color of leaf, flower, and fruit challenge the gardener's ability to plan a landscape and "paint with plants."

Propagating by softwood cuttings is perhaps the easiest way to bring woody wild shrubs into the garden. The procedure is simple, no costly facilities are required, and neither the shrub nor its environment is damaged. This method of propagation, in which pieces of young stem are rooted in a moist and well-aerated medium, is especially practical if many plants of one kind are needed.

It is difficult to specify exact dates for taking cuttings because elevation and climate affect the ripening of the wood. As a rule, a stem is ready for cutting if the wood breaks with a snap when bent. If it merely crushes between the fingers it is too young; if it bends without breaking it is too old.

There are always exceptions. Some plants root more quickly from young, pliable material. This is a desirable quality in deciduous shrubs such as serviceberry (*Amelanchier alnifolia*) and osoberry (*Oemleria cerasiformis*), where the roots must hold enough nutrients to allow them to break dormancy in spring and start new growth.

Most wild shrubs, however, are ready for cutting about one month after flowering. If in doubt about the ripeness of the wood, take cuttings immediately after the shrub has flowered and several times thereafter at two-week intervals.

The length of a stem cutting varies with the kind of plant. Ideally, a stem cutting should not exceed four inches. Use a sharp knife or razor blade to cut the stem at a slight angle just below a leaf node. On shrubs such as heathers and huckleberries, which develop many short side branchlets from a main stem, pull a branchlet down

Berries of salal, Gaultheria shallon

and off the main stem, leaving a heel of old wood at its base. This is known as a heel cutting.

Remove leaves and thorns from the part of the cutting that will come in contact with the soil. Also remove spent flowers and flower buds. To encourage more rapid root growth, wound the stem at its base by removing a one-half-inch to one-inch-long strip of the outer layer of wood, using a sharp razor blade. This step is not necessary if the stem is thin or fragile.

Prepare a container for the cuttings and get all necessary materials ready the day before you go out to collect. You can obtain plastic flats from nursery supply stores, but it is easy to build a wooden flat from a few pieces of scrap lumber. A standard flat four inches deep, fourteen inches wide, and sixteen inches long will hold many cuttings. For drainage, leave eighth-inch-wide spaces between the bottom boards or drill holes in the wood.

Fill the flat with a well-mixed rooting medium of three parts coarse sand and one part peat, vermiculite, or perlite. Soak the flat and contents thoroughly with water, let it drain, then tamp the soil with a brick or block of wood to remove air pockets. The flat is now ready to receive cuttings.

Collect cuttings in early morning when stems are full of water and before the leaves become wilted in the sun. It is preferable to insert them in the rooting medium immediately after cutting, but they will stay fresh for several hours if kept cool in a damp plastic bag.

Dip the cut end of the stem into a mixture of root-inducing hormone and fungicide (some brands of rooting hormone incorporate fungicide). Then, using a nail or pencil to make holes in the soil, insert the cuttings about two inches and space them in rows one to two inches apart, gently firming the soil around each.

When the last cutting is in place, moisten the leaves and settle the soil with a fine spray of water. Leaves that are large or have a tendency to droop can be bundled and held upright with a rubber band to keep them from touching the soil or shading other cuttings. Identify each kind of plant on a plastic label marked with waterproof ink.

Since cuttings need even humidity, they should be enclosed in a tent of clear plastic. A half-hoop of strong wire at each end of the flat will hold the plastic a few inches above the tops of the cuttings and allow air circulation. Secure the plastic around the edge of the flat with cord. Store the flat in a sheltered, well-lighted place, but not in direct sunlight. Check it every few days to remove decaying leaves and ensure that it is remaining evenly moist.

The time required for cuttings to root varies considerably. Some species, like mahala mat (*Ceanothus prostratus*), root within three weeks, while others, particularly the rhododendrons, azaleas, and ledums, may take longer, even as much as a year. Expect some disappointments. For reasons unknown, a few cuttings may decide to rot instead.

Rooting can be speeded up by giving the cuttings bottom heat. A propagating mat, which plugs into a standard electrical outlet and is regulated with a thermostat, permits the flat to retain a constant temperature that stimulates quicker rooting and higher rates of success. Flats can be stacked three or four deep if they are offset to allow air circulation. Safer than the old heat-cable systems, the propagating mat is available from many garden centers and nursery supply companies.

Rooted cuttings should be removed from the flat and placed in a pot of soil so they receive the nutrients needed for top growth as well as further root develop-

Left: Cassiope
mertensiana*;
below: kinnikinnick
(*Arctostaphylos
uva-ursi) *in fruit*

ment. Mix together a potting medium of one part peat, one part sand, and two parts rich garden soil. Use clean three- or four-inch diameter clay or plastic pots with drainage holes in the bottom. Fill a pot halfway with soil and firm with your hand. Use a table fork to lift a rooted cutting from the flat and transfer it to the pot. Dribble soil around the roots and tamp gently, then fill to within one inch of the top. As you finish potting each cutting, set the pot in a pan of water until the soil is thoroughly moistened. The potted cuttings should be placed in a cold frame until the following spring or fall, or until the plant is well developed. During this time they will need some care—plenty of moisture, removal of debris, and protection from frost—but propagation tasks are essentially finished.

There are some plants that make their own "cuttings," and the enterprising gardener can take advantage of this fact. The long, spreading branches of ground covers like kinnikinnick (*Arctostaphylos uva-ursi*) often form roots where a branch is in contact with the ground. Simply cut the rooted branch from the parent plant and transplant it to a pot or to a permanent place in the garden.

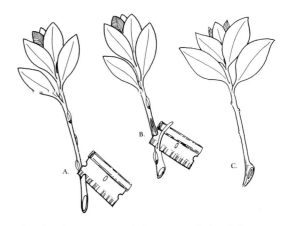

A: trimming a stem cutting at an angle just below a leaf node; B: wounding the stem by removing a sliver; C: side shoot pulled from the stem to form a heel cutting

With ground covers or with upright shrubs that have low, drooping branches, such as salal (*Gaultheria shallon*), you can encourage this natural means of starting new plants through a method known as layering. Over a foot-long trench about six inches deep, bend a branch to touch the ground about a foot from its tip, and with a sharp knife, make a small slit at the bend. Keep the slit open by inserting a matchstick or tiny pebble. Dust the cut with root-inducing hormone powder, then hold the cut

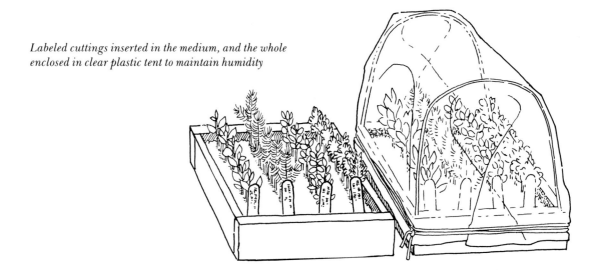

Labeled cuttings inserted in the medium, and the whole enclosed in clear plastic tent to maintain humidity

portion in the trench and cover it with a soil mixture of equal parts coarse sand and damp peat or vermiculite. A rock placed over the buried stem will keep it in place and conserve ground moisture. A year later the layer should have developed a healthy root system, ready to be cut from the parent plant and transplanted to the garden.

When it is time to move new plants into the garden some thought should be given to the conditions they prefer in nature. For example, those adapted to extreme summer drought are unlikely to thrive near a regularly irrigated lawn. Natives of foggy coastal areas planted in inland gardens may be well suited to such a spot. Similarly, small plants from woodland areas may prefer a little contrived afternoon shade, while chaparral shrubs from the hillsides would resent it.

Growing wild shrubs from softwood cuttings is a challenge and a pleasure. Once they become established in the garden these natives give many years of beauty and require little maintenance. With an initial investment of a little labor, you can then sit back and relax.

Stem cut with pebble inserted ready for layering, and the stem with roots formed, ready for severing from the main plant in preparation for moving the following season

BARROW MUCK

GEORGE WATERS

Sir Albert Howard, a pioneer of scientific agriculture, spent many years at the beginning of this century experimenting with the large-scale manufacture of compost from vegetable and animal wastes. He was distressed by the loss of soil fertility in industrial countries brought about by monoculture, the decline in mixed farming, and dependence on chemical fertilizers. He saw that to restore fertility ways must be found to return natural wastes to the soil.

His work was done in India at Indore, 300 miles northeast of Bombay, and the method of composting he advocated is known as the Indore process. It relies upon mixing all available vegetable scraps with water, animal manure, soil, and wood ash in heaps five to six feet high and wide.

There are now many variations on the Indore process.* The most important of these enable gardeners with insufficient

*The Indore process is described in detail in Howard's *The Waste Products of Agriculture* (Oxford University Press, 1931) and further elaborated in *An Agricultural Testament* (Oxford University Press, 1940). Notes on Howard's life and work, much information on composting, and the opinions of compost-makers in many parts of the country are found in *The Complete Book of Composting*, Robert Rodale, editor (Rodale Books, 1970).

material for a six-foot heap to succeed with a smaller one. Small heaps remain cooler than large ones because they have greater surface area—through which heat is lost—for the volume of material they contain. A simple answer to this is the New Zealand box, a slatted container about three feet square without top or bottom and with one side removable. The slats (boards of any convenient width) have gaps of about an inch between them to allow air to enter the compost, but provide sufficient insulation to retain much of the heat that would be lost from an unprotected heap. The box will also reduce the loss of moisture.

Few of us have supplies of animal manure for our compost heap, but good compost is made without animal manure so long as there is variety in the vegetable remains and the amount of fresh greens and other nitrogen-rich stuff equals the hard and woody. Without a good supply of nitrogen the bacteria will be unable to attack the tree leaves, paper, and other hard things that, finely divided, are important ingredients of any heap. An insufficiency of nitrogen can be corrected with additions of blood meal or a similar fertilizer. Any animal manure that comes along, no matter how little, is best included if it is from herbivores; small quantities are of little use alone, but in the heap their value is multiplied.

Organisms in the heap need moisture and air. Decomposition does occur in the absence of air, but it is a smelly process and is inferior, from a gardener's point of view, to that which results from an abundance of air. In building the heap, then, ingredients should be moistened, if necessary, and piled tightly—even pressed down—but not compacted.

As decomposition proceeds the temperature at the center of the heap rises to about 140–160°F. and then falls. At this stage more air and new material at the center will allow the process, now slowing, to speed up again; turning the heap, bring-ing material from the outside to the center, will achieve both aims. The more often the heap is turned the faster decomposition occurs. Dr Raabe, an enthusiastic maker of compost, turns the heap daily at some stages in order to have compost ready for use in two or three weeks. Dr Raabe anticipates the cooling process and turns the heap before heat builds up and a temperature is reached at which the organisms die; more air is provided and decomposition continues at greater speed.

Dr Raabe's compost differs from that left to molder in a corner in entering the soil while many bacteria, fungi, and enzymes are still active and before such nutrients as the compost contains are washed out by rain. And because his method is quick, several heaps a year can be incorporated into the soil, providing in quantity what Fred Loads, that wise old gardener of British radio, called "barrow muck," distinguishing it from store-bought "bag muck" by the sneer reserved for the latter. Fred encouraged gardeners to feed the soil and let the plants look after themselves.

SKELETONS IN THE
GARDENER'S CLOSET

IAN JACKSON

HORTICULTURAL grave-robbing is a less spectacular crime than body-snatching, which probably accounts for the scant attention paid to it by historians. Bones interest the gardener more than flesh and blood, of which they are merely the residue. In the last century, stray cats and circus animals that happened to die on tour were apt to find their way under a grape arbor or undernourished fruit tree, but there were no human carrion borders in the garden—such a practice verges on cannibalism; the usual ingredient was horseflesh. Those who are upset by the thought of human bone meal generally fail to note this fact and do not separate the flesh from bones in their ruminations, but it is an important distinction, for when human bones are used as fertilizer, they are usually well aged and bone-dry (one can indeed thank the sometime sentimentalist for this) in contrast to the nauseating semi-decay of animal remains that have not merited a preliminary churchyard rest. In his autobiography, *The Story and the Fable* (1940), Edwin Muir (1887–1959) gives a harrowing account of his two years as clerk in a bone factory near Glasgow, where the Catholic and Protestant workers fought each other with maggoty bones and the air

of the entire town was fat with decay. The occasional human skull or forearm that turned up, white and dry (and as lost as the poet) among the rest, is perhaps the only homely thing in his account. Human bones are certainly the least repugnant form this grim manure may take, and they supply an element essential to the right appreciation of fertilizers, one that is quite lacking in modern proprietary mixtures—a vague sense of awe and ceremony. Plants grown over them acquire a churchyard potency: the old herbalists botanized in the grave-yard, believing that the consecrated soil increased the virtues of any medicinal plant that grew there.

The cemetery, with its constantly stirred surface, has remained a sort of *refugium botanicum* (to use the pleasant title of an old work), and nowadays, with its purer air, a lichen oasis in built-up areas; not a few botanical discoveries have been made there. Robert Fortune found *Anemone japonica* in a cemetery near Shanghai, and 'Granado', an old carnation described by Parkinson, was rediscovered in a vase on a grave in a Norfolk village churchyard. Judge Clinton of New York, an amateur botanist and son of DeWitt Clinton, died while botanizing in a graveyard, and Lester Rowntree

(1879–1979) confessed to having stolen (with a gunnysack in the dead of night) her specimen of the very rare Franciscan manzanita (*Arctostaphylos franciscana*) from the now destroyed Laurel Hill Cemetery in San Francisco.

Churchyards produced the richest grass; villages in England and New England leased them as meadows. Later ages, with a more exact understanding of the value of bone meal as a fertilizer, dispensed with the notion of consecration and found the mere knowledge of the dead below enough to make the flesh creep. Lafcadio Hearn (1850–1904), who had a taste for cemeteries and frequented them wherever he traveled, in New Orleans, the West Indies, and finally Japan, reflected, as his railway carriage rolled past the picturesque cemetery of Spring Grove near Cincinnati, "The very richness of the verdure made you shudder. What made that grass grow so very, very green? What gave to the flowers a richer coloring? What nourished the roots of those somber and luxuriant evergreens? Surely they could not have gained such ghastly vitality in another soil!" Exiled in Egypt with Lawrence Durrell during World War II, Robin Fedden allowed the mummy-rich Nile mud to induce a similar shiver in the musing British expatriate. He found the soil "bursting with corpses" and offering an "almost indecent stimulus" to vegetable growth.

The history of human bones as a manure before the nineteenth century is sketchy. Battlefields provided bones in quantities large enough to impress the farmer from an early date, for even without thought of fertilizing, there was a pleasure in plowing one's enemies under, and, as the *Marseillaise* points out, irrigating the furrows with impure blood. To quote again from Lafcadio Hearn, this time from his exhaustive *Notes on the Utilization of Human Remains* published in the Cincinnati *Commercial* of November 7, 1875, "The bones of the Teutons slaughtered by the legionaries of Marius, near the present site of Aix in Provence, were so utilized, it is said; and the traces of that vast massacre are apparent even at this day, according to Ampère. The spot was called the Place of Corruption for years, and the name of the village of La Pourrière is said to be a corruption of *pourriture* (putridity)." Elsewhere, their use must generally have been inadvertent, although some Greek tombstones warned the farmer to keep his distance, and others (probably literary exercises) lamented the fact that the grave had already been turned up by the plough and that if this became standard agricultural practice, the farmer himself would not lie undisturbed. When the wayside tomb fell out of favor, and the dead were gathered into cemeteries, they could enjoy what Joubert called a pious uselessness until their eventual desecration. Many parks and gardens were laid out in abandoned cemeteries. The Oxford Botanic Garden, for instance, the oldest in Britain, stands on the site of a medieval Jewish cemetery, appropriated when Edward I expelled the Jews from England. The gardens at the London Charterhouse were said to have owed their luxuriant vegetation to the enrichment of the soil by the many thousands of plague victims buried there in 1348–49. The Scottish nurseryman Grant Thorburn (1773–1863) built his hotbed and pits in an old Quaker burying ground in the heart of New York City, probably more for the space than the bones. Several nineteenth-century clergymen laid out gardens, and even small metropolitan nurseries, in their city churchyards, a practice institutionalized toward the end of the century in London by the Metropolitan Gardens Association through the Disused Burial Grounds Bill.

As Wordsworth observed in a sonnet of 1822, the border between garden and churchyard was often difficult to discover.

Where holy ground begins, unhallowed
    ends,
Is marked by no distinguishing line;
The turf unites, the pathways intertwine;
And, wheresoe'er the stealing footstep
    tends,
Garden, and that domain where kindred,
    friends,
And neighbours rest together, here
    confound
Their several features. . . .

By the early nineteenth century, the other advantages of churchyard gardening were beginning to be appreciated, and bone dust became one of the many links between gardening and cemetery reform. Loudon devoted the last years of his life to the study of churchyard and cemetery planting, and in his usual thorough manner paid careful attention to the benefits to be derived from buried bones. Portions of workhouse grounds, he thought, might be used alternately as cemeteries and gardens. This revolutionary form of crop rotation was too far in advance of its time; many thought the subject might better be ignored. Loudon's proposal, in his *On the Laying out, Planting and Managing of Cemeteries, and on the Improvement of Churchyards* (1843), "to convert paupers into manure," as a hostile reviewer summarized it, was perhaps a little tactless, and moreover reminiscent of the communal burial pits at Naples and Leghorn, although the fact that the book was published posthumously gave the suggestion a certain authority *d'outre tombe*. (It is only fair to add that even the visionary Loudon recognized that people had feelings, and tended to make a distinction between their remains and those of animals: his *Gardener's Magazine* refers frankly, and occasionally with relish,

to the dung of bird and beast, but the place where humans were supposed to put theirs was always indicated as the w---r cl---t.) His remarks on the use of bones as a manure are characteristic of a contemporary of Coleridge and De Quincey, for in his usual helpful way—explaining unfamiliar principles by analogy with everyday experience—Loudon noted that the gardener might learn from the opium eater who wrapped his pills in paper for prolonged action, and apply that principle to gardening, burying bones entire for more gradual effect than was obtainable from bone meal or dust.

While Loudon's paupers may not have been openly converted into manure, a surreptitious trade in their remains certainly did exist. G. A. Walker reported in his *Gatherings from Graveyards* (1839) that "many tons of human bones are every year sent from London to the North, where they are crushed in the mills constructed for the purpose, and used as manure." The contents of the charnel houses of north Germany were said to have been shipped to Hull at about this time. The Philadelphia botanist and nurseryman Thomas Meehan (1826–1901) recalled that as a child in the Isle of Wight, probably in the late 1830s, while investigating old cellars near a churchyard, he found "heaps of human bones which occasionally went to the mill to make 'dust' to fertilize the English turnip crop." A degree of persecution tended to bring the remains of a community into commerce; in America it was Indians and occasionally Quakers, in continental Europe, the suppressed religious orders, and in England, dissenters of every kind (whose deathbed conversions were sometimes prompted by nothing stronger than a desire to rest in the comparative security of legally consecrated ground). According to *The Queen* for April 1880, soil from the

Whitfield Tabernacle was being "sold at eighteenpence a bowl for forcing mignonette and flowering geraniums" to florists in Camden Town. Florists were of course well known for their taste in bizarre fertilizers and the viler garden concoctions; it would indeed have been strange had human bones not appealed to their arcane sense of propriety in manures. Any reverence for the bones of the pharaohs had long since vanished by the nineteenth century, and fragmentary mummies were regularly imported to England from Alexandria in the 1870s. This was an indignity felt chiefly by the educated; a writer in *Notes and Queries* quoted Sir Thomas Browne (in whose day mummy was a drug and pigment) and observed, "What an instructive commentary is here presented on human preparations and insight into the future! The remains of the great and mighty of a famed and historical country, after lying undisturbed for thousands of years, dug up and transferred to a distant land to be spread for dung on the face of the earth!"

Bone manure seems first to have been deliberately applied to fields in the neighborhood of Sheffield in the late eighteenth century, but was not much used until around 1810. To what extent this was due to the Napoleonic Wars is an interesting question. Waterloo teeth have a definite place in denture history, and certainly the bleached bones of horses and soldiers from the trenches of Waterloo and Leipzig found their way into the manure trade; according to Henry Stephens (1795–1874), author of that useful compendium *The Book of the Farm*, the Russian battlefields contributed their store as well. The Scottish gardener Archibald Gorrie (1779–1857) was disturbed to find human bones among the usual animal remains scattered over turnip fields, but contented himself with observing that "those farmers whose feelings allow them to hasten the process of converting the bones of our brave defenders into vegetable matter, may find a powerful ally in bone dust, with little 'expense of carriage.'" Such farmers were easily found. Sir John Bennet Lawes (1814–1900), founder of the Rothamsted Agricultural Experiment Station in 1843, used Waterloo bones in his early experiments, dissolving them in sulphuric acid to dress his turnip fields. He later branched out into the manufacture of other sorts of fertilizers. That Waterloo played an important part in the popularization of bone manures in general (and not merely human dust) is borne out by a story in Augustus Hare's autobiography:

The country round Sherborne was the scene of innumerable battles in Saxon times, commemorated in the names of the fields and farms, which are supposed to owe their fertility to the carnage with which they had been covered. This supposition makes the peasants eager for the use of bonedust, which they believe to be imported from the plains of Waterloo. If a field, after having been thus manured, still yields no crop, they say "Waterloo bean't no use here!"

Farmers were developing a taste for military archaeology. In a letter to the Quaker poet Bernard Barton, Edward FitzGerald took note of the confrontation of historical reverence and go-ahead practicality over the bones at the battlefield of Naseby, which he was investigating in the fall of 1842 for Thomas Carlyle's book on Cromwell.

Two farmers insisted on going out exploring with me all day: one a very solid fellow, who talks like the justices in Shakespeare: but who certainly was inspired in finding out this grave: the other a Scotchman full of intelligence, who proposed the flesh-soil for manure for turnips.

It may in fact be doubted whether any other bones but those of man would have gained acceptance for bone manure so quickly; sentimental associations were of course a drawback to the use of human bones, but the "unknown soldier" had the advantage of being reverenced by all, but mourned by no one in particular. His remains might, in a vague way, be expected to do great things. The contrast with other kinds of bones was bathetic. George W. Johnson (1802–1886), editor of the *Cottage Gardener*, wrote in 1850, "Many of our readers must have heard, as we often have heard, the contemptuous query, 'What! old knife handles good for manure?'" Whatever one might think of old Waterloo veterans, they were not to be dismissed in the same breath with old knife handles.

Human bone manure likewise played a leading role in the early days of the cremation movement in England. The article by Queen's surgeon Sir Henry Thompson in the *Contemporary Review* for January 1874 marks the beginning of the controversy. His chief argument in favor of cremation was perhaps unfortunately chosen. It was the economic one relating directly to manures: to bury human bones in the lower rather than the upper soil was "absurd, if not wicked." Over half a million pounds a year were spent on imported bones when domestic might do as well; "Few people," he wrote, "have any notion that these importations of foreign bones are rendered absolutely necessary by the hoarding of our own some six feet below the surface." The ashes and bone-earth resulting from cremation "may be preserved in a formal urn, or may be scattered on the fields, which latter is their righteous destination." As the fertilizing power of human bones (and the insalubriety of improperly rotted flesh) was Sir Henry's central argument, so it was this that particularly angered his op-

ponents. Philip Holland, Medical Inspector of Burials in England and Wales, who replied in the next issue of the *Contemporary Review*, was appalled at Thompson's "suggestion that we should use our fathers' ashes as turnip-dressing, which would be worse than 'to botanize on a mother's grave.'" Those blasted turnips again! If only it had been some less plebeian, more picturesque vegetable, or better still, a cypress or rosebush. In fact, it was not until turnips passed out of the picture, leaving the field to urns and parks, that cremation became a generally acceptable form of burial.

Turnip farmers, like gravediggers, may kick old skeletons around, and treat bone dust with scant reverence; it is for poets and parsons to muse on them. Sir Thomas Browne touched on the matter in one of his commonplace books, noting that when the charnel house of St. Paul's in London was demolished, the bones were used as landfill in Finsbury Fields, the more than a thousand cartloads raising the ground for three windmills. He concluded with a memorandum: "To make an epigramme or a fewe verses upon this subject or of a windmill upon a mount of bones." Until the later era of satanic mills (when grim verses might have been written on bone flour and wheat dust) Browne's suggestion would be unlikely to inspire anything more biting than:

Here lies, beneath these grinding stones,
A parish of redundant bones;
Cast-off indeed, but useful still:
All's grist in God's sepulchral mill.

The meal of human bones would seem to be an ideal subject for minor versifiers of a moralizing turn, but, strange to say, the theme has attracted hardly anyone. Dante Gabriel Rossetti in *The Orchard Pit* and Andrew Young in *The Swedes* associated human bones with apple trees and rutabagas, but neither of them was minor or moralizing, and in both poems the fertilizing aspect is incidental. William E. A. Axon (1846–1913), the vegetarian antiquary of Manchester, is the only poet known to me to have tried his hand at bonemeal verse, in stanzas entitled *Priestcliffe Low*:

> Upon the sloping side of Priestcliffe Low,
>> Where now there wander slowly cattle
>>> sleek,
>> Ere yet the first of Peverils knew the
>>> Peak,
> In the pre-Roman days so long ago,
> A chieftain famed for his death-dealing
>> blow,
>> Fear of the strong, protector of the
>>> weak,
>> Whom death had made as women, mild
>>> and meek,
> Was buried 'midst his vassals' tears and
>> woe.

> They laid him with due reverence in the
>> earth,
>> But grasping hands have since dis-
>>> turbed his rest,
>>> And spread his bones above the nar-
>>>> row field,
>>> To make the soil a richer harvest
>>>> yield,
> So may his ancient valour have new birth,
>> And glow for truth and right in modern
>>> breast.

The subject seems tailor-made for flower sermons too, but a casual search through the published texts of those delivered annually under the bequests of Thomas Fairchild in London and Henry Shaw in St. Louis has yielded no reference. It is therefore tempting to offer this as a tip to clergymen, who, to judge from the sermons recently offered in the neighborhood—"Is Christ too good for us?" and "In an Evil World why bother to be good?"—must often be at their wits' end for attractive subject matter; but quite probably bones would make no impression on a modern congregation. We are no longer familiars of the graveyard, and there are plenty of "gay pageants that breathe that can with a dead body compare." Whether human bones are still ground to dust, I have been unable to discover. Who knows but that we may yet use them in the garden; the manufacturers will not say, no doubt rightly thinking that with so few garden moralists among us the information would be wasted on the purchaser. Discoursing on false relics in his *Small Talk at Wreyland* (1926), Cecil Torr wrote:

Down here a man remarked to me one day, as he was gazing across some fields, "It be a wonder-workin' thing, that Consecrated Bone." I began to think we had a relic here. But he spoke of concentrated bone manure."

Whatever the truth, one can still believe.

HEARTS AND FLOWERS

PATRICIA TALBERT

FRONTING a highway outside Victoria, British Columbia, are three tiny stucco cottages huddled together and cut off from similar houses by institutional buildings at either end. In the front yard of each grow tall-standing, old-fashioned, single-flowered hollyhocks. Not common red and pink hollyhocks. These are peach-colored and palest lemony yellow.

They clearly were not planted to any plan, but randomly scattered and interspersed with drying weeds. Never had I dreamed of such gorgeous hollyhocks. My first thought was to run to the three doors to ask about them. But these houses, something told me, were lived in by quiet, private people. Better that I write to them than startle them at their own front doors.

I recorded the addresses, and within hours I was penning individual pleas to the hollyhock cottages. Not knowing the residents' names, I thought for a long while about the form of address I should use. If I simply addressed them to Occupant they might be thought junk mail. I could address them to The Person Who Grows Flowers. But these hollyhocks seemed rather to grow themselves. Finally I settled upon addressing each to The Keeper of the Hollyhocks.

I knew they would write back. Surely no Keeper of Hollyhocks, however accidentally, could not write back. But perhaps these cottages are lived in by people who don't like gardens. Maybe they don't know these are hollyhocks in their yards. Maybe the hollyhocks have always been there, maybe they are considered weeds, maybe the owners had even tried to get rid of them.

Impatiently I waited. Would they understand that someone, a stranger from California, really wanted and needed their seeds? Would they dismiss my request as idle, believing their seeds to be common, available from any store?

Not two weeks later an envelope arrived from Canada. The enclosure read: "I received your letter about the yellow hollyhocks. The ones you saw were all from my garden. I will send you seeds when they are ready. I also love gardening but am now nearly eighty-seven and am not able to take care of my garden. I would very much like to get some of your seeds. It may be a change. I have one plant which bears flowers pale yellow with a vivid pink center. Would you like some of those. Sincerely, Una Hillier."

Would I like some? Indeed! Dear Mrs

Hillier, I was so afraid you wouldn't answer my letter, and I am so anxious to have some of your hollyhock seeds. Yes, of course, I would like the pale yellow one with the vivid pink center.

A few weeks later a second letter from Canada arrived. Again the writing was old-school swirly: "In answer to your request for some seeds from our hollyhocks, my wife and I are pleased to enclose herewith some yellow and cream seeds. Thanks for your offer of some of your seeds but we will very likely not be living here next year. We trust that you enjoyed your visit to Victoria." It was signed Bert and Hilda Ralph, Keepers of the Hollyhocks.

Mrs Hillier wrote a second time, more chatty now. She had not forgotten. "I have enclosed the seeds you wanted. They were a long time maturing because we have had so much rain. I must tell you that these yellow hollyhocks do not always come up yellow. Some years they have been pinkish. I do not know what causes this unless it is the bees. I have them all over the garden and they have come up in my neighbor's garden. Do you know anything that will kill thistles. I have more each year, have tried everything, even gasoline. Thank you for the seeds. Una K. Hillier."

Enclosed were two odd little hand-folded and pasted envelopes labeled "pale yellow pink centers" and "yellow."

Dear Mrs Hillier, thank you for taking the time to share your bounty with a fellow gardener. I'm sorry that I do not know how to kill thistles.

From the third cottage there had been no word. Maybe they've moved. Maybe they aren't interested in seeds or seekers of same. Maybe the third house talked to the first and second houses and already knows that seeds have been mailed. But Mrs Hillier doesn't seem to have spoken to Mr and Mrs Ralph. As close as they are, squeezed together between the fire department and the highway, they apparently don't discuss their mail.

Months went by with no response from house number three. Then one day a fat, securely taped envelope arrived. The note inside was succinct: "Here are the yellow and pink hollyhock seeds you wrote for. I wish you success with them. I am not much of a gardener. They were here when I moved in. G. Parsons."

Those three letters were every bit as good as three valentines. Gardeners always respond. I think they can't help it. Ask a gardener what that lovely little gray-leaved plant in his windowbox is and you will soon be growing a gray-leaved plant yourself. Ask a gardener where he came by that tall lily and chances are that, lickety-split, he will dig you up a clump, wrap it in damp newspaper, bind it with string, and thrust it into your hands before you have managed to catch its name.

I tell this story about the hollyhocks to remind us all of an honorable tradition. Visit or write to a gardener today. There's just no telling what will grow.

INDEX